Safe Suicide

Safe Suicide

NARRATIVES, ESSAYS, AND MEDITATIONS

DeWitt Henry

RED HEN PRESS | Los Angeles, California

Safe Suicide: Narratives, Essays, and Meditations
Copyright © 2008 by DeWitt Henry
All rights reserved

Book design by Mark E. Cull

ISBN: 978-1-59709-100-8
Library of Congress Catalog Card Number: 2007941168

The City of Los Angeles Department of Cultural Affairs, Los Angeles County Arts
Commission, California Arts Council and the National Endowment for the Arts partially
support Red Hen Press.

First Edition

Published by Red Hen Press
www.redhen.org

To Connie, Ruth, David and Eva

Acknowledgements

The following essays appeared slightly different form in *The American Voice* ("Memoir of My Father"), *Cottonwood Review* ("Odd"), *Nebraska Review* ("Subversions," "My Dog Story"), *The Iowa Review* ("Bungee," "Gravity," "Improvisational," "On Aging"), *The Harvard Review* ("Forces of Nature"), *The Berkeley Fiction Review* ("Beautiful Flower"), *The Missouri Review* ("Wide-eyed" under the title "Wide-Awake"), *The Green Hills Literary Lantern* ("Arias," "Besmirched"), and *Agni* ("Innocents Abroad"). My thanks to these publications and their editors.

"Wide-eyed" from *Fathering Daughters* by DeWitt Henry © 1998 by DeWitt Henry and James Alan McPherson. Reprinted by permission of Beacon Press, Boston.

Special thanks to John Skoyles for help with editing; and to Jack Smith for proofreading.

Contents

Each time it tries to say more than this
The tip of the tongue must wrestle a leech.

—Bill Knott, *Lines from Future Poems*

Memoir Of My Father

My father came home each night from the factory at six or six-thirty (seven was late and we'd be starving, dinner held). He carried a briefcase, full of mail; used the upstairs bathroom; then settled down in his living room easy chair, both before and after dinner, to open and read all the mail and toss the envelopes and unwanted letters on the floor around him, where I was expected to pick them up and stuff them in the nearby wastebasket, which he disdained to use. He seemed perpetually brooding, silent and withdrawn; and I feared his angry reprimands, often when I went against my mother somehow; feared his apoplectic red face, his bulk, and his stentorian voice, which at its most violent pronounced a "damn" or "hell," but never any other curse. Early after our move from Wayne to a new house in nearby St. David's, in imitation of my older brothers Jack and Chuck (and keeping up to their legends was my pattern), I stole forbidden matches from my mother's desk and sneaked outside at night to the dark and hidden path within the rhododendrons, stuck matches in a row in the ground, so one would ignite the next, then lit one and watched them go. I wasn't caught at that, but felt so guilty and afraid of being found out, and especially of Dad hearing, that I went on my own to confess to Mom, and begged her not to let Dad know, as if his punishment would be as swift and merciless as Calvin's God's. And she scolded and warned me and as if sharing my fear of Dad and his outrage, she promised not to tell and didn't.

Also, as far back as I can remember Dad, there was the oddness—long before I had any explanation for it—and tension that he couldn't drink anything alcoholic, even desserts that had a mint liqueur, but that on special occasions Mom, and then later my brothers, could. Out for dinner or at another grownups' party, there would be, when he was offered cocktails or whatever, a stiffened refusal, almost angry, and right there, a sense of odd and shameful difference from "normal" parents. Liquor was the ultimate forbidden, not so much as sin, though there was that element too, but as a poison, something that led to unthinkable damage and ruin. The slightest taste of anything alcoholic and he would, I was made to feel, fall instantly and terribly ill. Assumed also was his difference in other ways, that he was maimed somehow and withdrawn from society—though Mom "loved" people—with the exception of immediate family, his mother and sisters, whom we'd dutifully and regularly visit and be visited by, and some very old business friends; that he was sulking and remote and demoted from any family authority, except as ultimate punisher. At the same time I have another early St. David's memory of sometimes being woken in the night by violent thunderclaps and lightning, and groping terrified out of my bed and down the hall to be with him and Mom, to crawl into their beds—his bed (they had twin singles), which was nearest the door—and sleep with him for protection. I know he welcomed me, gently, warmly, reassured me, and I was afraid of the long, awful scar on his left leg, where the flesh folded in. He had had an infection that involved his bone marrow as a teenager, and a piece of bone had been taken out—at least that is the garbled version I squeamishly absorbed—and he reassured me it was all right, but I was afraid of somehow falling into the scar. I ran to them three or four times this way, and then was made to feel I shouldn't, that I was too old for that, and it was more manly not to need them; and I don't remember being scared of lightning after that and felt proud that I wasn't, though I did have other night-time fears. A recurrent one was of some kind of intruder, who would climb up on one of my windows and I would see his dark form against the lighter night, or somehow an intruder had gotten in and was looking for me in the dark, and in panic, trusting the darkness itself for protection, I would lie still, afraid to breathe, then having to breathe, as soundlessly as possible, through my mouth, and fearing he could hear my panting heart.

⸙

Two obvious things about Dad were his weight and emphysema. He varied between two hundred and ten after a rigorous diet and two hundred and sixty, from a forty-four inch belt to a forty-eight—the belts seemed long enough to me, absurdly long, to use as pretend whips. His pants and jackets I was utterly lost in; two of me could have fit in easily. His shoes were also, for a long time, boat size to me; then as I grew older, a little pinched and small, but I could wear them, and did, especially his castoff loafers and golf shoes, with cleats. He also wore felt hats and the closet was full of them, all of which swam down over my ears. His workday costume consisted of loose boxer trunk underwear (my brothers and I grew up wearing jockey shorts, so these always, again huge, seemed outlandish), some striped, some polka-dotted, some plain, a cotton undershirt with shoulder straps, then nearly knee-length dress socks, which he had to fix with garters, then a starched white shirt, and one of several fine suits, brown, pin-striped, gray, and a matching tie, then polished brown shoes with wing tips. As he got dressed, he would sit in his chair up in the master bedroom, and one of us would bring him his coffee. He would shave—he had a coarse beard and used all current shaving gimmicks, a procession of single-blades, double-blades, self-ejectors, and electric razors of different designs—and then put on scented aftershave. He'd have a full breakfast at the dinner table, and leave finally around nine, sometimes as late as eleven. Weekends, he wore causal clothes, slacks and a jacket, a sport shirt, a wool shirt, and in summer, golf shirts.

When he reached the family candy factory, he usually took off his coat, hung it on a hanger, and put on protective white overalls over his executive clothes—he did this even when we'd go visit the plant on deserted weekends.

The emphysema came from his smoking—he was a chain smoker of Luckies and Camels in prefilter days, and smoked three to four packs a day, waving off any nagging objections. They had taken away liquor, he would say at different times, but they weren't going to take away his cigarettes. Some poisons he reserved the right to subscribe to. Anyhow each time, or third time, he lit up, he launched into a deep, bellowing, prolonged and helpless fit of coughing, during which his face reddened darkly and his eyes bulged, and I—all of us—cringed in some degree of fear, afraid he would have a heart attack. But if we said anything or even if he saw us looking with concern, or if we had kept talking with consternation or aversion, he'd turn angry, waving us away, waving away any notice. We were to live with these eruptions the same way he did, as if they were normal, as if they weren't there.

Fat from the beginning symbolized, through Dad and his mother, Nana Henry (who was enormous and pigeon-breasted), a kind of weakness, corruption, and gluttonous eating that we scorned. Typical Christmas or birthday gifts to Dad, when they didn't involve smoking or golf, were fat man jokes: a yardlong shoehorn, a quivering, Buddha-shaped doll on a scale. Part of Dad's problem, it turned out, was diabetes, which he contracted by sampling too much candy as he walked around the factory over the years. But there was no fat on Mom's side; in fact, she was put on weight-gaining diets and rarely weighed more than one hundred and five. My brothers, Chuck and Jack, like Mom, were effortlessly and naturally skinny, at least in their later teens—Jack would come in and eat a whole loaf of white bread;

Chuck would make ice-cream sundaes for a snack. Judy, on the other hand, was determined to lose weight and went on obsessive diets, always dieting, eating nothing but salads and Melba toast, until Mom grew concerned for her health. Going through my lumpy pre-teens, I was most self-conscious about my large rear-end, which I dreamed of slicing off. They teased me: "peanut!" "rumble seat!" And Dad would caution me solemnly later, you're the one most likely to get fat.

∞

I don't remember at what age, except it was early on, when I was nine or ten, that Mom told me officially that Dad had been an alcoholic and what that meant. I don't recall the way she told me, except that it was serious, an adult confidence, and the feeling communicated was one of shame and tragedy. That alcoholic was something unspeakable to be—actually I think my terror at the first werewolf movie I saw on TV—it was Lon Chaney's *The Wolf Man*—bore my sense of that monstrosity, of a loved and recognized man suddenly changing into a terrifying and unrecognized beast. I do know that my brothers and sister never discussed it with me, though by Mom's account, they had all been "hurt" by it.

Much, much later, after the legend of this family shame, of why we were isolated, why the boys and Judy were shy of bringing home friends, why my parents never entertained, why we all seemed withdrawn from the "normal" world—after all that was boringly assumed and rote—Dad himself took me aside for an official father and son talk. We were alone, out on the sun porch leather couch, and I felt nervously embarrassed for him. I must have been seventeen, maybe older. There was no new information in his telling, but his tone was part apologetic and embarrassed, part bravely level, part dismissive, like all of this was long ago and over with and settled, and no longer painful to him, and it shouldn't bother me, but he wanted me to know and to hear it from him. That alcoholism was an "illness," something constitutional, and that you couldn't help. That some people could take a drink and it wouldn't trouble them; but that other people, and he was one of those people, but hadn't realized it for a long time, the alcohol did something to their systems, and they just couldn't drink, that's all, without it taking over. That for a long time he had been drinking like that, and it had burned out his brain—in fact, he insisted, part of his brain had been permanently damaged, which was why he was the way he was now—that their friends and people around Wayne and at the Golf Club had seen him like that, and some still remembered and didn't understand, and that finally he'd been hospitalized and treated by Dr. Apple, the psychiatrist, and dried out, and he'd never touched a drop since. And that the worst time had been hell on Mom (it was afterwards she'd gone to Bermuda on doctor's orders to recuperate), and "your mother stuck with me through that"—he emphasized with some wonder and pride— "a lot of women wouldn't have, couldn't have, and I'll always be grateful to her for that, we should all be grateful. She's one woman in a thousand."

An odd genre among our family snapshots mocks drunkenness. One of Mom and Chuck—taken by Dad, I have to guess—has Chuck in white bucks and a top hat, holding a long-stemmed beer glass in one hand, while his other arm is around Mom, who has hers around his waist and is slumped against his side. Her eyes are closed, a cigarette dangles from the side of her mouth, and at the end of her free arm she holds a rum bottle by the neck and braces it against her knee. In another, which I took on my eleventh birthday party, Judy, cone-shaped party hat awry on her head, eyes half-closed, a sprig of mint in her teeth, toasts the camera with an outsized brandy snifter, which we normally used as a vase.

One Christmas I bought Mom and Dad a set of eight glasses called "Name Your Poison" (a problem was that gift shops themselves were devoted to this genre, so when it came to Father's Day or similar occasions, many of the neater things had to do with drinking). Each had a death's head on it and then its own special label: "Arsenic," "Hydrochloric Acid," "Strychnine." When we served drinks to company—we always made a show of doing so, cordially, and company, from Aunt Kitty and Uncle John, to Aunt Peggy, to the Hayn's, to the Hinkel's, to the Watson's all accepted heartily—Dad enjoyed serving highballs in these glasses, which particularly amused him and always drew a comment.

Dad slept much of the time he was home. Often, it seemed, he only woke up and got dressed in order to eat and then fall asleep again on the living room couch, or sitting up in his chair. And when he slept, he snored.

I took a black and white photo with Chuck's telephoto lens, when I was sixteen or seventeen, which sums up my feeling about my father then. He looks dead, as in some part of my heart I wished him to be. He is on our chaise lounge, out on the patio where Mom and Judy used to sun. The picture is just of his sleeping face, half-covered by his hand, on which his head rests. The little finger pushes up on his forehead. The eyes are sunken. The features look as collapsed, slurred down, as a mud-slide; a deep cheek crease runs down from the nose, whose nostrils slant, joining another from the corner of the mouth. The mouth is darkly gaping, slack. The flesh is coarse and porous, like pigskin on a billfold, and stubbled over and around the mouth. The image, like death, is of utter flaccidity.

Odd

The oddest adult in my suburban Philadelphia childhood was a retired prizefighter, a man blinded in the ring, but someone who had had a serious career and earned a fortune, so that he lived with his sister and his German wolfhounds in a forty- or fifty-room mansion that we, my friends and I and other schoolchildren, passed each day walking to and from school.

For me, the walk home each afternoon was one mile, the length of Midland Avenue from Louella, past the single-floor "modern" house with picture windows on the right, past the Catholic school where tough kids hung out, past Bob Teal's house on the left (his father, Mr. Teal, was the high school music teacher and band leader, and Bob's two older sisters were cheerleaders), then the long uphill block to St. David's Avenue. Mostly I walked with Dale Wilson, who lived in the new apartments on the corner of St. David's Avenue and Lancaster Pike; we walked, careful not to step on sidewalk cracks, and talked about how babies arrived. Dale had the idea that it had something to do with "fucking," but I disagreed, horrified at the idea, and said what my mother had said, which was that when a man and woman loved each other and were together for a while, then a baby happened. We were ten. 1952. TV was still a luxury. At school we practiced air raid drills in basement hallways lined with civil defense boxes and canisters. At home, one of my favorite toys was a model of a B-52 bomber that released an atomic bomb when I pushed a button on top.

There were kids, other ages, who walked the same street, and the legend had spread that halfway up the long uphill block was the house where this retired fighter lived, who loved kids. That any afternoon if you braved the white gate between the solid bank of hedges and pine trees that sheltered the view of his home from the street; if you ventured up his strange front walk to the wooden porch; if you braved the first floor windows flanking the front door; if you rang the button bell and had the nerve to wait, as if for trick or treat—first, there would be the dogs barking, throaty woofs muffled by the house, then, perhaps, a woman's voice:

"Quiet! Quiet! Just a minute, I'm coming."

And the sounds of her presence, a blurred face peering, the unlocking and opening of the oak front door into a paneled vestibule.

Dale had done it twice before he told me. Other kids had taken him. As we came up the hill, he urged me to try; did I want a candy bar or not? For that was the prize.

The lady who answered would be gray-haired, tall, formally dressed. She would materialize before you, questioning, as if she had no idea: "Yes?"

And you would say that you had heard that the man here liked to meet children.

And she would answer: "Yes, yes, just a minute."

Perhaps from the strange depths of the inner hall and the house's reaches and darkness, a deeper, gravelly man's voice would be calling: "Sonja. Sonja? Who is it? Who's there?"

"It's some children!" she would call. And then to you: "Just a minute. He'll want to meet you."

There would be a shuffling behind her and this man, casually dressed, a handsome man larger than any father, broad shouldered, broad faced, wearing slacks and an ascot and with neatly combed white hair, would emerge, and she would make way. You would be scared but at the same time fascinated to look: the face, the eyes, the blank, cloudy, unseeing eyes. The face handsome otherwise, like Wallace Beery's, the actor's, or like Ralph Bellamy's; an educated and distinguished face. And he would be tapping with his cane and groping forward.

"Hello," he'd say. "Are these the children?" And then to you, "Hello," he'd say to space, the space where you, the unknown, waited. "What's your name? How many, two? What are your names?"

And you might find the nerve to answer, or your friend might; for no kid would ever try this alone, except for maybe Shaner, the older kid who had first brought Dale here, and from whom, perhaps, the man's rumored history had begun. Whatever first had led Shaner here, a meeting on the street, some door-to-door solicitation, Shaner had had the nerve to ask: How did you get blinded? In the ring, the man answered. Perhaps Shaner had been inside. Were there trophies inside? Pictures on the walls? Clippings in a scrapbook? How did we know the lady to be the man's sister?

"Have you been here before?" the man would ask.

"No, never. Just some kids told us we should stop and ring the bell."

"That's right," the man says. And then: "And you? What's your name?"

"Dee," I say uncertainly, for I *am* there; but at the same time I relax, because so far this all seems rehearsed, a customary thing, and going just the way Dale has said.

"Tell me some things you like to do," the man says. "Do you like sports?"

"Football."

"Hmmm," he says. "You an Eagles fan?"

"Sure am," I lie.

"What are your favorite subjects in school?"

I say art. Dale says math.

"Hmmm. Here's a riddle for you. Let's see: What goes up the chimney down, but can't go down the chimney up?" He turns his face expectantly from one of us to the other.

I have heard the riddle before, but never really understood the answer.

"C'mon, guess. You've heard this one."

"Santa? I don't know."

He chuckled. "An umbrella."

Dale and I look at each other.

He smiles broadly. "You're good children. I can tell," he congratulates us. "Can I feel your faces?"

I stand confused, for Dale has never mentioned this, but I can't refuse, or probably the man won't give us the candy. So I let him touch, his coarse fighter's fingers drifting delicately over my features.

A lifetime later, that blind man's gentle, rapid touch, searching my features, haunts my imagination. Dismissing any suggestion of perversion (as our parents must have dismissed it then), I have come to think that for him the touch was redemptive.

Perhaps sixty at the time, he must have fought as a young man some thirty years before, in the era if not that of Gentleman Jim Corbett, then that of Jack Dempsey, Gene Tunney, and the Frenchman Georges Carpentier, and those very hands, as fists, had beaten men senseless, scores of men, men who had been intent, too, on battering him unconscious, all for the diversion of thousands of fans in echoing, smoky arenas, on from the 1920s into the Depression years.

I try to imagine such a man's life. Whether his wealth was partly inherited and he had come from a privileged background (and if so, what had driven him to fight, what buried rage, or what further need to prove his superiority against those who challenged it in physical, rather than in social terms). Whether he had gone to a private men's academy, like my older brothers, and started boxing in school; then had gone on to college at some place like Yale, Cornell, or Princeton, and boxed there. Had moved from school to amateur bouts, had turned professional and worked his way through ranks of street pugs and men from backgrounds that offered no means for livelihood or gain but this, men fighting for survival and advancement.

Or whether he himself had been poor. Had never been to college. Had labored and battled and suffered like the prizefighters in Hollywood films. Had from teens through his twenties battled not only opponents' fists, but also the greed of gamblers, molls, and promoters. Had had the sense to save and invest his winnings. And then what fight had ended his career? Perhaps he hadn't been blinded in the ring at all. Perhaps some gangsters had blinded him.

Somehow, I imagine, his money had cost not only his eyes but also his dignity; that he had felt some shame for his past. Perhaps in years of bitterness he had come to reflect on the squalor of violence. On the savageness of man.

He was a man without a wife and children. The house and grounds, in our town, must have been worth $60 or $70 thousand at the time—hardly an estate, but evidence of respectable fortune. He and his sister lived reclusively so far as we could tell. Why had they moved here, and when? Where was romance in his life? Had he lost a woman? What was his sister's story?

Perhaps they traveled regularly to Europe. He must have books in Braille, but otherwise little business in his day, little to amuse him. There he sits, listening to the radio, or to the phonograph. Perhaps he listens to recorded plays. Perhaps his sister reads to him.

For myself, I am troubled by the ugliness. Not the ugliness of his sightless gaze or searching touch; not the violence he had caused and suffered; not his adult pathos and mystery, all of which he exposed to us in his need. But by my own ugliness of submitting there to the oddness so that I could get my candy bar and escape.

⟨∞⟩

"You are good children," he repeats. "Here is a candy bar for each of you." He gropes back into the hall. The sister has vanished. There is some sort of basket, and he offers me my choice. A Hershey's? Or a Clark Bar? Or a Mounds? I ask for the Clark. Dale takes a Hershey's. "Wait," he says, "you're such good kids. I can tell. Let me give you each two."

He does, both Hershey's this time.

"Now you come again. Come back again!" he says, shaking our hands. Patting our shoulders. Then releasing us with a wave and smile into nothingness.

"Come again."

We never do, or at least I don't, though I do tell some other kids. And later, other times, when my mother drives me on this street from school, or on our way to or from errands and shopping, I would see him sometimes from the car. He'd be out walking, with his cane, and wearing his dark glasses, his arm in his sister's, and the two wolfhounds straining on leashes. He would be dressed dapperly, scarf, cap, overcoat.

Subversions

My nephew, John Friedericy, a painter and sculptor, attempted a correspondence with me as his uncle, the writer, in the late 1970's. "I have just realized that you and I are in the same business," he wrote, "making art." Among the color slides he sent of his paintings was a self-portrait with my father, John Henry, his "grampa," for whom he was named. My mother and father had flown from Philadelphia to Los Angeles several times over the years to visit my older sister, Judy, and her family and my father had reveled in his grandfather role.

John's portrayal of my father suggests partly my sister's view of my father as a recovering alcoholic and as a candy manufacturer and partly John's conscious difference, in terms of parallel male identities, as an artist and as a homosexual.

At the viewer's right, my father sits in a throne-like wingback upholstered chair reminiscent of one from home. He is sixty-eight and obese, mostly bald, but with a thin, white crown of hair. He sits slope-shouldered, his belly rising as a flaccid gut, piled upon itself, hanging over his lap; his arms droop and hang like paws, with long-fingered, claw-like hands. He wears a collarless button sweater over a white button shirt and cowboy string tie. The right side of his face is in shadow, the right eye piercing and stern, mouth tight, cheek tense, while the left side, like a quarter moon, is brightly lit, relaxed and oddly wondering and innocent. He is the father that my sister called "the old monster"; he is also the predatory capitalist, his claw-like nails suggesting cartoon portrayals of robber barons. His weight seems the curse and prize of his very corruption, a self-burdening appetite. And above all, he sits impotent and fatigued.

John, at eighteen, sits beside him in the center of the painting, carefully imitating my father's posture, but sitting sideways on a spindle-backed chair, muscularly vibrant with youth, arm braced, rather than drooping, on his thigh. John is lean and long-necked, hair close-cropped and brown; his left eye is vigilant and wary, his right melancholy. The lines and rhythms of the two figures oddly cast the viewer's eye to the left third of the painting, where there is only empty space.

I did not know of John's homosexuality when I first saw this painting (he would die of AIDS at the age of thirty-four), but having struggled imaginatively with the figure of my father and my own relations with him throughout my life, I felt oddly jealous and usurped.

⟋⟋⟍⟍

I overheard no fights, ever, between my mother and father, though there were many teenage sulks, tantrums, and shouting matches between Judy, especially, and Dad, and Mom, and the rest of us (I was no angel); nor was there any sense of Dad and Mom ever sleeping together, sexually, at our St. David's house—of physical affection between them. My mother later denied this, but it was my perception then. They had separate single beds, twins, the master bedroom, and Mom complained that Dad's snoring was so loud that she had to move into the guest room to sleep. And his snoring was loud. We could hear it rooms away or when he was sleeping elsewhere, on the sun porch, or on the living room couch, or even nodding in his chair: it was as stentorian as his voice bellowing in righteous rage; his mouth would hang open slackly and he would breathe through his mouth; there was that rasping snort of intake, then wheeze out, the sound building through a series of breaths to a crescendo that we thought surely would wake him and maybe did a little, but then the snoring would subside back to its lowest pitch, only to build up again. If at first Mom moved "just to sleep," later the move proved permanent, with the guest room bathroom her bathroom, filled with all her feminine things—powders, bottles, lotions—and then the guest room closet and dresser holding most of her clothes.

⟋⟋⟍⟍

I am eleven, perhaps, when Mom asks me to rub BenGay on her back, which aches. She lies face down on the guest room's twin bed nearest the door, loosens her belt, blouse, waist of her skirt, baring the midsection of her back, and tells me to rub, so I put some ointment on her skin and start, shyly, not wanting to look and not liking the loose, mealy feel of her flesh. She tells me harder, more, and I feel queasy, and even angry, rubbing as high as under her brassiere strap and as low, at her insistence, as the top of her buttocks and buttocks crevice. I tell her I'm tired, I don't want to do anymore. And she says, please, just rub it in; that feels so good. And then, sensing my discomfort, says that's enough, asks me to cover the area with a towel (I have the memory still of gritty, blemished flesh, somehow unwholesome). Thank you, she says. Go on, I'm sorry I had to ask you, but there's no one else home to help.

I leave her, then, feeling guilty both for my refusal and for my disgust.

—◦◦◦—

Judy, six years older than I, and four and six younger than my brothers, Chuck and Jack, would make her mark during these years at The Baldwin School for Girls in Bryn Mawr—academically, in English; creatively in writing and in art; and athletically, after a try at lacrosse, in swimming, and in water ballet. Her social life involved some crushes, few dates, and centered mainly on her Baldwin schoolmates, who shared in these activities, and in the summers, on the local swimming club's swim team, where she became a star, working tirelessly with an older coach, Jules Provost, who would later teach me Science at public school, and who served, according to Mom, as one of several "surrogate fathers" for her.

Judy wrote to Jack, shortly after he left in 1952, about Dad (she was in 11th grade): "I just picked up this letter again. It is now morning and I am determined to say everything I can possibly think of NOW and get it mailed. . . . This past weekend Mother and Daddy entertained some weekend guests, the Goodlaw's. It is the first time that Daddy has let himself or Mother entertain since Dee was born. The experience was good for him and a welcome break in routine for Mother. . . . Poor Daddy. I have gotten to the point where I have no feelings but pity and disgust for him. He must live the most unsatisfying empty life with no real interest beyond his own welfare. I used to think I really hated him, but he is so pathetically like a little child, weak, and helpless, that I couldn't hate him. It would be horrible to be a man physically, and practically a baby mentally. It sounds silly, but if you could see how he craves pampering, and nearly has a tantrum when things cross him, or how he frets and worries over every little thing . . . I really shouldn't be writing stuff like this. Quite unchristian and very childish. Nevertheless, I do feel this way about the old monster . . . I've often wondered if you really hated him. I think you did for he nearly ruined you. I, fortunately, missed almost all the sordidness. . . . Good lord, what a depressing subject to waste time writing about—Please excuse me—."

At Baldwin, they told Judy to work on her posture. She slouched, had curvature of the spine, and needed to improve her walk. She was to balance a book on top of her head, and of course, we all joined in to imitate her, as she practiced walking, sitting, and rising, all with a volume of the Britannica on her head. Judy's favorite thinking place was the Walton Estate, where she would go alone or sometimes take me, out through a path in the dense woods behind our back neighbors' houses. By this path, which I retraced with my school friend John, often, when he visited, Walton's was ten minutes or so away—you waded and pushed through overgrown bushes, ferns, and hanging branches, with dankness, cobwebs, and with shade from the branches interlocking and arching above, while woodpeckers hammered, echoing, and cicadas whirred. You'd come out, then, following a creek, above the smaller of two ponds, set in the estate's open expanse of lawn, gardens, driveways and walks. A big white house, lived in, was to the left, far off was the gatehouse and wall, and far to your right, the castlelike main mansion, deserted now. Judy's spot was at the spillway from the upper, main pond where a picturesque waterwheel was attached to a stone cottage, a mill, actually, with a wooden door and tilting tile roof, and inside, through a mesh of antique gears, a millstone crunching round and round on a pedestal. Though miniature, the waterwheel and mill were "out of a story book," an illustration brought to life, say, from the Brothers Grimm, and all the more appealing for being deserted and in disrepair. There were flat boulders to sit on, where water poured and splattered over the wheel, the wheel creaked, turning, and a channel began that fed into the lower, smaller pond, across the road. When we couldn't find Judy at home, usually she'd be here, writing in her notebooks or diary or drawing sketch after sketch. Mom would sometimes drive here searching for her.

We shared a bathroom, with one door opening in from the backstairs landing where the door to my room was, and the other door, with a full-length mirror on her side, opening in from her room. The main door to her room opened in from the second floor hall. The connection of our rooms, and their isolation, in a way, from the front of the house, separated us both from Mom and Dad and from the boys (when they were home) on the third floor. Judy had put toilet paper in the keyhole of her hallway door, to discourage peeping, of which she told me later, both Jack and Chuck were guilty.

Our bathroom was yellow; Dad's was blue, Mom's pink. Judy left hairpins all over, and had a habit, too, of cutting her hair over the toilet, so there would be strands and snips of hair everywhere. She took bubble baths. Once she left her diary on a shelf by the tub and I looked through it, but when I teased her about Tom Eglin, or someone she had written about, she was deeply hurt that I invaded her privacy and made me swear never to look in it again, even if I happened to find it. We would play on her bed, rocking cat's cradle, back and forth, or scratch each other's backs.

She had her wisdom teeth out and swelled up horribly and was bedridden for a week with ice packs on her head. Her mouth was bruised where they had clamped it open.

She had a reputation for eating leftovers off our plates, so a legendary joke has me walking into the kitchen, stamping on her foot, as if it were the lever for a garbage can, and when she opened her mouth to yell, shoving in a leftover piece of chicken.

She dieted perpetually, worried that she was fat, especially in the caboose, and she sunbathed for hours, too, out on the patio, which I found mindless and boring. She would baste herself with lotion and just lie there, sleep, sometimes read.

⦿⦿⦿

Given the presence of my teenage sister and older brothers, I was remarkably unaware of sex in the house until I discovered it for myself. Vaguely, there was some teasing talk among Judy, Jack and Chuck ("Boy, I'm glad we don't get periods," Chuck once said and Judy blushed and threw something at him). Privacy was the rule; bathroom doors were closed. My first glimpse of adult nudity was changing into swimsuits with Dad and Chuck, or later, at Martin's Dam, the local swimming club, in the men's lockers with other grown men. I was uneasy and shocked at the size of their genitals and overall hairiness, but that was about all. Information about and interest in sex came from outside home, from friends at school. We heard about fucking early on as something dirty and revolting that older kids did, and made no connection between that and having babies. My friend John Barnett as early as second or third grade played an undressing game with a girl who lived up the driveway from his house on the farm, where his father was a dairyman. He told us (this was third grade) that girls looked "like this," and drew a circle with a line down the center, which looked like a rearend if anything, and Kit Wilkes agreed, his sister looked like that. And then Susan Epps, according to Kit, had shown him *hers* during rest period (we were eight). Kit and she had spread out their blankets in the cloak closet, which had accordion doors that closed, and she had told him she had a bad bruise on her leg, high up, and he'd asked to see it and she'd shown him. So the question became, whether, if we asked nicely, "Can we see your bruise during rest period?" she would consent to show John and me as well. She did, half-heartedly, and we went into the closet, but then she changed her mind. We never saw it.

As for John, he continued to play with the girl up the driveway on the farm, in her house, in her room and in the attic, and she regularly showed him hers, and wanted to see his, and then one day, playing Mommy and Daddy, she asked him to put his in hers, and he did, and he *peed* inside, he told us, giggling, like this was a big joke. We never got to see her ourselves; like Susan Epps, she was shy of newcomers. (A year or two later, John's mother caught him doing it with her in their attic, beat the bejesus out of him, and forbade him ever to play with her again.)

I had been going to John's, as his best friend, for afternoons to play at the farm long before Kit joined us as a third friend—Kit's father had just been promoted at Sealtest and with their new affluence the Wilkes' had moved to a new house and big yard out Church Road, near John's farm. It was Kit who instigated our own "show me" games; he, John and I, with some giddiness of the forbidden, the idea that nudity itself was forbidden, mysterious and private, and with only the vaguest idea of sex, would pull down our pants, one at a time, to show our rear ends to the others. The main place for this was the hayloft in the dairy barn, where we built a secret fort or clubhouse with bails of straw. We lost interest after the first few times, or maybe John became more preoccupied with the girl up the road, but also Kit stopped visiting. His parents didn't like him coming home smelly and dirty, and he didn't really share John's and my pleasure in the fields and woods; there was also the class issue. I was socially acceptable as a playmate, pretty much (though the Wilkes' were too young and society-oriented to feel at ease with Mom and Dad), but John was impossible.

Also at John's, though forbidden by his parents, we hid in the hayloft and peeked out louvers in the cupola at the bull, with his flopping pink penis and huge balls, mounting abjectly passive cows that had been herded into the breeding pen with him. The cows had large, grayish folded vaginas— we probably called them "cracks," because I lacked the proper word until much later—where they appeared both to piss in gushing streams and to drop their cow pies, too. I failed to see an analogy to humans and did not understand John's excitement, except for our not being supposed to see this.

Any connection between fucking and babies came much later for me, in fifth grade, when I was walking the mile home from school with another friend, who said that he heard that fucking was how you made babies. I refused to believe him, naw, you got babies by "loving each other and being together," that's what my mother had told me, and, some other time when

I'd asked, she had begged the question and told me what it felt like for a woman to deliver a baby: "like you're trying to make a job, a big job, and you have to bear down." My notion was that having babies had something to do with kissing hard and a lot and some mysterious process, like osmosis, which happened when a man and woman were together for extended periods of time.

Troubled by my friend's assertion, I asked Mom again.

We were in her bedroom, and she took me into the bathroom and shut the door, in order to talk seriously and privately. To my muted horror, essentially she said yes, that what Dale had said was how it happened, that "fucking," which was not a nice word for it, was how the man's seed got inside the woman and fertilized her egg; and, yes, that was what she and Daddy did, to have each of us.

But fucking was such a dirty and disgusting thing, I said: "People must really love each other, to be willing to do *that*."

Mom said, yes, but that it really wasn't all that unpleasant.

⸺⊗⊗⊗⸺

One weekend, when Dad took Mom, Judy and me to a business convention at Buck Hill Falls, Chuck had a party in the basement playroom at home, evidence of which Mom and Dad found everywhere on return, beer cans, garbage, cigarettes, and probably a bleary-eyed and hung over Chuck. They were furious at him for not asking permission and for letting things get so far out of control. The neighbors had complained, Dad learned, and the police had come. Chuck was forbidden to have another party at home for some time.

Nonetheless, the playroom became his special project. He rehabbed the bar, scrubbing, sanding, staining and waxing the wood. He polished its brass rail. From behind the bar, over the sink, he took apart a sixteen-inch web speaker, the "best" in its day, which had been built into the wall; he patched a hole in its paper cone and with great satisfaction hooked it up successfully to his forty-five record player. His favorite party records, besides Doris Day, were Glenn Miller, Benny Goodman, Spike Jones and the Firehouse Five, Tex Ritter; but he also pioneered, where Henry tastes were concerned, a passion for the classics, especially once he'd gotten a new turntable and patched together a real hi-fi for the newly developed 33 and 1/3 "LP"s. He would listen loudly and raptly to Beethoven, Rachmaninoff and Tchaikovsky, urging our appreciation. For Christmas at some point he tried to involve Jack, who shied away, thank you, by giving him an LP, *Classical Music for People Who Can't Stand Classical Music* by the Boston Pops.

Chuck was also instigator, with Mom, of our mural project in the playroom. On either side of the window well, where we kept our eight-inch TV, matching leopard skins from Bloomingdale had been hung; these came down, all the walls were painted mint green, and in keeping with other nautical touches (the wall fixtures were brass sailing ships holding pretend candles), we sketched and painted undersea murals, using gray, maroon, white, and some touches of black paint.

Mom and Judy took the largest wall, beside the fireplace, painting a gray undersea centaur figure, with flippers instead of hooves, a muscular horse body, and an equally muscular man's torso, with red hair and flippers for hands. He was accompanied by naked red mermaids and their cupidlike babies. The females had legs that became serpentine only at the knee and ended in fins, so one, swimming down, had naked buttocks, as well as breasts; and the other, lolling back with hands behind her head, had breasts with nipples outlined in white, and a suggestive, though hairless, crotch. One of the babies, imitating its father, rode a serpent. On the near side of the adjoining wall, before it was broken by the windowwell, Chuck painted a seagriffin, with horns, a dog snout, duck feet, and a fish tail; then on the far side, Judy painted an even more sexual maroon mermaid, fish from the hips down, but with large, nippled breasts and long, sweeping hair. All of this was permitted as "art," and out there, as it were, for prurient perusal, which it surely got, from me, Dad, and my friends; we were all coyly proud of it, both as evidence of family talent and, somehow, of our liberation and daring. My own contribution, on the remaining bit of wall, towards the stairs, was a Donald Duck.

—∞∞∞—

After fifth and sixth grades, in the summers, I went for two weeks to a Boy Scout camp, somewhere west of Paoli. All the Troops belonging to the Valley Forge Council joined us there. We had cabins with double bunks built in and tarps that rolled up for ventilation. The dining hall was up the hill, where exhaust fans beat in the walls and we sang "Mrs. Murphy's Chowder." An infirmary was across the lake. I bought a stool weaving kit at the camp store and made a stool for Mom. We had casting lessons and contests. Other memories: an open "church" area surrounded by rocks, where we held nonsectarian meetings on Sunday; the swimming area; fog off the lake at dawn, when reveille would be blown; the mysterious "Flaming Arrow" ceremony, which frightened me. Everybody lined up, as for inspection, or Taps, at attention in front of their cabins, making a big circle in the dark. Then, across the lake, we'd see a torch bobbing, which was somebody running; there'd be a long, uneasy wait as he disappeared and was going around the lake, across the bridge at the far neck, and up the trail on our side where we couldn't see, and then he came, sweaty, panting, naked except for a loin cloth, face and body done up in war paint, and the torch hissing as he ran with it over his head, rippling and hissing with a whoosh as he ran past, moccasins going slap slap, and ran around the circle, inside, to our faces. We were supposed to keep looking straight ahead. Then without warning he would stop and hit somebody—one of the older scouts, usually—in the chest, knocking him backwards; there would be a scuffle, and then he'd run on, and stop and hit again, tapping the candidates indicated by the brothers in each troop, and secretly elected by them. The boys tapped would disappear for three days, and when they returned, were sworn to silence for a day, and never told what rites they went through, but now they were official "flaming arrows," and wore a red sash that said so. John became a "flaming arrow" the summer after sixth grade.

By then John was more distant from me as a friend, and he had distinguished himself both for his woodcraft and physical strength among the scouts; he had passed Star and was on his way to earning Life rank (he would later earn Eagle as well as serving as a patrol leader). This year at camp he had grown notorious for being able to get an enormous, adult hardon, which at the time none of us had seen, let alone discovered on ourselves. Word went out one day that he was getting one in his bunk and you gotta come see this. And half in embarrassment, half in pride, giggling, lying in an upper bunk, with a crowd of boys watching, he had a shockingly big one, big as a man's, and said if he kept working on it he could get it shoot jit (his word). The tone of the whole demonstration was like a circus act, a curiosity, not anything dirty or perverse, except that we didn't want the counselors to find out. Actually someone said the only other guy in the troop who could get one up that big was our older Explorer Scout counselor, Boris. John was respected for this ability, and wondered at, as if he had crossed some pale beyond us.

Christmas vacation, 1954, the night before Judy announced her engagement to Hans Friedericy, whom she'd met at Swarthmore College and who was sleeping in the guest room down our hall (and, I realize now, also she was pregnant, with her heart full of complex emotions), I had worked up my courage to ask to see her naked. She was nineteen, soon to turn twenty, and I was thirteen.

Before this time, before she left for college, her grown-up woman's body increasingly fascinated me as mysterious, beautiful, and more important than those of girls my age. We shared the bathroom. She sunbathed at home; and at Martin's with the bathing suits, my friends and I were always trying to look down the tops of suits, hoping one would slip down with a dive, or imagining what if we could climb a tree, or sneak on the changing room roof and peek in through the skylight. At home, I had noted paintings in Mom's art books. Judy, of course, always locked the bathroom door, but after a bath or shower she would unlock it then go into her room to dress; and, seemingly innocent a few times, I had tried to time her actions, then barge in when I knew she was still naked, and she had shrieked, angry, clutching a towel or dress in front of her, "Get out!"

But here she was now, gone to college, leaving, my beautiful sister, whom I had missed, and I felt it was abnormal, and a failing or handicap somehow that I had never seen a woman naked, and that included little girls and even babies.

⟨⟨⟨⟩⟩⟩

I knocked on her door from the bathroom and heard her call, "Come in."

I opened the door a crack.

"Come on in, silly. Come in." She was lying on her bed, dressed, reading a book. We'd all gone to bed; I was in pajamas. "Come sit down here beside me. Now what's wrong? You're acting so funny."

"Nothing," I said. I was embarrassed and grave, sorry to have come.

"You can't fool me."

"All right. I have a problem."

She watched me intently, melting into all consideration and kindness when she saw how serious I was, and I felt hot, my heart thudding.

"It's about sex," I said, my voice cracking.

My hands were trembling and I tried to make them stop, but I was trembling all over.

"All right. Is there anything I can do to help? What do you want to know?"

I asked her what "coition" was, and "climax," and she did her best, clinically, to explain, all adult, wise and knowing. Then I couldn't say it. My eyes filled with tears and I tried to whisper, but my mouth was dry and my heart plunged:

"I've never seen a woman without her clothes on—I wanted to ask you to let me see you."

She frowned, and I felt as if I had thrown myself off a cliff, was still falling.

"No, I don't think that would be a good idea," she said, but I was looking at the floor, overcome with having it settled, over. "Why, you're shivering! Don't be afraid!"

"I knew it was wrong," I blurted. "I'm sorry."

"You wouldn't look in keyholes like your brothers. You wouldn't sneak. You came and asked me honestly and I respect you for it," she said.

I wanted to get away and leave it settled. I didn't care anymore.

I said good night and left her and went to bed, at peace, glad for what I had done, that I had failed. I lay in the dark, everything forgotten, almost asleep, when the bathroom light came on and I heard a sound and I knew Judy must be coming. But I wasn't sure; then it really was her and she came in and whispered, "Dee?" She sat beside my head on the edge of my bed, beside my pillow, and reached out and touched my brow and swept my hair. I looked up at the darkness of her and waited.

"I've been thinking," she said. "Will it really help, do you really think it will help you to see me in the nude?"

My heart beat, but I blinked and stammered, "Yes."

"Well, turn on your light," she said calmly.

I could hardly move, but I reached and turned on the light beside my bed. I looked back up and saw her smiling. She stood up smiling, kindly and serious. She wore red silk pajamas, and in silence, she reached to her throat, undid the first button, and slowly the next, and I began to see the looseness and swell of her breasts, and the next, and then she took off the red silk jacket, and I stared, my eyes fixed on her breasts and nipples (the size of female nipples I had never imagined), and I could feel my eyes straining larger and I struggled to keep calm and to look at her so I would never forget what I was seeing. And while I stared at her breasts, she unsnapped the pajama bottoms and they fell from her and she stepped out of them and she was naked. I was shocked by the sight, because I had never imagined it. And she stood watching me, kindly, patient.

"Have you seen enough?" she asked, after seconds had passed.

"Can I see your vaginnia?" I asked.

"Vagina," she said, and put one foot up on the bed to part with her fingers the hair and discolored fold, showing me more than I had understanding to see, really.

She dressed again, then, and I was calm too. We had been through something together. My heart burst with gratitude and wonder, and she came back to sit on my bed. I reached my arms around her warm neck and she held me, while I sobbed with my face hidden in her hair, and she held me.

"Good night, now," she said. "I'll see you in the morning."

"Good night. Thank you."

She was gone; I turned off the light and lay back looking up into the darkness. Something had broken in me, and I was grateful to her, loved her.

But then the guilt of our encounter intensified, when, next morning, I felt a little scared of facing her first thing, and as I came downstairs, Mom met and told me to come into the sun porch, where Judy and Hans had something to tell us all, which proved to be the engagement announcement.

That night, helplessly, knowing I shouldn't, but needing to, I went back in and asked to see her again, but she said no. That wouldn't be a good idea. She said that she had talked to Hans about it, and he had said it really was not a healthy thing for me at my age.

—⊷∞⊶—

From then on I struggled to remember, to recapture, to find pictures to approximate what Judy looked like, the first of which was a postage stamp sized ad in *American Artist*, with a woman artist painting a nude female model, and this was a photograph, I told myself, with the added shock of the real, and the model had large nipples like Judy, though the picture was so small and the dot pattern so coarse that they were difficult to see for sure. I was studying this picture in bed one night, later that spring, and trying to imagine intercourse, what it might feel like; it occurred to me to make a ring of my thumb and forefinger and push my stiffened penis through it—maybe intercourse felt something like this—when something awful happened, something like throwing up or diarrhea, where the body convulsed beyond control, a hot flash like that, too frightening for pleasure, and my penis spilled some sticky, thick liquid, which wasn't urine, and which I felt, watched, and then examined with horror. I had harmed myself somehow. Mom had warned me about wet dreams, in the vaguest of terms, and in eighth grade they had shown us a human reproduction film, all diagrams and cartoon drawings, that depicted the event as something that happened to boys my age, just as menstruation happened to girls, and not to worry about it, and there had been John's demonstrations at Camp Delmont, but I made no connection. I was afraid I might not be able to pee again, or that I had become infected.

My impulse on all bodily matters was to run and tell Mom, but I didn't this time. I waited, sickened, instead, to discover that I was all right the following morning; and then, of course, to experiment again, once my fear of consequences passed, though experiment and my other excuse of maybe making my penis larger and longer by exercise soon gave way to the mixed need for and struggle against this new pleasure, as something shameful, sinful, and addictive, all signs of which I had to hide.

—⊗⊗⊗—

"Don't you ever talk back to your mother!" Dad fulminates, no room for protest, and I am silenced, hot-faced.

He does and will endure our teen-age sarcasm towards him, but at the slightest sign of disrespect to Mom, who might defend us otherwise, his full anger is sanctioned. She is "sainted Mom," by contract, almost; it is on her command that he allows, against his own judgment and grain, all sorts of liberties, including disrespect of him.

—⊗⊗⊗—

"What's that, the salt over there?" Dad would ask.

"Yup. That's salt. Would you like me to pass it?"

"What's that, salt over there?"

Dad would never ask directly, please pass anything, gravy, butter, salt, rolls, but always, and deliberately, asked what the thing was until we had to pass it to him. This was his special mockery of manners, but it would not work in reverse.

"What's that, the butter?" I would ask him.

"Umhm, that's the butter." He would smile, and he would not pass it until I asked, "Pass the butter, please?"

The centerpiece and candlesticks were between him and Mom, each sitting in the chairs with arms at opposite ends of the table, and they would have to lean to look and speak around them. Dad, however, at table rarely spoke.

He never excused himself, but got up when he felt like it, and left his napkin in a heap beside his plate. He put his elbows on the table, too, when he felt like it. Corn on the cob he ate like a typewriter carriage, buttering the whole, then tucking his napkin in his collar (to protect the silk ties that Mom regularly had to have dry cleaned) and gnawing across, row after row, then wiping his face and picking his teeth afterwards. He slurped his coffee, always, one eye squinting, the other open wide, eyebrow raised, and his pinky out as he held the cup.

After dinner, after dessert, after the coffee and the cigarette or two, which launched his red-faced coughing fits, after the dishes were washed, he might return noiselessly to the kitchen; there might be the tell-tale ring of the dome on the cake dish (quickly smothered) or the muffled whump of the refrigerator. Other times we would simply discover half a cake missing, or others, brazenly, proudly, Dad would enter with his "snack" to join us watching TV: a ham-and-Swiss sandwich, say.

"I never want to be like Dad," I told Mom, as she drove me home from school or shopping; we were in the Buick, rounding a curve down towards the St. David's Road intersection with the Pike. "But one good thing is I know I'll be a good father. Because I'll know how not to be."

"You should never say that," she admonished, though I could tell she agreed, and in a funny way was pleased by what I said.

Fall, 1955, Judy, at twenty, married with Hans and keeping their Harrisburg apartment, and still using Chuck's car, had her baby, John Christian Friedericy. Her pregnancy over the summer had fascinated me. Now there was a baby and Mom, Dad and I would drive the hour on the turnpike to visit.

Children to Mom were sacred and she spoke rhapsodically of childbearing, her own role in creating and in nurturing life. Through this sentiment, as well as through my own brother love, I viewed Judy's pregnancy as a family miracle. So much was centered on it. I was taking pictures, John as my model, with Mom and Judy overly appreciative of the results. John barely sitting up with a cap on his head, big smile. John in a bouncing sling chair. John, after they had moved from their apartment into a trailer in Harrisburg, smoking

Hans's pipe upside down as he tottered in an outside crib. John in Dad's lap, held at arm's length while Dad mugged at him.

Dad was in his way as excited about John as Mom was in hers; for him, I think, this was proof of redemption, proof of life going on, with the next generation the start of a new role for him as grandfather, a role where he would bear no guilt or resentment.

My parents moved to their retirement home, in Villanova, in 1965, after I had finished college. During my visits, after the preliminaries of how my life was going, graduate school, teaching, writing, my car, health, bank account and taxes, Dad would retire to his chair in the corner of the living room, the same wing-backed chair in which John would later imagine and paint him. This was his place of state. Often he fell asleep here, sitting up. He worked here too at business letters, and at planning his finances, filling page after page of yellow tablets. A time of peak pressure for him was the selling of the family's candy factory, and his planning of how the death of my grandmothers would add to his and Mom's estates, providing enough income from investments for a comfortable living. But his favorite preoccupation in this chair was to rehearse the situation of each of his four children, and of each of their children, their problems, and inevitably, their successes, their happiness. He gloated, given the near-disaster of his alcoholism, at how well things had turned out.

Jack had his construction business in Colorado, had married June and adopted June's children, Larry, Terry, Dale; Chuck had his medical practice in New Jersey, had married Nancy and fathered three boys, Chucky, Bobby, Scott; in Hans, Judy had found a loving and practical provider, a stress engineer who progressed in career from building bridges in Harrisburg to teaching engineering at the University of Virginia to working for McDonnell Douglas in Los Angeles and, later, Tucson. Judy's children were busy and doing well, Johnny, Lucia, Bonnie. Dee and, well, who knew, until Connie; he'd done well at Amherst, gone on the Harvard, switched from Harvard to the Writers' Workshop at Iowa, then back to Harvard; he had his studies, his teaching, his writing. Each had troubles, but each was sound and steadfast. When I was home, he would rehearse this litany with me, leaving me for last.

He died unexpectedly in 1976, still dreaming our lives. No flaws, no weaknesses; he believed that we had all proven to be equal to life, a credit to our mother and her gifts, but a credit to him also, and to his recovery and unswerving devotion to family. By then I, too, had married, though thanks to an unforeseen depression in the Humanities, I would not find a full-time teaching job until 1984. Dad had advanced us money "on my inheritance," and Connie, my wife, was just managing to support us with a day care job, while I taught composition part-time, worked on my first novel, and volunteered my time in starting up a non-profit literary magazine, *Ploughshares*. We were subsisting at the poverty line. Nevertheless my marriage itself came as a relief to Dad, proof that I was no longer sowing wild oats and living "just for myself." He and Mom came to visit: "Don't worry about jobs," he assured me. "Persevere. You'll make it."

⁂

Several times, in worrying about my reluctance to settle down, Dad had warned me: "Just two things about your mother. Don't expect a woman to be like her, because nobody can live up to her. She's a truly remarkable woman. Whoever you marry, don't measure your wife by her." And the second thing: "Your mother is a wonderful person, but you have to cut the apron strings. I'm telling you for your own good. She won't mean to hold on, but you can't let her, either."

Still later, after I had married, Dad returned again to the theme of Jack's life, emphasizing with satisfaction that time heals all wounds, between both man and wife, and father and son. Jack, as the eldest, had experienced Dad's illness at its worst. I knew from Jack's accounts and from Mom's of these years that at the age of sixteen he had assumed the role of rescuer, that at one point, in order to protect Mom from Dad's drunken rage, he had even threatened Dad with a loaded squirrel rifle, and had been ready to shoot, if Dad hadn't backed away and left. That, for years to follow, Jack had felt the obligation not only of "being there" for Mom, but also of serving as a substitute father for Judy and especially for me.

Now, Dad was telling me, as if by recounting the story of Jack's release, he was hoping to free me, too, from any worries about him and Mom; that on the night before Jack's wedding in 1961, Jack had been out with the boys and come back to the motel where he was staying with Mom and Dad. That Mom and Dad had been sleeping in the same bed, in each other's arms, and that their rooms had been adjoining or connected somehow, so that Jack had to tiptoe past them in order to get to his own bed. That Dad had been awake, but had pretended not to be. That Jack had stood at the foot of their bed shaking his head, "Well, I'll be damned," he'd repeated, "I'll be damned."

⎯⎯⎯⎯

Was John Friedericy damned or freed, I wonder now?

During John's childhood, I felt some rivalry. He had replaced me as the focus of Judy's nurturing love and attention. Also Hans and Judy proudly presented him to my parents as the genius, the prodigy that we each had aspired to be. Even Mom, I felt, turned her foremost dreams from my promise as an artist to John's.

John had picked up painting at the age of five from Judy, who imitated Mom in working with oils. She did a child portrait of John. They painted side by side for a while; then John refused to do more, intimidated by or jealous of Judy's adult talent. A local teacher was so impressed by the drawing and painting that John had done that Judy made a choice, then, to stop painting herself so that John would feel no competition and would go ahead to work freely, which he did. He started attending adult sketching sessions at the University of Virginia while he was still in elementary school and sold his first painting, a floral still life, at age nine. When I visited, in the summers of 1964 and 1965, his sisters tiptoed around him while he painted, read alone, or practiced the violin, and they deferred to his imagination in their play. They had a whole room for play on the first floor, where they had painted splashy murals, and where they dressed up in costumes and performed plays, and where John had made a puppet theater and they put on puppet shows.

Without my saying anything negative, Hans let me know that he supported John's violin playing, that that was okay, not "sissyish," and that this was a cultured, European broad-mindedness contrary to the Huck Finn style boys' lives made legendary by my brothers. It was okay not to be athletic, okay to be sensitive, in love with reading and with stories, to play chess, and to practice violin rather than, say, trumpet, drums or sax. They had turned their rambling house into a hermetic arts colony, removed from the conventional world, and protected from it by Hans's wage earning.

At the time, I felt that Hans and Judy over-insisted on John's genius because of their mutual need to believe that they were themselves exceptional. After they moved to California, Judy kept Mom posted on John's progress, and Mom would share the letters with me. John graduated from Palos Verdes high school with honors in 1973, continued his education in fine arts back at the University of Virginia, where he earned an AA in 1975. When he was sixteen, in an effort to build common ground, I published a portfolio of his pen-and-ink drawings in my literary magazine, *Ploughshares*, including an image of a young man weeping in the arms of a stronger, older man that I took to be a tableau of father and son. He earned his BFA at Otis Arts Institute in 1976 and a number of gallery exhibitions of his work soon followed, the newspaper reviews of which Judy forwarded. Mom treasured little soap sculptures he had done on visits to Philadelphia of Indonesian dancers entwined with snakes, as well as some mannered watercolors of ships mired in sand.

Dad's was his first, felt death, and from that point on his paintings became preoccupied with images of death. Before, in the dated slides he sent me, he had painted academic, sexual nudes, female and male, reminiscent of Gauguin; one painting, especially poignant to me now, is of the exterior of their Tucson house, and in the upstairs is the face of an imprisoned, teenaged John.

I could not then, and cannot now, imagine John's sexual awakening, except that it was kept secret from us, and apparently from Hans, who had his own secrets and subversions. At the time, I assumed from John's clinically detailed paintings and sculptures, that he had had, in Hans's European, hedonistic manner, his experience of women. He painted his sisters, as well, in elegant Renaissance costumes and postures, like princesses.

If Mom knew or suspected that John was gay, she never shared that confidence with me. She loved his work, nearly all of it, but pointedly did not like his posthumous portraits of Dad.

She died, after nine months' struggle with heart failure, in the fall of 1985. A few months later, Hans staggered Judy with his surprise determination for divorce, forcing her to start over at the age of fifty-two. This was followed by the news, in course of a phone call, when I suggested that she travel east, and that maybe John could travel with her and something about his having a girl, or someday getting married, that: didn't I know, John was gay? That that was news that Hans had been unable to take.

In 1987, I saw John and his work in San Francisco and met Bruce, his friend and lover since teenage years, with whom he then lived, sharing a house on Divisadero Street. Then he learned a few months later that they both had AIDS.

He felt deserted and failed by his father, I know, and Judy related to me one of John's typically wry accounts about Hans making the gesture of visiting him and Bruce, of Hans trying to explain and justify himself to John, when John asked how he could leave Judy for a younger mistress ("Mom, she's just a bimbo!") and how he could turn his back on them all as a family. Hans's answer was: "I don't know, son. I can't explain. It's just something physical." A similar answer might have served for my father, at the point when he was still drinking and had determined to leave the family.

In those last years, as his illness worsened, John became more productive than ever, painting and sculpting his best work. He returned to the image of the older and younger man embracing with a lived sense of tragedy, no longer (if ever) father and son so much as fatherly, protective and commiserating lover and broken, grieving lover.

I am confused by these connections. I can't entirely grasp what John sought and found in Dad, as Grampa. My guess, though, is that in Dad he imagined destructive passion in the ordinary life, unredeemed by artistic talent, the revenging Mr. Hyde against all social rectitudes, especially against those enforced by women. By contrast, in himself, he imagined the daemonic side as redeemed by art, rather than by life. Something like that.

I grieve my nephew. I never knew him well enough. I am proud of his art and of the spirit, familial and original, that speaks so richly through it. His wish for us all is expressed plainly by the painting one first sees now in entering my sister's home. Entitled, "To my family, Easter 1980," it shows a skull on a plate, and from the eyes, nose hole, and mouth, grow a profusion of lovely flowers.

Arrivals

My ambivalence about having children was instructed in some way by my mother, who had sacrificed worldly talent and what she referred to as "self" for her children's sakes—and whose frustration we children felt as deeply as we felt her love. My father's instruction had to do with providing. Your first responsibility was to family, to earn a living to protect and empower them, regardless of whether the act of earning was anything you liked or wanted to do. A *man* provided.

Born in 1941, I grew up in a conservative suburb west of Philadelphia romanticizing children. My sister was first in our family to marry, first to have a child (in fact she had been pregnant before deciding to marry). Later, my ex-steady high school girlfriend, separated from her college husband, had her baby, which could have been my baby, I felt, home with her. I wanted to be a father, as a visceral act of adulthood. At the same time, the same girl in an early false alarm with me, had had me staring at the prospect of missing or delaying college if we had to get married; and once I was in college—Amherst College in far off Massachusetts—and discovering myself apart from home and family, all my efforts were directed at having sex without having babies.

After college, as I went on to graduate school at Harvard, then at the Iowa Writers' Workshop, then back to Harvard, accumulating draft deferments until I reached the draft-free age of twenty-six, I was attracted to pleasure-seeking, adventurous women, who did not want marriage and babies, at least with me. I thought such women would increase my experience and understanding of life. I still did not want to get trapped.

By the time I met Connie Sherbill, I was worn out from serial, casual relationships, and I knew that I needed permanence. At one point, when pulling the spread up over my bachelor pillows, I wept at the thought of the pillows being babies, which I was burying. I thought I knew myself at age 30, and that, having had my vanities chastised, I had learned to value the goodness of a woman's heart.

Connie and I met at a Cambridge party, partly involving my writer friends, and partly, for Connie, Boston University students. She was from Miami, her parents recently divorced. We slept together on our second date, and she was over at my apartment when her older sister called—one of Connie's roommates had offered up my name or number—to tell her that their father had died. I drove her that night to her sister's apartment in Waltham. I had no idea where we were going, out streets and through towns strange to me. We arrived, and suddenly I found myself in the midst of Connie's family, her sister, her sister's husband and baby, her sister's in-laws, and her older brother, too, who happened to be visiting. I didn't shy away. They greeted me as Connie's young man, allowing for my goyishness; and putting on my best behavior, I did my best to share in their love, and their loss.

Connie had just graduated from Boston University and found work as a Headstart teacher in Allston-Brighton. She loved children. She had a strong, Jewish sense of family. She was funny. She was sexy and beautiful, in an openhearted, wholesome way. She loved and wrote poetry, but she had majored in art history, and mainly wanted to draw and to paint. After the break-up of the apartment where she had been living with four other B.U. students, she took a room in Cambridge for appearances, but essentially moved in with me. Later my parents would visit Cambridge and would meet and welcome Connie as a girl I was "serious about," but with no idea that we were living together; on Connie's side, however, her mother and family had no problem with our arrangement, but later as we visited and met her various relatives around New Jersey, we were gravely lectured by one of her uncles to consider our status as a mixed couple, Jewish and Goyish. "You are nothing," he pronounced. "Neither one nor the other."

On finishing my Ph.D., the winter of 1970, I felt cheated to discover that there were no jobs in the Humanities. I had volunteered with a group of local writers to start a literary magazine, *Ploughshares*, while I was lucky to find even part-time teaching at Simmons and Harvard.

Before long, rent increases for my Central Square apartment forced Connie and me to look for a new apartment, which, thanks to Connie, we found in East Cambridge, a third-story walk-up, where we would live for most of our first, childless five years together.

The move was an agony for me, books boxed, furniture disassembled, two or three entrepreneurial students who called themselves Turtle Movers doing our heavy loading and unloading. I would have the second bedroom as my study; Connie would take a third, back bedroom for her studio. We were married in 1973, and continued to live there in the midst of Cambridge's sexy, rowdy singles' culture, until the summer of 1976. Connie was the breadwinner. I stayed home to correct papers, prepare classes, and to work on *Ploughshares* or on the novel that I thought would be my key to a full-time job and a stable future. She was working from early morning until six at the Headstart classroom.

On either side of actual marriage, sex for us there became strained. Connie seemed on edge—before marriage because we weren't married, and after marriage because we put off having children. I kept, always, a distance between us, as a form of self-defense. I had to keep free, I thought, for my writing.

At the same time, I had the sense that my "life" was an adventure for her, and that she shared in its excitements and promise. Besides writing my novel, that "life" was *Ploughshares.*

Shortly before meeting Connie, I had pledged myself to a partnership in starting up, editing, and administering *Ploughshares* with Peter O'Malley, a tall, black-haired Dubliner, who was a few years younger than I was. He and his older brother, on arriving in America, had invested some family money in an Irish-American corporation called Clonmacnoise, whose initial venture had been to convert a seedy corner bar one block down from my bachelor apartment into a stylish Irish pub, which they named The Plough and the Stars. They hoped the pub would serve as an artists' gathering place something like Dylan Thomas's famed White Horse Tavern in New York. Local counter-culture journalists, poets, and fiction writers hung out there, along with musicians, painters, and unabashed bar-flies, all of who, it seemed to me, were attracted by Peter O'Malley's flamboyance and charm as bartender. Ostensibly, in composing music scores, Peter aspired to models such as Lucas Foss and Gunter Schuller, was finishing his master's at Berklee College of Music, and insisted on playing classical music stations as background music for the bar. I had been drawn in, partly on recommendation of a woman I dated, who had also dated Peter, and partly in response to a poster in the window inviting submissions of poetry and fiction for a broadside. I left a story, and Peter told me some months later that he liked it, but that rather than publishing a broadside, the bar was now pondering whether to publish a magazine. He asked if I would like to work on such a venture. I said yes, I would, having run and edited the literary magazine for three undergraduate years at Amherst College. Peter convinced the bar to put up cash for the printing bill, and I put up my time and brains—though later, too, I put in $800 from my meager savings.

So began my literary life. A life of meeting, reading, socializing, and combating intellectually with the other young writers (all male, initially) who joined the original editorial board: George Kimball, Aram Saroyan, Bruce Bennett, William Corbett, among them. I brought my friends and heroes in as contributors, Richard Yates, say, Brian Moore, Andre Dubus. They brought theirs: Ted Berrigan, Fanny Howe, Anne Waldman, Sam Cornish, Russell Banks, Paul Metcalf. Peter had begun dating Ellen Wilbur, whom he married before I married Connie. Ellen was the daughter of Richard Wilbur, one of my poet heroes, and in addition to her own talent as a writer, she brought her family's standards to our task and reinforced Peter's commitment to the magazine. Before long, she joined our editorial board, and we would meet in Peter's and her apartment. Aside from editorial matters, there was also a life of business and legal worries for me that involved my substituting resourcefulness for resources. I chased around Cambridge, Boston, and the South End on production chores, getting type set, selling and getting copy for ads, and eventually pasting up pages and opaquing negatives at the printer's.

I needed Peter mainly as an icebreaker, an emotional prop, and a sounding board, though from the first I guarded myself against his seeming recklessness and his ready attendance on operators in the business world.

After the first two issues/years (we called the magazine an occasional of the arts), our new financial partners became federal and state arts agencies, to which we applied for small grants, and which both demanded public accountability. Peter's attitude was up the system; bluff your way through. After we triggered an audit by the National Endowment for the Arts concerning matching funds, where Peter could only plead loss of our check book and good-intentioned ineptitude, and we narrowly escaped having to return the grant funds, I demanded control over the checkbook if I were going to remain involved. Peter grudgingly conceded.

From then on, I did the grant writing and reporting, I policed the bank account, and I dealt with our pro-bono accountant, who was also accountant to the bar. Again, as granting agencies required us to incorporate as non-profit and to win tax-exempt status, after some failed attempts by Peter's lawyer friends, I ended up learning non-profit law, and with help from the agencies, wrote and won an appeal to Washington to reverse a turn-down by the IRS at the district level. This also entailed our surrender of private interest in *Ploughshares*, and the formation of a board of trustees, at least on paper, at whose pleasure Peter and I would serve as "co-directors." As for trustees, Peter and I agreed on Daniel Aaron from Harvard, Barry Spacks from M.I.T., and Bernard McCabe, Chairperson of English at Tufts, primarily friends of Peter's.

After five years, I felt that I had outgrown Peter. On my own, in 1975, I organized and incorporated a non-profit trade association for small presses and literary magazines, Book Affair. A poet we had published, Joan Norris, had been hired as public relations director of a local bookstore chain, Paperback Booksmith, and she offered to teach me p.r. and to persuade Booksmith to distribute *Ploughshares* chain-wide, thereby doubling our circulation. I directed Boston's first two small press book fairs, first at B.U., then at Harvard (where we had 200 exhibitors, and a three-day attendance of 10,000), having arranged sponsorship by the alternative weekly, *The Boston Phoenix*. In the grants world, a war between "populists" and "elitists" had broken out. For some years federal funds had been subgranted through The Coordinating Council of Literary Magazines in New York, which had 350 members ranging from the venerable *Paris Review* to the dada-mimeo rag *Strange Faeces*. Grants panelists were elected from this membership, most of which did not vote. As the "populists" began to campaign for slates to dominate the panels, I wrote to magazines I respected all over the country to campaign for panelists who would support "serious literature." I was elected to one panel, which met in Austin, Texas, and met my antagonists face to face. Eventually a "populist" slate prevailed and caused an outcry by giving an equal, small amount ($600) to every applicant. Polemics flew back and forth.

In addition to being a writer, I began to see myself as bound to the mission of reforming literary culture with *Ploughshares*. I would be an arts activist. I would organize a new literary community, a peoples' literary community, founded on real and engaged merit, rather than on fashion or commerce. I felt my mission with self-sacrificing fervor, a fervor guided and driven by my education.

For several years, Connie had given me the time and space to try my luck.

Not only was she bread winning, but she shared in all my efforts. She helped me with the backstage arrangements for fiction and poetry readings at Matt Talbot's, a South End bar newly opened by Clonmacnoise and managed by Peter. She carried boxes. She read manuscripts. She cheerfully sat at the sales tables at book fairs and other sorts of places. She had been the one, through a connection at Head Start, to discover the Massachusetts Council on the Arts. She slogged around on foot with me a day before the 1976 book fair, putting fliers on car windows in Harvard Square. When an issue was printed, she allowed ten or fifteen cartons of *Ploughshares* to be delivered and carried up for storage in our closet or foyer; then helped to carry cartons back down and rode shotgun while I double-parked to unload them at the Booksmith warehouse and at bookstores in Cambridge.

We socialized with Peter and Ellen. I met Tillie Olsen, who was in residence at M.I.T., and who came to our apartment for dinner, recognizing and praising Connie for her sacrifice and tenacity in both our marriage and our work on *Ploughshares*. James Alan McPherson visited us, hand delivering a story in manuscript. Robley Wilson stayed overnight. Elizabeth Bishop called me there several times. Sam Lawrence, the publisher, called, surprise, in the middle of one day, to say he'd liked the excerpt of my novel he'd read in the first *Ploughshares*, as well as the interview I'd done with Richard Yates in the third, and he would be happy to read my manuscript.

Connie's own life, apart from mine, centered on her Headstart job and on her friends there. One of these was an elderly man named Roland, who was owed favors by Boston political cronies, and who tried to get me hired by the state college system. She was also close to her younger brother Ray, who was going to B.U. When the landlords tried to raise our rent, she got together with others in adjoining buildings and formed a tenants' union. She appealed to the Cambridge Rent Control Board, refused to pay our rent, pooling it in escrow, and deducted hourly wages for herself for regular custodial work in our building. I had visions of our being evicted, and was skeptical of the organizers, of their type; reluctantly, I sat in on one meeting, while they all sat cross-legged around a table with a candle on it, drank wine, sang folk songs, and planned strategy.

Ellen and Peter were pregnant before long; a son was born. Peter needed steady livelihood, and leaving *Ploughshares* largely to me and my devices, he took a nine to five job with a friend at the Middlesex County District Attorney's office.

Connie wanted us to move. This phase of our lives, she felt, had run its course; the future of rent control in Cambridge was doubtful. Cambridge was a city of transience, youth, and the singles culture, symbolized perhaps by the girls who sunbathed topless on the roof across from our bedroom windows, if not by the barmaid who lived downstairs and who cried out so loudly when she had sex, that Connie jumped up and thought someone was being assaulted in the street below.

The suburbs, by contrast, were for families, and biologically, she felt, she couldn't wait any longer to start one.

She searched the towns west of Cambridge, primarily Watertown, a working-class town, where the rents were low. Through an agency, she found two apartments in our range and had me drive the five miles out Mt. Auburn to see. The apartment we liked was across from a junior high school, with a playing field with basketball and tennis courts and a tot lot. The landlord, Michele Timperio, was first generation Italian and spoke a thickly accented, broken English. He was a contract plumber and construction worker, sporadically employed. His wife, Dorinda, was also first generation. They had three young boys. The apartment was on the first floor of a nicely kept two-family house, with the Timperios living upstairs. Where our rent in Cambridge had worked its way up to $250, we could live here for $275. There would be no lease, just an honorable handshake, old-country style. We moved in that August 1976.

Although we had moved to have children, I remained defensive; just a little longer. Connie cajoled: "Please, please. I'll take care of the baby; I won't ask anything of you; this is all I'll ever ask; you'll love it, you'll see."

But I still did not have a real job. We were scraping by somehow on Connie's salary (which we'd lose with a baby), plus my token salary—some $2000—from *Ploughshares*. Connie's attitude was to start a family regardless. We'd find some way to get by, because we'd have to.

My father died unexpectedly in October 1976, and soon afterwards my mentor and friend from Iowa, Richard Yates, moved to Boston. I don't recall my father's death influencing my choice. But I do recall confiding my misgivings about parenting to Yates, who believed in my work. Yates had warned me all along about wasting my time on *Ploughshares*. Three years before, Connie and I had visited him overnight with his second wife, Martha, and new baby, Gina. Since then, he and Martha had been divorced, and he'd been living alone in lower Manhattan, struggling with the novel that would become *A Good School*. He'd survived a fire in that apartment with burns over most of his body, and once healed, had moved to Boston to put the memory behind him, to be closer to his publisher, Sam Lawrence, and, I flattered myself, to be near Connie and me as friends. "Think of the girl," he advised, regardless of my fears: crucial advice for me at the time.

Connie and I made love without contraception for the first time. Our lovemaking was ceremonious and ardent, lit by candles. Connie had a miscarriage by January; then was pregnant again in March.

❧

Who would it be? What would it be? How could we cope with it? What would it be like? Were we adequate? Was I adequate, given my distractions? My way of dealing with the coming child was not to deal, but to deny, one day at a time. The baby wasn't born yet, so forget it, don't worry, go on as normal. That notion, the going on as normal was key for me, normal meaning life as understood, life as having been proved possible. And all along my fear was our instability—our poverty, however much a function of my pride, when it came to borrowing or asking for money from my mother; our just getting by without extending our vulnerability.

Besides birth classes at Mt. Auburn hospital, where I had promised to go despite my "normal" schedule and where I was reprimanded in one exchange for referring to our unknown baby as a "creature," by which I meant an unknown life form and experience—the doctor, self-importantly, had jumped on the idea of monster, of negativity, thank you; besides Connie's day by day growth, from normal to larger, to larger, with this hard lump pressing against her organs, and our lovemaking getting more awkward; there was the gradual accumulation of baby things, a crib that we put in our dining room, which was to be the nursery, a battered changing table, likewise diapers, clothes, toys. It was all fixed up as if somebody lived there, as surely as we did ourselves, except we didn't know who yet (and always the nightmare fear that something might go wrong), or even what gender —I jokingly preferred the female, I said, because it would give me a Freudian advantage.

Breathe hee, hee, ho, we had been instructed, or he, hoo, to help master the pain. We had paired off, the group of maybe ten or fifteen couples, to practice. Husbands coaching wives: hee, hee, ho. Fix your eyes on a spot on the wall, on a corner, somewhere definite. Hee, hee, ho, blow on the ho. We had watched a birth movie. Wives had been told to practice Kegeling (sic), as if they were trying to pick up a ten-dollar bill with their vaginas. Quote, unquote. This would develop important muscles for the birth.

The ordinary day of those months consisted of my retreat to the air-conditioned second bedroom, which was my office for writing, for *Ploughshares*, and for Book Affair. Lacking file cabinets, the room was cluttered with piles of books and papers. I worked on a typewriter, eking past the two thirds mark on my novel. Predating computers, and lacking even a hand-held calculator, I tallied numbers for *Ploughshares* and Book Affair on ledger sheets over and over. Each day or so, I drove six miles into Central Square, Cambridge, to get the mail from the *Ploughshares* post office box (an address so well established that despite O'Malley's and my moves, we felt we shouldn't change it). Meetings with Peter or with local writers and editors grew more difficult, given the distance. Connie commuted by bus to Newton Upper Falls, working now for an after-school program, where she befriended a single mother who was a freelance designer and who helped me design the *Ploughshares* covers.

I bought a light box and began pasting up photo type in our living room, hours and hours, like an engraver or an architect. We had recently changed from local printers to a low-cost, large-volume company in Ann Arbor, Michigan, whose Boston representative came to pick up the paste-up of each issue at my apartment; and that same winter, I received the first delivery of the finished magazine, a fiction issue that I had co-edited with Tim O'Brien and which included the opening chapter of his soon-to-be-published, National Book Award-winning novel, *Going After Cacciato*. Some three weeks later, to the astonishment of my landlord and the entire neighborhood, an interstate tractor trailer pulled up, barely missing overhead telephone lines, wheezed to a stop, and the driver and I proceeded to unload, carton by carton, off of two shipping skids, 3000 copies packed 80 in a carton. Half of those cartons, Michele, the landlord, helped me to carry, or to roll on his plumber's wheelie, from the front sidewalk through a side door, through his finished basement, to our small, closed-off storage area; the other half I carried up the front steps to our living room.

For the next two weeks Connie and I would stuff copies into mailing bags, staple the bags, hand address, and put stamps on perhaps 1000 copies to subscribers and 100 to contributors. Our couch, dining table, chairs, every available surface would be covered with stacks of copies. I'd drive boxes-full to the post office or stuff them into collection boxes. I'd drive one whole carton to O'Malley. Six cartons I'd send to our national distributors. Six cartons I would drop at the Booksmith warehouse. Besides working to clear our living area, I'd work in a euphoria of sharing, and then the phone would ring: first congratulations come in.

Michele, the landlord, cast a doubtful eye on all this, except that he respected hard work and gathered that this was our way of earning the rent. A baby was another matter, however. We had agreed: no pets. We'd put off telling him until Connie began to show, and we felt uneasy about how he would react. He wasn't pleased, I gathered, when we did tell him officially: "Bambino?" We overheard long discussions in Italian, rising, falling, through our floor between him and Dorinda. From their tones, Dorinda seemed to convince him in the name of family values to accept the idea of a baby. We would all get along. His favorite axiom was "one hand washes the other," and we lived uncomplaining in the envelope, upstairs and down, of the Timperio family life. Through our floors we heard their family meals and most of their TV time, spent in the finished basement playroom and second kitchen, including loud quarrels between the boys as native speakers of English and their parents; through our ceiling, late at night, we heard the ferocious, rhythmic banging of the parents' sex.

Connie had grown big and tight and solid by the pregnancy's term in mid-December, 1977. We had given up sex for several weeks, and before that had tried in ways that her girth and burden would permit. She was sitting up in bed watching TV with me—the TV was on top of a counterpane we used as a bureau across the room. It was after dinner, around seven; another average night, though she was about a week overdue. We were rehearsed and ready, with her bag already packed. I had practiced the quickest route from Watertown to Boston Lying In, in Brookline. She had had contractions before, without their proving to be the main event. Again, as instructed, we wrote down the time of her contractions, and when they came at shorter and shorter intervals, five minutes perhaps, we called in, and the doctor said to come on in. Though her water had broken as she sat up in bed, and she grew more and more excited, panting with the contractions, for some reason neither of us believed that this was really the beginning of the birth. We joked all the way to the hospital about this probably being another false alarm, and continued joking even after, at maternity admissions, she was put in a wheelchair, and I rode with her up the elevator. "They're going to be mad at us," she said. "They're going to send us back home."

But in the birthing room, where Connie was the first of several women in a row of rooms to be examined, we were told: "This is no false alarm. You are at three fingers." She was my hero, I was thinking. I was to time and she was to endure the contractions, as we had been instructed. Husband was to work with wife, ice on the lips, count, encourage, tell her to keep her eyes on a fixed point, hee, hee, ho. She was vivid with the effort and excitement. This was the life-risking, life-fulfilling mission of her being; what she was meant for. Her high was like a combat high. Next door another woman screamed and cursed in pain.

Brede Sibley appeared, Connie's Irish friend from Head Start, who happened also to be an obstetric nurse at Boston Lying In. She had come in especially, or had extended her shift in order to help Connie. The regular nurse, who had just come on duty, was impatient and rude. There was no sign of a doctor.

Four fingers dilation. Five.

Connie wanted to push, but they told her not to, to hold off, and hold off. Then they told her: Go! The baby had dropped and descended. She pushed, in agony. Feet in stirrups. There was no shame here. I saw through the distended vulva, like a bladder pressing through a cut in a basketball, the top of the baby's head, distinct black hair. I was thinking that this was what vaginas were for, as if that were a lifetime's revelation. This was what sex was for. She had been shaved, disinfected.

An hour passed, two. The doctor had come; not Connie's obstetrician, Dr. Shirley, who was on vacation, but another doctor, who was covering for him. We had come in around seven. It was midnight now. Connie was exhausted. They were checking the baby's heart rate too, and the baby was exhausted.

Go was for a forceps delivery.

No time to waste. They were in an emergency mode, decision made. They had real concern for heart irregularities in the baby. Connie was lifted onto a gurney and rolled out. I was given a doctor's smock and mask and paper covers for my shoes.

They had resisted giving Connie a spinal anesthetic; now they did.

In the operating room I watched a miracle: consummation shining in Connie's agonized face; pain with the fullest meaning, giving life; the scalpel's quick, deft slice, widening her vagina, the red blood welling and flesh parted like meat at the butcher's; forceps; now PUSH, that's it, it's coming, look! Straining, searching in the overhead mirror: "Oh, I can see it!" she gasped. And then, like a rabbit, a slick, bloody rabbit, out of a hat, zip, whoosh, the baby was out, and held by the doctor upside down, gasping its first breaths, dark eyes open, seeing for the first time. The doctor said, "It's a girl!" And Connie: "Oh, she's beautiful!" They placed the baby, cleaned up, on Connie's breast, Connie beaming beatifically. They would sew Connie up, they told me, directing me out; then I could see my wife and daughter in the recovery room. There was also some concern about the baby's heart rate, an irregularity related, they thought, to the prolonged birth trauma, but they wanted to make sure.

I took off the white smock, mask, and shoe covers, and was led, after a wait, to an area with beds on wheels, and curtains, which was just a temporary recovery place, before the patient was moved to a room. Connie was exhausted. It was 2:30 a.m. or so. The baby—we'd decided on the name Ruth Kathryn for a girl—with its startling, full head of black hair, looked like me, my baby pictures, the Henry jowls. It was asleep, and would be for some time, recovering. I was to call everyone, Connie's mom, my mom, and they could call the brothers and sisters. "We're fine," Connie told me. "I love you. Go on home and get some sleep. They said we were a great team."

Whatever our differences and difficulties, I had never loved her more completely. I thought of that other moment of seeing her as a bride, on her way towards me.

I drove back to visit my wife and my daughter at nine the next morning. They were in a room now, in a different wing, shared with another mother and baby. I had my camera and took the first pictures of Ruth. Connie wore the hospital name-tag on her wrist. She was sore, but radiant. Ruth weighed something like seven pounds. She was, full length, no longer than Connie's forearm and hand. She was asleep and wouldn't wake up for me.

Dick Yates, whom I had called to tell, showed up one visiting hour unexpectedly, the first visitor other than me, tall, stoop-shouldered, and shy, bearing a bouquet of roses for Connie, a gallant gesture I had failed to imagine or make myself. Throughout the wing new mothers were shuffling to and from the bathroom, or otherwise in the corroder, knock-kneed.

Connie had stitches where she had had to be cut, and wore heavy dressings; but all the pain had meaning. I can't remember a first querulous look from infant Ruth—Baby Girl Henry, yet to be named—at me, her dad; I do, the wide, dark eyes, staring and taking in. The baby fingers clutching. The toothless baby yawns. And perfect little ears, toes, all the parts. And that she looked like my baby pictures, and everyone remarked, "She looks like her dad!" Round-faced, puff-cheeked. That Connie was tripping, exhilarated, even when weary and half-comatose. Directive: get this, need that, call so and so.

Two nights later, then the day I brought them home. We were discharged. I pulled the Chevy II around to the front entrance. Connie with Ruth out in a wheel chair (December 21 by now, cold); plus a newborn basket of diapers, bottles, and promotional whatnots. Settled in the car, that car, old and rattletrap, with floorboards rusting out. Our first trip as the three of us. Then pulling into the driveway at the apartment in Watertown, and Ray,

Connie's younger brother, who was working at UPS while finishing B.U., greeted us from the back door. Later Connie's mother, Hazel, would come for a week to help, up from Manhattan.

The crib and bassinet now had its occupant, who lay on her back wriggling while cheerful and awake and watching the crib toys overhead, or the faces of her mother and me; or who was lifted out to ride on our shoulders, or be cradled in our arms, or to be breast fed, or changed. Moment by moment, I was astonished at how natural and possible parenting was; that we were coping; that we were doing the right thing; that we had common sense and good instincts and a well of proud love that bore us through sleeplessness and two- and three-hour feeding schedules; that baby shit was just shit, as blood was just blood, vomit, vomit: you cleaned it up; you were competent, direct; you had your purpose.

Our income for 1977, Ruth's birth year, was $6500, $4500 of which Connie earned from the after-school program, and the rest of which came from my self-employment (fees for editing and for production tasks on *Ploughshares*), along with interest on the $9,000 my father had given us, "as an advance on your inheritance," when we got married. For 1978, we somehow lived on my part-time teaching at Northeastern, as well as my *Ploughshares* fees, and interest, a total of $5800. The pre-stagflation dollar was worth three times what it is now twenty-three years later, and for a while my mother also helped us with checks for $100 each month, but we were living at daily risk. Next to rent, our highest expense was a non-group Blue Cross family plan. We had no dental or other insurance. My eleven-year-old car, with its floor rusted out, had been kept running by a sympathetic mechanic.

1979, 1980, and 1981 were banner years, however, thanks to state and federal grants. After several years of applying and being rejected for NEA Fellowships in Fiction, I was now awarded one—$10,000—for a portion of my novel. For my editing, I also received one of the first Editor's Fellowships from CCLM for $5000.

Through Book Affair I had designed a three-year library project funded by the state arts council at $30,000 each year and providing a $6,000 administrative salary for me. I catalogued small presses and literary magazines in the state, then offered vouchers to 256 public libraries to order them, collated the orders, and paid the publishers (including *Ploughshares*, which gained 100 new subscriptions); I drove around the state to librarians' meetings;

I carried displays of books like a salesman; I sent promotional packets to each library. I generated coverage in local papers. I wrote a column reviewing literary magazines for *The Wilson Library Journal.*

Ploughshares was paying its way in earnings and in grants. I prided myself on turning every small grant into earned income in our fiscal base. We now had a $26,000 budget. Starting in the fall of 1976, I successfully applied for the first three-year, $30,000 "Literary Magazine Development Grant" from the NEA, without which we couldn't have continued, and with which, for the first time, we published four issues each year, begged and bought national ads, invested in direct mail and evolved as a business. We also undertook a series of benefit readings and parties. By 1982, our budget was $56,000.

For some time Peter O'Malley had been abroad and out of touch, but after *Ploughshares* received the Development Grant, he became re-involved, especially in promoting the benefits. We worked well again together, I felt, showing off for each other, coup by coup. He respected my editorial, political, and business acumen, as measured by the magazine's prestige and budget. I respected his blustery charm, his energy, his good intentions, and his ability to ingest opinion and advice from both the literary world and from the Boston political and business world. He mixed with a set of Irish American lawyers and businessmen in downtown Boston and saw the membership of the Boston Eire Society, which included judges, lawyers, doctors, insurance executives, and trustees of Boston College, as a moneyed, cultural and social bloc comfortably separate from literary Boston, which remained primarily Yankee. We set out to play on that cultural opposition: Irish, Catholic, and B.C. on one side; and Yankee, Protestant, and Harvard on the other.

For our first benefit, in Harvard's Sanders Theater, Robert Lowell (Harvard Brahmin) read with John McGahern (Irish novelist); for our second Richard Wilbur with Brian Moore. Lowell had agreed to help, thanks to his friendship with poet Frank Bidart, who had edited an earlier, remarkable *Ploughshares* issue. McGahern, whom both Peter and I admired, and who taught at Colgate, I had written to. Thanks to Stratis Haviaras, a Book Affair director and curator of the Poetry Room at Harvard, we got use of Sanders Theater, as well as of the Poetry Room for a reception afterwards. We did a mailing. Peter made personal phone calls and asked twenty or thirty wealthy prospects to underwrite blocs of tickets, which they were then responsible for selling. We gained an audience of 900, much publicity and good will, and a net profit of nearly $2500. The Richard Wilbur and Brian Moore event in 1979, to a slightly smaller audience, netted a similar amount.

Then Peter set off unilaterally, which alarmed me, given our public trust. I took him at his word, however, that he would personally protect *Ploughshares* from liabilities. In Ireland, he had been a friend of Siobhan McKenna, the actress. She was coming to the states to tour a one-woman show, *The Branchy Tree*, a medley of passages about women from Yeats, Synge, O'Casey and others. She would do a Boston performance to benefit *Ploughshares*. Peter had gotten the function floor on top of the Parker House Hotel in Boston, as I heard it, in collusion with the Parker House publicity manager. The costs, however, incurred all on speculation against funds yet to be raised, proved to be staggering, some $12,000. The function was black tie, had a cash bar (proceeds to the hotel), and tickets were $100 each, including a dinner that cost $60 per plate. Peter's style was to go for broke, and to plead, stall, borrow, and worry, hoping that he sold enough tickets to cover expenses. In fact, starting with his own brother, he let in people he trusted to pay later, people he would be badgering for months to come. Rain the night of the event was torrential. Peter kept ordering and canceling plates until the last minute, and ended up having to pay for a number we never used. Stephen Mindich, publisher of *The Boston Phoenix*, took me aside, chuckling, "This is no way to raise money." The performance, however, was brilliant. The audience was wealthy and glamorous. McKenna was pleased. But when all accounts were settled the *Ploughshares* bank account received a check for only $1000. I insisted again that Peter and I work together, and that any fundraising for *Ploughshares* operate through our bankbook, managed by me.

We went on to hold other large-scale readings, which made us friends and helped to build our reputation. Others who read for us on later occasions included Seamus Heaney, Elizabeth Hardwick, James Merrill, Ray Carver, William Styron and Frank Conroy. In time the audience that we had found had been over-solicited by other sponsors, so Peter attempted two benefits out of town, the first on the estate of a friend of Peter's on Martha's Vineyard, the second the SoHo loft of a painter whom this friend patronized. Again, the events were glamorous, but the money they raised for *Ploughshares* was negligible. A picture from the SoHo party, where Seamus Heaney had been the reader, shows Peter at the cash box, hands up and screaming.

Thanks to the notoriety of *Ploughshares* as well as to the progress with my writing (I finished my novel, or thought I had, just days before my 40th birthday), I was offered the Writer-in-Residence job at Emerson College again for 1981-82, followed by a three-quarter time appointment for 1982-83; and at last I was hired there as full-time, tenure track faculty in fall,

1983. For the first time Connie and I had security, including health and dental benefits. Our family income had jumped to $26,000. *Ploughshares* was able to move out of our second bedroom to a rented storefront a half-mile away, thereby making room for Ruth, who had spent her early years climbing over book boxes, and watching Connie and me staple, stuff, bundle and bag *Ploughshares* issues for subscribers. Given that I must absent myself for teaching, a local poet, Joyce Peseroff, agreed to help me part-time at the storefront as our first managing editor.

⸺⸺

Once we had Ruth, things began to change between Connie and me. One thing was romantic privacy, gone forever. Another was Connie's change from deference to my career as the key to our family life to questions of her own self-esteem. She wanted a second child immediately and was in her mind dedicated to parenting above all, and where I had been defensive about a first, I was not ready—in terms of providing livelihood —for a second. The world, I felt, even after my hire by Emerson was not endorsing me.

I had expected instant success upon finishing my novel in mid-1981. I had had encouraging early readings of the manuscript by writer friends. I had published excerpts over the years, thereby interesting several trade publishers. I found a prominent agent, who saw the book as a property and sent it out to three different houses simultaneously, hoping to start some bidding; it came back, and after a year's trying with ten more submissions, she gave up. Difficult times for first novels, especially literary novels, I was told. Good book, but unmarketable. I tried another ten submissions on my own, with two close calls and a citation for third place in a contest in England. I found a second agent. More submissions, more rejections. Clearly, the book would not be published overnight, if ever; and clearly it was not the redemption I had counted on, especially in terms of recognition and livelihood.

Connie and I had started trying for another pregnancy, nevertheless, in January 1980. Labor Day weekend of that year, after nine months of trying, my testicles swelled, and I went to the Emergency Ward with epididimytis, a viral inflammation of the network of vessels through which new sperm cells travel to the prostate. I was treated with antibiotics and referred to an urologist, who, in a follow-up appointment, found my sperm count to be in the infertile range. A man who resembled Don Rickles, he blandly asked whether I was sure that Ruth was my daughter. I sought a more sensitive and tactful urologist, who specialized in infertility; Connie also started having examinations and treatments for infertility with her obstetrician. We went through a gamut of procedures that were starkly unromantic and dehumanizing, including a self-induced wire up my urethra, pulled scraping out, in order to provide tissue for a culture. For me, masturbation went from being a private vice to a public, or at least a medical, obligation. I was to deliver samples within an hour of producing them to my doctor's office in Gerber baby food jars. My doctor put me on a fertility drug, saying it worked about 20 percent of the time. I had a few promising counts (18 million per cc, 40 percent motility, 60 percent forward progression was my personal best). We kept trying through 1982.

During this time, in the winter of 1981, immediately after I had taken four-year old Ruth alone to her first movie, Disney's *Cinderella*, in a theater packed with sneezing and coughing children, she contracted myocarditus, a heart virus that threatened her life (again the figure of 20% was cited to us, this time as the fatality rate). Connie was terrified. Suddenly Ruth was gasping for breath. We rushed her to the hospital and she was in intensive care for the next week, with an oxygen mask, IV's, monitors, the works. Our sense of powerlessness was harrowing. The doctors were younger than me, and I felt, however earnest, similarly inexperienced and fallible. Yet we had no choice but to surrender Ruth to their care. Connie lived at Ruth's bedside, sleeping over, as much as she could; I went home to sleep, deliberately, so that I could come in and take Connie's place. As Ruth improved enough to move into a room, we were surrounded by distressed parents and sick children, to whom Connie and Ruth reached out empathically to help, cheer, and befriend.

Given our struggle with infertility, the month by month possibility of pregnancy, and still other procedures to consider (such as artificial insemination with my sperm as concentrated by centrifuge), Connie reasoned that if she couldn't have a second child right away, while Ruth grew to school age, then she was not going to be left at home with Ruth and nothing else, no teaching, no art. She corrected tests at home for a business consulting firm. In 1982 and 1983, she earned one thousand a year by teaching shul at Temple Beth Israel in Newton, a way, she felt, of getting back in touch with her religion as well as with her older brother, Danny, an orthodox rabbi in Illinois, who was married with his first baby daughter and already expecting a second child. Otherwise, she began to put her energies into volunteer political activities.

One of her first friends in Watertown was Glenda Alderman, whom she met as part of a play-group that was forming, and who had had her first baby, Jesse, the same month that Connie had had Ruth. Glenda was a social worker, and her husband, Pat Farren, was an anti-war activist working for the Friends' Committee. Glenda knew Joan Krauss, a fervent local activist, whose youngest son was also Ruth's age and whose husband was a carpenter. Also nearby was a wealthier young mother, Barbara Ruskin, who had a house, not just an apartment, and whose husband did grant-funded medical research. With toddlers of an age, one bond was the forming of the play-group, where each member would watch the children for a different day, and the other members would have time for work or other activities. Another bond was the fledgling Watertown Citizens for Environmental Safety, an organization that overlapped with and led to friendships outside the playgroup.

Although Connie, in making local friends of her own, hoped to interest me in her friends as readily as she had been interested in my *Ploughshares* friends, I found myself suspicious and resentful of their influence and their claim on her time, which increasingly became a claim on my time. I was skeptical of their pretensions. They seemed to me half-baked, self-promoting and sentimental. During the by-gone era of Vietnam War protests, I surmised, they had found solidarity and passion and some sense of taking part in big issues, but now they lacked any cogent cause for which to organize. The environmental movement at the time seemed to me an obscure and forced occasion, even when focused on preventing the construction of a nuclear power plant, say, in Seabrook, New Hampshire. As for acting locally in Watertown, the group sought abuses in public policy concerning lead paint, asbestos, lead pipes, winter road chemicals, and radon. But given that the military industrial complex had had a significant presence in Watertown, the likeliest suspect was the Army's Watertown Arsenal, which during World War II had been operated at full tilt, employing most of the town, but which had been decommissioned sometime in the late1950's, and then, except for a few laboratory buildings that the Army still used, deeded over to the town. Recently the town, after years of political indecision, had moved to develop the site partly as a huge mall, partly as housing, and partly as a public park. Once one of the most ardent WCES members, Susan Falkoff, and Connie started to investigate the Arsenal, they learned that the Army had conducted nuclear research there connected with developing the atomic bomb, that the remains of a small nuclear reactor existed on the grounds, and there might be nuclear wastes in the soil. They demanded documents from the Army, received back dismissive replies, wrote back again, wrote Congressmen and Senators, and finally got the Army to give a contamination report, which WCES then verified by hiring an outside examiner. Nothing much came of the effort. There was residual radiation in the area of the park's tennis courts, but according to the outside examiner, it was below a level that posed any real hazard. The reactor building was duly dismantled. Susan was featured on the cover of a Sunday supplement as a citizen crusader; she posed, arms crossed and severe, outside the Arsenal gates.

—∞∞—

1983, 1984, and 1985 were our most difficult, strained years as a couple, culminating in our resolution to adopt an infant from Korea and with my mother's death in the fall of 1985.

My sperm count was still the likeliest cause of our infertility, and our conclusion, which Connie accepted before I could, was that factors on both sides—age, low count, irregular ovulation—rendered hope for a birth child pretty much impossible. Also that hope became less important as time passed, and as Ruth grew four, six, eight years distant from a new sibling. More than Connie, I had to work through stages of anger, grief, and resignation and grow free of that loss before I could know my desire for another child.

By the end of 1983, I felt that Connie didn't love me enough to sacrifice her dream of a second child on any conditions. I wanted her to say that she was happy as we were, or that she could live with just Ruth. She had given me an ultimatum that we would continue trying for a pregnancy for six months more, and then we would adopt. Deep down, I wanted her to sacrifice her needs so that I could match her sacrifice with mine, but freely: okay then. Urging her. Let's go ahead and adopt.

What, I felt at that point, were my choices given that I felt I had no choice? Either I went forward with our marriage without a second child, which meant that Connie would divorce me; or I went forward with a second child that wasn't my birth child and that I wanted to it be, which risked my resentment, and my divorcing Connie.

Starting in June 1984, Connie and I had a few counseling sessions at the suggestion of our infertility doctor. The counselor, a woman, listened to us separately and together, and helped me to verbalize my feeling that, "I need to know that my case is hopeless before I can consider adoption." She also warned Connie that I needed time, that I felt pressured into deciding; and that if Connie continued to ignore my feelings, it would be natural for me to turn to other women; that Connie could lose me.

Ovulation by ovulation we were pursuing AIH (artificial insemination from husband), and as with each cycle the AIH failed to produce a pregnancy, we began to discuss, along with various adoption strategies, AID (artificial insemination by donor).

Donors were donors, medical students, usually, paid for producing each sample. We would never know a donor's identity, but if he were a medical student then probably he was intelligent, and at least a token effort would be made to match my own physical characteristics—dark hair, medium height and build—so that neither family nor anyone else would ever have cause to doubt that the child was mine by birth.

Adoption could be similarly covert. One plan was for Connie to wear a pillow, pretending to be pregnant, and to fly to Brazil, where a Caucasian newborn pledged for adoption would be switched for the pillow at the hospital, and then she would fly home, mother and child. There would be expenses for this operation, but they would be less than for a legal adoption, and the secret would be kept from the child and from the world. Legal adoptions cost from six to ten thousand dollars—if not beyond the limit of our means, then at the limit. Massachusetts had a state program, that held couples on a waiting list for as long as three years, longer than Connie felt we could wait, and the placements of state wards were random, rather than selective. There was also a state foster care program, with immediate placements for older children, often disabled or retarded, but the children could be taken back by the state at any point.

In the light of these options, AID, covered by our health plan, involved no legal costs, and at least, I told myself, the child would be genetically Connie's, and for medical purposes would have a genetic history. As a placebo, they could also mix in some of my own sperm during insemination, so there would also be the possibility that Connie's egg, having been battered by the donor's sperm, had been finally penetrated by one of my own. Partly as a result of counseling, for my own part, AID seemed preferable, though I felt the preference as I would, say, for gas over hanging, given the necessity.

Still, I stalled, and come summer, Connie insisted: if we were doing AID we had to do it now, because she didn't want the procedure conflicting with her job. At the same time, in case she still failed to get pregnant, she wanted to initiate an adoption application with a $500 fee. I wanted the aggravation to be over. AID was unnatural for me, emotionally. I felt angry inside. In keeping with our counseling, I tried out the positive feelings that AID couldn't be done without my consent, that it was a choice to be proud of, a choice that took manliness itself, and that was a gift of strength. Connie also tried to respect my feelings and calmly spelled out for me why August was the rational starting time. She asked me if I felt I needed more time. I couldn't answer right away. Again, a few days later, she casually asked me what she was to tell the doctor's office. I answered: "Wait." At which she burst into tears and turned into another room, leaving me, as she didn't come back, and then I heard the front door slam, to bear the burden. Alone, I wavered. I wanted to make her happy. What difference did waiting make when I was going to consent anyway? But no, this was not about AID, I told myself; this was about counting, about mutual wanting rather than a contest. When Connie asked again, a month later, she said that the choice was mine, and that she would love me in any case. I said I wanted to wait for our counseling appointment the following week, and then to schedule my okay for mid-September. From sweetness and smiles and normality, instantly she went to terrors, like that: anger, tears, and a sleepless night for both us, as I sifted and resifted. Why couldn't I consent? I did, finally, in mid-October. Then after two, and on the eve of a third AID session, in mid-December, Connie urged me to start adoption efforts. AID was not working. Seven-year-old Ruth urged me as well, shortly after I had taken her to see the movie, *Annie*. How much farther does one go, I asked myself?

During this same time, Richard Yates needed my friendship. He was having breakdowns, where he would grow progressively manic, drink constantly, quit taking medication, and then would end up out of control, hallucinating and raving, a mental condition aggravated by alcoholism and by epilepsy, both of which afflicted him, but distinct from either. He had described this condition in his 1976 novel, *Disturbing the Peace.* I was shocked to learn that he had a history of such episodes, which were triggered by anxieties over meeting deadlines for the advances that were his only livelihood, and then after publication by the pressures of publicity and negative reviews. In this case, his one-time friend, Anatole Broyard, had scathingly dismissed *Young Hearts Crying* in *The New York Time Book Review.* Andre Dubus called me and said that he'd just been talking to Dick on the phone and that Dick was raving about being poisoned, something about rat poison and the CIA and being kicked out of his regular bar, The Crossroads. I tried calling, then drove into Boston, and no sign of Dick, talked to the owner of The Crossroads, Mike Brodigan, who was a friend of Dick's, who respected Dick's talent and understood his condition. Yes, Dick had been unruly, shouting; yes, he'd told him to leave; but that was two nights ago. No sign of him since. Brodigan had been worried and had even tried calling Dick's daughter, Monica, in

New York, but she hadn't heard anything either. Two more days, then Peter O'Malley called me and said that the Cambridge Police had called him, that Yates had given them Peter's name; that Yates had been picked up in Harvard Square and then kept at the station until they turned him over to a drying-out facility. I tried the V.A. hospital (Dick's only medical coverage was his V.A. benefit, dating from World War II), but Dick wasn't there. I was at a loss on where and how to act as Dick's friend. Among writers in Boston, Dan Wakefield had become Dick's close friend too; he advised, just let it be.

Eventually, Dick called me. He'd been released, but he was soon drinking again. I was teaching *King Lear*, the mad scenes on the heath, and as I met Dick in the Crossroads, and then convinced him to go back to his apartment, a block away, and get some sleep, his short-tempered, fragmented ravings reminded me of Lear's. He asked me if he was making sense. I told him, no, but that I could see he was in pain, that he was ill. The next day Wakefield called, distressed, and asked me to come with him to Dick's apartment, that Dick was in the midst of an episode; we had to get him help. There was heavy rain; Wakefield met me at Emerson and I drove from 100 Beacon down Beacon to Dick's apartment near Massachusetts Avenue. Dan rang and Dick buzzed us in, but after we climbed the stairs to his landing, he shouted to us that his door was locked, that someone must get him out, he couldn't get out himself. He had the keys and he would shove them to us under the door, but someone had to get him out. A key slid under the sill and Dan let us in. Yates, in baggy pants and an undershirt, greeted us with crazed, speeding, and brilliant invective, which we took. Memory blurs. The room was a mess, clothes, money, and papers strewn around, spilled ashtrays, bottles and beer cans. Wakefield kept saying, "Dick, you're not making sense. Have you had anything to eat? Do you have anything to eat?" Dick sat hunched on his couch, shakily smoking, while Dan and I sat facing him in folding chairs. Dick turned on me: "Get high school outta here! What are you looking at? Those eyes!" He pointed at my rubbers: "My mother taught me to take off my rubbers in the house!"

We got him to eat; got his doctor's number, called the hospital; the hospital said they would have the police dispatch a squad car to bring him in. "You're calling the cops on me! You're calling the cops!" Dick kept raving, in disbelief that friends would betray him so. Two patrolmen did arrive, took charge, and experts, we supposed, with all sorts of derangement, they calmed Dick and got him to gather keys, money, i.d.'s and things he'd need in the hospital. Dan and I left. Later, Dan said, Dick would thank us for calling for help. It was right thing to do. He needed care.

For Yates, I remained on call; and indeed, he did call from the hospital pay-phone a few days later, making all sorts of apologies and asking me to bring him a carton of cigarettes. I told him, sure, forget it. I got directions, bought the cigarettes, found my way and parked. I felt that I was braving hard circumstances as I passed through the worn lobby, checking at a security desk; then up an elevator to the 12th floor, Ward C, a floor sealed off for mental patients and for detoxing drunks. Another security station: I was visiting Yates, Richard. An orderly led me through doors down a bleak hallway. Dick was in his room, in pajamas and a robe, just waking up. He had been writing steadily with pencil on a yellow pad pages and pages of *Cold Spring Harbor*, much of which, in fact, he finished while in the hospital. He was greedy for cigarettes. As a social gesture, he led me down the hall, saying hi as we passed other patients, to an open lounge; we visited a while, as he smoked and coughed, and he started to tell me about one of the other patients, who was eating a bowl of soup across the room. The guy had been a famous jockey at some point, and I forget the rest, except the jockey sounded like an apt subject for a Yates story. I left, feeling glad to have visited and to have found some open rapport with Dick that allowed for his illness and our friendship.

I was glad, also, having turned in my grades, to escape and to leave with Connie and Ruth for Christmas at my mother's in Villanova.

As we returned, with the new year we moved relentlessly towards adopting. Connie pushed for a dinner visit with a local librarian and her husband, who had just adopted a racially mixed baby. We heard through this couple of a nearby international adoption agency. The agency had an information session and Connie insisted that we go (including Ruth) "only for information." Newly adoptive parents spoke honestly of their experiences, while their infants and young children, of varying ages and national origins, played or clung to them. They spoke of the difficulties, the waiting, the differences with relatives about race and religion, health issues, cultural issues; they spoke also of their love, and, through what I saw at the time as pathos and defeat, their gratitude. This was not me, I thought; this couldn't be.

Starting in the fall of 1984 with the anticipated publication of a book, *The Ploughshares Reader: New Fiction of the 80s*, edited by me, and with the prospect of articles attendant on its publication in *The Boston Globe, The*

Philadelphia Inquirer and elsewhere, concerning the history of *Ploughshares,* my strife with Peter O'Malley grew serious. In his own non-literary circles, I heard, Peter had been representing himself as an editor, especially on the fiction side. Given this supposed expertise, he'd been assigned by the Middlesex District Attorney to help line up literary witnesses against the x-rated movie *Caligula.* He was a friend of a prominent Boston literary lawyer, Ike Williams, who was planning to start a literary agency, and who would specialize in movie deals and in scouting new talent the likes of Tim O'Brien's and Jayne Anne Phillips's. Then, I also suspected that the cadre of business friends that Peter had cultivated as *Ploughshares* patrons, and with whom he socialized, had begun to notice my claim to primary editorial credit, and to pressure him to confront me.

I moved to develop *Ploughshares* as an organization, precisely to keep Peter accountable, and to protect the honor of the collective efforts of all the guest editors, writers, and genuine donors. I needed a court of appeal to which both Peter and I would be answerable, and with which I could share the responsibilities of fundraising and of running the magazine. I called for an organizational meeting at the Cambridge home of Anne Bernays and Justin Kaplan. With the help of Joyce Peseroff, I sent out invitations to Peter, Ellen, our trustees, our patrons, and the local writers who had served as guest editors, and perhaps as many as thirty people troubled to attend. The *Ploughshares* issue that Bernays and Kaplan had just edited was proudly displayed on their mantel. We socialized a bit, and then, having waited for Peter for over an hour, although Ellen was there and assured us he was coming, we started our meeting. I handed out an agenda. We had begun discussing suggestions for new trustees, when there was a commotion in the hallway and Anne announced that Peter had arrived. He proceeded, in apparent innocence, to disrupt the meeting and turn it into a party. He'd been waylaid. Business matters. Traffic. Hello, old friends—direct social friends to him, regardless of their part in *Ploughshares.* He went into an adjoining room and started playing the piano. Anne Bernays rolled her eyes. We couldn't go on with the meeting, so we gave up on discussing *Ploughshares,* and after some uneasy smiles, thanks, and regrets, people left. I left.

I was furious, and for a while we stopped talking. I did speak to Michael Connelly, a book editor, mutual friend, and a *Ploughshares* patron, and said: "I'm through carrying Peter. I've carried him all these years, and I'm through." Connelly said: "I wish we could get you guys back together."

Not only Michael Connelly, but Ellen herself tried to make peace between us. I loved and respected Ellen as a person, a writer, and a kindred spirit. She assumed that I loved Peter too, and all this was a family matter, to be settled in private somehow.

We had a meeting, which Ellen arranged as Sunday brunch in their kitchen. Connie, as my wife, and as partner in my life's sacrifices for *Ploughshares* was not invited, and was never acknowledged to have a legal role (Ellen had been designated corporate clerk). In the friendliest, low-key way, over coffee, eggs and bacon, Peter explained his point of view. He had his own history of *Ploughshares* to write, which disagreed with mine. He should have been given credit as co-editor of *The Ploughshares Reader*. He had resented a 1979 article about me in the *Amherst Alumni Magazine*, in which I had been described as the primary director, editor, and sustaining force of *Ploughshares*, and he had not been mentioned. He had let that go, but now he heard that *Harvard Magazine* was contemplating an article about *Ploughshares*, angled on me as an alumnus and on other Harvard faculty and alumni who had been guest editors. This he would not stand for. He demanded equal credit, a separate interview, and a combined photograph, where any future articles about *Ploughshares* were concerned.

I replied that he was free to write any history of *Ploughshares* that he might want to, as long as it corresponded with the facts. That I had been generous to him in my own portrayals of his role; that, in fact, he had never edited anything, other than some material he had brought back from Ireland for the first issue (most of which our first committee had rejected); that he had, yes, through his friendship, involved Cambridge literati as guest editors and most recently he deserved full credit for involving Seamus Heaney and the Kaplans. And where, I asked, had I ever claimed credit for his primary accomplishment, that of developing our private patron base? As for *The Ploughshares Reader* and the upcoming *Ploughshares Poetry Reader* (edited by Joyce Peseroff), they are one editor's accomplishment, which should credit others in the introductions. I had been spelling out *The Ploughshares Reader* for better than a year, and I had never heard a suggestion or objection from him until now. He was misrepresenting his credentials at my expense, if he was trying to sell himself as an editor. He was not respecting my work or Joyce's, for which we were not paid, really, and for which recognition was the only reward. His contribution to *Ploughshares* needed to be spelled out as distinct from mine; otherwise he was calling into question the whole thing that kept me going. We needed a corporate structure.

We agreed to meet and talk more regularly. Peter insisted again that he be involved in any upcoming interviews concerning *Ploughshares*; and I insisted that he pursue no more contacts with university sponsors, such as Brown or Boston College, which he had attempted recently, without involving me.

Connie and I filed our "Application for Adoptive Home Study" on May 6, 1985.

We had a home study, three visits with a social worker; Ruth was seen by a child pyschologist; we had Korean culture classes. In our application we stated that we pursued international adoption out of positive feelings about differences in background and race. That we believed in pluralism as a social goal. Also that there was something in having the ideal of adoption out front, the ideal of helping the state of things—which differences of appearances would emphasize, where a like-to-like adoption would seek to hide itself as an adoption. For my part, I felt that a non-white child would deepen the commitment to our balance of cultures, Jewish and Christian, in the minds of both our families.

The International Adoption Agency offered a choice of programs among 1) Indian, which we were told some couples preferred because Indians have Caucasian features; 2) Asian (Cambodian, Korean, Filipino); and 3) Central American (Salvadorian, Guatemalan). I favored the Korean program, with its system of orphanages that had been in place since the end of the Korean War. The health of the babies was said to be excellent; also education was highly valued in Korea, and Connie and my both being teachers promised our acceptance. But mostly I told myself I would study my child's culture with him or her, and that one day, perhaps, we would visit there. I was attracted to Asian cultures because of my impression of their history, religion and art, and because my sister's husband was half Indonesian, half Dutch. Also my brother Chuck had served a postwar Army tour in Korea, been moved by the plight of orphans at the time, and had taken hundreds of slides; a surgeon now in New Jersey, divorced, with three grown sons, he supported our choice.

⊸∞∞⊶

We had heard from Chuck in February 1985, that my mother had suffered heart failure and been hospitalized, but was all right now. She hadn't wanted to tell us or have us worry. By the time we filed the adoption application, her heart condition had worsened. I visited her alone in Villanova after my classes had ended, but neither Ruth's nor Connie's had yet. She was in decline, as she would be throughout the summer.

The adoption process of that summer did not feel like an opportunity to me, so much as another tightening of the noose. And it made me feel crazy, out of control, and lonely. There were all the noose tightenings: my mother, my trouble writing, the claims of Emerson, the troubles with Yates, the deepening hopelessness of *Ploughshares*.

At the same time, I was deeply grateful for Connie's loving care and sacrifice for my mother. That counted. Mom could no longer live alone, and for periods there was an expensive, live-in companion, whose smoking, and whose personality Mom detested.

From adult distances, my sister Judy, and brothers, Jack and Chuck, would visit as they could. Connie and Ruth took the longest visits—Ruth even enrolled in a summer camp in Bryn Mawr—leaving me in Boston to deal with *Ploughshares*.

Still I wrote to myself at the time: "I don't know how much more I can take. I don't know where to find me. How to act out of whole values, full self, all energy directed against outside problems rather than wasted fighting against itself, inside." I turned 44, past imagining at 24.

Judy was visiting from Arizona to stay with Mom in August; Mom had just had another episode and gone back into the hospital at the time when a big article about me, *Ploughshares*, and the anthology appeared in *The Philadelphia Inquirer*. I had known an article was coming out, but I hadn't seen it. Judy and she joked on the phone that there was a full-page picture of me with the caption, "DeWitt Henry is co-director of *Ploughshares*, conceived in a bar in 1970." Mom was proud and showed the article around to nurses, doctors, visitors and other patients.

September 2, a week before she died, I called Mom in the hospital, and she was "feeling high...junkie Ma." I told her that I wanted to hear her voice, that I wished I could be sitting close, that these distances weren't there. I told her about Emerson, about Connie's work at the Atrium School, and the Watertown schools starting, about the new issue of *Ploughshares* due for delivery, about our house hunting. I told her that the love goes on, always; that we—we Henrys—had a torch of talent, vision and spirit that is more than any of us, a privilege beyond us, and that it had been passed from her to the rest of us. No waste, no loss.

<hr/>

My share of my mother's estate, at least as estimated by Chuck, who was executor, allowed us to house hunt. None of the houses we looked at in

Watertown entirely pleased Connie, but in December, I pushed for the purchase of a three-bedroom cape with a furnished basement about a mile away from our apartment (a mile and a half from the *Ploughshares* storefront), and only two blocks from the Atrium School. The price was $169,000. Connie, for her part, conceded, though she made it plain that this was far from being her dream house. Michele Timperio actually helped us to move, struggling with our queen-sized mattress with me up the stairs of the new house.

We heard back from International Adoptions in February 1986. A male infant, born September 15, had been assigned to us. His picture arrived, passport sized; two pictures. His Korean name was Jung Min, and we decided to name him David Jung Min Henry. He had been born in Seoul. He was healthy, but was recovering from croup. He had been with his birth mother for six weeks and then had been put in foster care, with a Mama San.

Connie studied and studied and showed the tiny pictures to all her friends.

Like a man told he has a terminal disease, like Mom when she was dying, I lived by denying. This hasn't happened yet. Even as the time grew closer. But then the expected call came April 24. Connie was jubilant, and Ruth echoed her excitement. Our baby was coming, was airborne, and would arrive at Logan Airport on a Northwest Orient flight direct from Seoul at 9:55 pm tomorrow night. Our chosen presenter, a woman from International Adoptions, would be there to meet us and would actually go on board for the baby.

Chuck called that evening and asked, "C'mon, tell me what you feel." I told him I felt prosperous, larger, I guessed; *more*. Life was going to be different, and probably, I said, I felt, shyly and tentatively, that it would be a difference of growth, of strength.

I didn't tell him that I also felt grief and bafflement, and that Mom's dying was part of it; that I had gone bicycling for distraction and exercise and found a cemetery and was drawn to coast through it, thinking of her.

The next day came. We put up a donated crib in Ruth's room, reliving the parallel of her arrival eight years before, and of her infancy, and of naturally meeting her needs. Night came, a soupy, foggy night. Connie and Ruth were excited, and I was too in my graver way. Connie had a friend meet us at the airport to use a video camera borrowed from the Atrium School to record the event.

We were late, in our minds, rushed and anxious in airport tunnel traffic. Where was the International Terminal? Where to park? We had some baby things in the car. The crib, bassinet, and other clothes were ready and waiting at home. We rushed into the massive, modernist terminal, with flags of all nations hanging from the vaulted ceiling, echoing announcements and voices, and we were disoriented at first, not unlike our final trip to Lying In, when Ruth had been born. Finally, far down the hundred or more yards of space, we saw a gathering of people we gradually recognized as officials of International Adoptions, other parents and prospective parents, perhaps forty or so. Hubbub. Comparing of notes. The clock said something like 8:39. The flight was on schedule, due at 9:36. There was a steep escalator to the unloading gate, which was itself out of sight.

We have the video, amateur, mono-color (a green/blue tint), with long static portions between sequences.

Ruth is bouncing around in a plaid jumper and puffy-sleeved blouse. Clock says 9:36. I'm there on my muted best behavior, jacket, vest and tie. Connie in a jacket and blouse is glowing. Ebullient. They talk to another mother nursing an infant, waiting also. Connie and I sit and Ruth climbs in Connie's lap. An announcement. The flight is imminent. Flight has landed. IAI staff joke as the greeters go up the stairs and disappear; they tell us to go out the gate passageway and into the plane, that this is called "the birth canal." What is so momentous for us is a frequently scheduled event for the staff, ho hum.

Squeals and applause, ripples of exclamation, flashbulbs popping, as the first greeters, men and women, descend the staircase with blanketed infants in their arms; the first several coming down are not ours, but then Connie and Ruth have spotted our greeter coming down and have surged forward into the crowd, until contact is made.

Connie suddenly has a blanket and baby in her arms, while Ruth pipes, "Mommy! Oh, oh!" And Connie croons, "He's perfect! He's beautiful!" Eight months old David peers drunkenly around, smiling, and studies Ruth's face.

"Hi! Hello, yes, cute little boy!" Ruth coos.

I shake his tiny hand. "How do you do, David Jung Min?"

Connie says: "This is Daddy, over here."

Ruth can't wait to hold him, and I am telling Ruth to keep back, to wait, but Connie says, "You can hold him. Gently. Gently, with your brother."

Ruth holds him and says, "Now I believe it! Oh, you are cute!"

And Connie: "Look at this guy. I can't believe it. Now I get to look at your face. Hello! Hi, David Jung Min Henry! Welcome to the United States!"

Someone in the background says, "Congratulations!"

The Greeter is saying, "Maybe he recognized you from the pictures. What do you think?"

Connie has him back, and then I take him, rock him. I am silently beaming.

Then Connie takes him: "Welcome to our family!"

⚬⚬⚬

Ruth had been alone in the small upstairs bedroom of our new house. Now she would share her room with the baby whose crib we put by the front window. Connie had networked our needs and borrowed nursery items, the crib, a bassinet, a changing table. We had a diaper service for a while, and all three of us, including Ruth, would change David in turns, cleaning him, rinsing out the cloth diapers, carefully pinning together the fresh diaper, fearful of stabbing him as he wriggled. Later we switched to disposables.

For the next two and a half years, neither Connie nor I had a full night's sleep. Ruth managed to sleep through David's crying rages and fits, and more often than not, we would keep him in bed with the adults, bonding with Connie, which made Ruth jealous, because she wanted him to bond with her. We fed him bottles of Similac.

The preflight report from the Holt Agency had described him as "babbles well...walks well in walker, crawls well, not shy with strangers, fond of coming out being carried on one's back, cries if no one is around him...curious, is a cute baby."

From our IAI counseling sessions, and from articles about adoption, we had learned that primary bonding would be with one parent, usually the mother. Also to expect the baby's grief and his fear of abandonment and loss, given the loss of his birth mother, and then of his foster mother, losses heightened even more by the shock of changing familiar sounds, language, and sights for a totally strange world. Night after night, as we heard his inconsolable cries, I felt we must be over-projecting our adult sense of his trauma, and that these were any infant's cries, given discomforts, for gratification: the dry diaper, the bottle, the rocking. But unlike Ruth, he had been deprived, separated from his birth mother's breast and body, and in our bed, I would hold him, so he couldn't writhe or kick as he raged and howled, wild and inconsolable, restraining him firmly with my reality and my love, to let him know I was aware of his anger, aware of his anguish, that it was okay, just noise, and that there was nothing I could do but what I was doing, which was to share and not let go.

We all loved him, and each of us in his or her own way, with our own emphasis, but together, also. Connie marveled. Ruth continued to compete with me for the second bond, to imitate Connie. Pictures. David sitting on Ruth's 7-year-old shoulders, feet around her neck. Ruth holding him grinning on her hip. David in his diaper, standing, arms propped on the back of the love seat by our front window, peering out—a favorite preoccupation, on the lookout for birds, squirrels, cars. Soon he was toddling, and we put up gates for his safety.

A photograph from 1986 shows Richard Yates in front of our house, one arm around Connie, the other around Ruth, who comes to Yates's waist, and who is holding infant David on her hip.

Connie took off work that spring, but in the fall of 1986 went back to the Atrium, half time, teaching first grade. She had found a day-care nanny, Lucille MacDonald, who lived across the street from the Atrium and who looked after ten or so children each morning in the furnished basement of her home. Ruth had transferred from the Watertown Elementary School to the Atrium after finishing second grade, so while I headed into Boston to Emerson, Connie would drop off David at Lucille's, Ruth at her Atrium class, and then start her own teaching day, which ended at noon, when she would pick up David. Through day-care, as she had through the playgroup with Ruth, Connie cultivated friends, with whom she traded favors.

The Atrium School had become for Connie what *Ploughshares* had become for me, more a mission than a job, and the social arena where she felt her talents most challenged and recognized.

The school had been founded in 1982 by Ginny Kahn, a wealthy educator, and initially it occupied space in an East Watertown cultural center. Connie had been hired there in 1983, thanks to the recommendation of a teacher who had worked with her in Head Start, and who now had a child at Atrium. Connie had stopped teaching six years earlier, when Ruth was born. Here she admired Ginny, and the hard-working director and his wife, and made close friends with her fellow teachers. She loved the school and loved teaching. In 1985, Atrium had relocated in the Browne School, a public school building that had been vacated by the town, and that was only two blocks from our house. Where classes had been limited to Kindergarten through Third, they now expanded to a full program, serving Pre-K through Six. They encouraged Connie to go back to school for teacher certification, which she did, at Emmanuel College, taking courses from teachers less experienced than she was herself. Her full-time teaching began in 1987.

One of my joys was to go out walking with David in a backpack, sharing nature. He would pull on my hair or ears, and we'd be talking all the way, unless he fell asleep. We hiked down the street to a one-hundred acre federal estate, Gore Place, where a trail led through woods, and there was a pen with sheep. When he had trouble sleeping at home, at night, sometimes I would walk him around the house in the backpack. Later, he could ride in a safe kid's seat on the back of Connie's bike, all strapped in. She would take him out, or we'd go out together; or I would take her bike and ride off with him.

He studied and imitated me, man-wise, when he could, from pretend shaving to practicing golf shots on our back lawn, to pretend mowing with his bubble mower. The playground across the street had a tot lot, with a slide and special swings, and David especially enjoyed being pushed in the swings and otherwise watching Ruth perform on the monkey bars.

⊶∞∾

Life went on, as life does. Just as we thought that we had reached one plateau, more setbacks would come. There would be the gauntlet of rejections of my novel, and the emotional link between my lack of publication and my infertility. The *Ploughshares* strife with Peter would continue. Where Emerson promised us stability, and where I expected to win tenure, along with chairmanship of the writing program—and a permanent shelter for the magazine—the tenure and chairmanship would be contested by a campus rival, and the Emerson affiliation opposed by Peter.

There would be strain on our marriage again, as away from home, Connie's and my lives divided more and more. Where I would need understanding, deference, and help, Connie would feel as a working parent that she needed logistical and emotional support as well. When it came to issues of time and domestic responsibilities, I would resent first having to meet teaching obligations, then having to sacrifice writing time in order to stay with Ruth and David while Connie went off to Atrium committee meetings, WCES, or to visit with friends. I would resent having my contributions resented as too little, too late. I would feel Connie's detachment now from *Ploughshares* and from my writing life, which she seemed to view more as my impossible dreaming than as my promise of publication or success. But what would sting me most would be the denigrating comparison of me to other fathers, other husbands, all of whom worked for their families first, it seemed—not for some grandiose ambition. Having worked their forty-hour weeks, their time and hearts would be their families'. They would take their children places, gladly parenting nights and weekends, while their wives had lives and activities of their own. At the Atrium, all the fathers would join willingly in activities that I would shun; all were able to, somehow: fairs, assemblies, picnics, clean-up days.

There would be more deaths. Dick Yates would move away to LA, then to Tuscaloosa, Alabama. The last time I would see him would be at the Indiana Writers Conference, the summer of 1990, when, even a needing a wheelchair then to relieve his lungs from walking long distances, he had been pursuing fiction writer Judy Troy with the expectations of a younger self. He and I both did readings, mine from new work about my family past, which he thought was as good as or better than my novel. He would call me periodically from Tuscaloosa, gasping to speak between breaths from an oxygen mask. Then would come a sudden call from Seymour Lawrence, his publisher, telling me that Dick had just died, November 7, 1992. There would be a memorial gathering in New York, followed by another in the Lamont Poetry Room at Harvard, on Dick's birthday. In eulogy, "Richard Yates," I would say, "will always be one of the 'few good voices in my head,' speaking to my aspirations as both an artist and a human being. I hear him saying, in essence: love life, live, what are you afraid of, be a father, be a husband."

Tragedy would visit family friends, the Farrens, beginning in early 1993: a two- year ordeal of their son's, Gabe's, dying of liver cancer, followed immediately by the father's, Pat's, three-year battle with brain cancer until his death. Where Gabe was David's best friend, Pat was his "second father."

Though I would get tenure, become Chair of the Emerson writing program, and after a bitter legal struggle with Pe.er see *Ploughshares* acquired finally by Emerson: at school, campus and department politics would undo me. Emerson itself would go berserk, with faculty and trustees divided on the transition from one Presidential regime to another. I would be voted out as Chair. I would lose control of *Ploughshares*. I would find myself marginalized in a world that I had largely created, or felt that I had.

Coincident with the troubles at Emerson, I would send out my second book with high hopes only to meet with more rejections—good book, unmarketable. I would come to doubt my own motives and validity. I would struggle with a drinking problem. I would become equally addicted to marathon training, driven by grief and anger. I would have the impulse to abandon everything.

My father's alcoholic breakdown had been in the decade of 1944 to 1954, when he had felt compromised in a corporate career by having to return home and take over the family candy factory for my domineering, yet ailing grandfather, who died soon afterwards. My sister's trial came with her husband's desertion right after our mother died, and then within two years, her son's death from AIDS. My brother Chuck's family life ended with divorce and estrangement from his three sons, and his career as a cancer surgeon ended with an early retirement that he blamed on the cost of malpractice insurance. He also had a drinking problem. My mother had stayed with my father "for the children's sake," but always had wondered what her life might have been had she chosen to leave "for self." In her last ten years, after my father's death, as much as we had meant to her, she felt that once we had grown and grown away, that she was left a widow in an empty house, where (as she wrote) she spent her time—that loved and magnificent person—"trying to justify [her] existence."

But now as I faced my abyss, my family would save me.

I would invest myself during that critical summer of 1993 in David. We would go biking, all nine miles to the MIT bridge and back (Dave's bike still on training wheels). We would stop at the bridge to watch far off the visit of tall ships to Boston Harbor. We would stop to buy lunch and eat it along the river. This was my running path. From the path we would see the Boston skyline first, far off, then nearer, especially the Prudential building. Along the river, canoes, kayaks and crew teams would row in shells. Then David and I would rent canoes. We would learn the Charles from midstream, watching, as motorboats washed us with their wakes, and as the scullers rowed past, the joggers, bikers, skateboarders and bladers along the riverbanks, who would be watching us. I would take David in to work with me, and we would go into the Prudential and all the way up to the Skywalk, where we would watch planes land and take off from Logan in vista, then using the coin-operated binoculars, search the meandering of the Charles north and west, along the very paths we had biked, until we spotted the red roofs of the Arsenal Mall in Watertown. We would go to fireworks on the fourth. We would go out to Walden Pond, the two of us, for the first time in years for me.

Down the years, friends would save me. Teaching would save me. Successive chairs and administrations at Emerson would build the writing program in the direction that I had envisioned; my adversaries would move elsewhere, replaced by genuine colleagues. *Ploughshares* would flourish, thanks to the dedication of my protégé and successor, Don Lee. I would go on to publish several more anthologies, and, after four revisions, my novel.

My children would grow. They each would graduate from the Atrium; Ruth would go on to Belmont Middle and High School, and then leave for Hampshire College; David would go to Beaver Country Day School. I would be absorbed in their struggles and negotiations with the world.

Where once my life had seemed impossible to imagine with children, now life would prove impossible to imagine without them.

But most of all, Connie's love and faith would save me. I would tell her in a 20th anniversary note: "At loving cost to yourself, you have brought me to places in myself I don't know about or imagine. I thank and salute you for that. As long as I have known you, you have never felt or acted mean-spiritedly or selfishly towards others. You have shaped our family. You have loved and cared for and supported your mother and brothers and sister, as well as my mother and brothers and sister. You have shaped other people's children as a teacher for the span of our time together. You have also proven to be a citizen of friendships, and of values in the world. I am proud to be your partner, lover, husband, and even more smitten by you and grateful for the luck of our finding and joining lives than I was waiting for you to join me in front of Judge Sweet. Even more because we are more, each of us."

I write this now in my basement study, same house. David's teenage music—defiant hip-hop—penetrates from upstairs. Throughout all my ambivalences, all my arrogance, my fears and angers and confusions, I realize in this time of outcomes, I was being split open by new life, myself out of myself. I was arriving as a fuller human being, with Connie's attending.

Bungee

She didn't like to do things where the trick was not to die
—Lorrie Moore

Here I am. I've decided. Actually I decided before the ascent, before the free ticket, before the swaying, crowded cable car, before the tundra and alpine wind, the high camp resort, the skating rink, the open swimming pool, the bar and bloody mary, when, down below, I had only heard about the crazy bungee attraction on the edge of a cliff, and how wind or mishap, and you would do a Gloucester, five ship masts down, where thou wouldst shiverist like an egg.

⸺

I am at the Squaw Valley Writers' Community. I am here for one week in August 1994, as the fifty-three-year-old founding editor of *Ploughshares* literary magazine. I have come all this way, 2500 miles from Boston via Denver to Reno, then a limo with congenial others past and through burning forest fires until we get to Tahoe City, and then to Olympic Village at Squaw. I am housed in a well-appointed sky lodge, steeply up an opposing hillside from Olympic Village, and just downhill from where the genius and organizer of the conference, novelist Oakley Hall, and his family live. My lodge mates are novelist Sandra Scofield, whom I published early in her career, and with whom I have had some correspondence; and Paul Mandelbaum, representing *Story* magazine. Sandra is a workshop leader. Paul and I are "outside readers," asked to read for publication and to comment on a number of pre-selected manuscripts by conferees. The weather is clear. Mountain nights cold and crystalline with swarms of stars, dawns chill, days hot by noon.

⸺

I have enjoyed repeatedly John Frankenheimer's film, *To Live and Die in L.A.*, which opens with a treasury detective bungee jumping for recreation off of a bridge. The character's jump, of course, becomes a metaphor. He is addicted to risk. That is why he pursues a brilliant and vicious underworld Willam DeFoe, who is a counterfeiter. The detective survives his bungee jump, but he is killed later in the line of duty. This happens to driven people, we opine, people attracted by danger and risk.

⸺⸰⸺

"Occurrence at Owl Creek Bridge" by Ambrose Bierce is probably another reference point. How could he have written this before bungees existed?

⸺⸰⸺

When, years and years ago, I trusted my older brother to catch me, as we sought to scare strangers with our act, I would simply fall forward, stiff, like a board, hands at my sides, and he would catch me, to others' gasps and thrills, inches from the swimming club's cement. I trusted him to catch me.

⸺⸰⸺

Forty-five dollars: that is the first dare, at least for Scottish/Irish me. If it were free, I tell myself, or if someone else sponsored me, but to sign away all liability on the one hand and to pay forty-five dollars for a thrill on the other, this causes pause. I sit with the conferees, two men, two women, witty, talented, sexy, young, with whom I have ridden in the cable car. We watch the jumping. A steady alpine gale blows in our faces and hair, not unpleasant. The surround is rocks and tundra. I think of Hemingway's epigraph to "Snows of Kilimanjaro": nobody could explain what a leopard was doing at this altitude. Here at some 8000 feet, over the valley base of 6000 feet, was a sports mall, a bar, a swimming pool, a skating rink, and as advertised, off one side, on a cliff edge, a girdered bungee scaffold (your basic erector-set, two verticals and a bridge, perhaps fifty feet high, a ladder up one side, with guy wires for stability). The resort managers called it "upper camp," and during ski season, when all those time-share lodges were filled with vacationing and well-heeled skiers, no doubt it thrived. The whole Squaw Valley thrived.

⸺⸰⸺

To Eastern, marathoning me, in mid-summer, the upper camp seemed surreal, some capitalistic caprice worthy of Citizen Kane, with down at the base every day at noon, a Swiss costumed trio playing "edelweiss" in the courtyard, and the big cable cars, right out of some movie, say *The Eiger Sanction* with Clint Eastwood, starting up. The cable car building, an edifice, had its own restaurants and shops, but especially, for a price, had a thirty-foot facsimile of a rock face that visitors could climb. People, adults and children, lined up for their chance. College kids on summer jobs hooked them up to rock climbers' harnesses, ropes and pulleys and monitored their climb up the plaster protrubences and hand and foot-holds that simulated a cliff face all the way to the sound-proofed ceiling, some thirty, all-weather feet.

I've heard, back East, of bungee disasters. In Portland, Maine, where I was on the staff of another writer's conference, there were fliers inviting takers. Apparently they used a crane in a parking lot, and there was some story of a jumper whose harness broke. Splat.

Something in me doesn't care if I die or not. I have lived my life. I have made my account. I'm insured. My wife and children are financially planned for. I trust, I guess, the "system." Hundreds of people take this risk, and surely the Squaw Valley corporation couldn't allow it if it really weren't safe. But something in me still is fatalistic, not caring at this point.

The drop is like a hangman's drop, an executioner's, but farther and longer, perhaps three or four seconds. It begins, once the harnessed jumper is in position on the scaffold, with the bungee master chanting over a loudspeaker, "one, two, three, BUNGEE!" At which point, the jumper, previously identified as Jennifer, say, is supposed to dive. The first woman we watched did so, on cue. Wheee! She fell, harnessed from the back to her thick umbilical, then hit the limit of its stretch and rebounded maybe two-thirds of her drop, down again, rebounded, two, three times maybe, before the resilience died, and then the bungee master lowered her into the big, inflated safety cushion underneath, and she thrashed and waded to terra firma, unbuckled and shouted again, whee! And came staggering back towards the bungee office, or stopped to have friends take her picture.

Some parent or guardian pays and sends a ten- or twelve-year-old girl up. She has the harness on. She climbs, hand over hand, the high ladder of the scaffold. She walks the transverse platform and waits her turn, waits for the Bungee Master to beckon and call, and to attach her harness safely to the bungee cord (imagine the job description here; he himself seems college age, nineteen or twenty; he is undoubtedly a bungee fanatic, a proven veteran). Lets him position her, counsel and calm her. Ready now? Stand there, I'm going to count, and then you jump, okay? She smiles wanly, swaying in that steady wind, trying not to look down except at the scaffolding itself and her feet, trying to feel the actual and rough and hard facts of her apparatus and of reason, avoiding the deep look below or the even deeper, vanishing look at the vistas of drop and sky and mountain ranges. Trying to be rational, be brave. But still her heart is thumping more loudly than ever in her life, her vagina and her rectum clenched. When here, this boy, not so much older than she, hair windswept, as casual as a high steel worker, as bored and ordinary as the bagboy at her supermarket, starts chanting, and the loud speaker echoing her name, Jeannie, and one, two, three, BUNGEE! Except she doesn't move. She can't. He doesn't push. He reassures, counsels, and tries twice more, before she says she can't, she wants to go back down, unbuckle, please, and climb back down. No refunds. Next?

Robert Stone is here. Richard Ford is here. Amy Tan, too. Al Young, authentic guru. Stone has bungeed into drugs and politics. I find myself worrying with the conferees about their tameness, their well-behavior. I want their skins on fire.

I think of skydivers and skiers. Of my Boston dentist, Ed Donle, an avid skier, who has, in fact skied at Squaw, as well as at Aspen, and someplace in Utah, where the skiers were flown in by helicopter, he told me (as he drilled my root canal), and were dropped on pristine mountain tops, with no way back but down, with no marked trails.

⟨⟨⟨

Fatalism is not the best of attitudes, but it is one I have increasingly acquired. My older sister and two older brothers as well. My mother too. Here I am tenured teacher of Shakespearian tragedy, thank you, at Emerson College in Boston; beyond stoicism, instance after instance, of accepting one's fate: "That's he that was Othello. Here am I." Or T.S. Eliot's favorite: "Ripeness is all." I feel that I am at that place in my life, not despairing, but not fearful either, not regretful or apologetic. I've given my account. "If it is not now, it will be later. If it is not later, it will be now." The chances of a safe jump, of something like a suicide, but not really, not literally, are high; the chances of an accident low: but still, they are, high or low, chances, risks. Why take them? Why the fast lane bimbo? Why the ten-year-old? I feel that I have nothing to lose, even though I do. All life is a surprise, I know.

⟨⟨⟨

Why not? We're all just—us—this paragon of animals, this quintessence of dust. Let me tell you. I gave them my Visa card. I read and signed the release. No heart problems, no. No medications. I was excited in a way comparable to buying magazines with nude pictures as a teenager, or condoms later. Hey, I am doing this. I am aware, thank you. I am showing off for you and for myself and for those here to witness and for those later I will tell about it, if there is a later. Stephen Crane stayed in a flophouse; Henry Miller went to Paris, Hemingway to war, to bulls, to fish, and to women. What am I doing here? What is this leopard doing at this altitude? I fit the harness on. The girl in the office checks it, adjusts and arranges it. They are used to "me" here, they know my type. There is a normative procedure here, just as there is, so boringly, on airline flights. Fasten seat belt like this. Oxygen masks will drop down. Lights will lead to exit. Here, we need to fasten this a little tighter. How's that. Raise your arms. Good.

⟨⟨⟨

I feel good, and foolish, at the same time. Good, as if I am braving superstition, whistling in my dark; stupid in that I am showing off, for myself, and for the conferees. Anyhow my money is spent, my border crossed. Fool, philosopher or what, there is no return for me as there was for the ten- or twelve-year-old, whose retreat I wanted to cheer and to applaud. I feel exposed. I start my climb hand over hand. Real weight. Real metal cold under my hands. Real distance, higher and higher. The wind feels stronger and I am more fragile, clinging to my ladder, climbing, not so far, and yet it feels forever, heart-pounding rung after rung. (Maybe this is suicide: maybe that is the power and pleasure, as I look down at my perspective-dwindled witnesses, my distant admirers, as I gaze off into the inhuman vastness and beauty of geology, the mountain rangings. Why not? Cleopatra: "There is left ourselves to end ourselves.") I reach the top, where College Boy is waiting. Climb up shakily, holding guardrails, to the catwalk, open like a sidewalk grate. I feel the scaffold tremble, vibrate and sway, yet here is this twenty-year-old, up here all day ("Yo! Lunch break, huh? John break?"), adept in cowardice, in folly, in measures. As knowing and solicitous in his obsessions as a bartender, mortician, or prostitute, and god help us, a writing teacher, in his/hers.

Where is my wife? Where my two children? Where my students? Where my dentist, my friends? Where my life back in Boston? They are no more part of this experience than Bunyan's Pilgrim's domestic and social lives are part of his Spiritual Progress. Except that all of my commitments have been plunges into faith.

Jonathan Edwards: "The God that holds you over the pit of hell, much as one holds a spider, or some loathsome insect over the fire, abhors you, and is dreadfully provoked . . . You hang by a slender thread, with the flames of divine wrath flashing about it, and ready every moment to singe it and burn it asunder . . . your most lamentable and dolorous cries and shrieks will be in vain."

I am performing for him now, Mr. Bungee Master. Eye contact. Sizings up. I am brave, savvy, stalwart, myself in his eyes. No fool, no problem. Me in my Carpe Diem 10K T-shirt, baggy shorts, and running shoes. Him round-faced, blonde, shorter than me and hefty, a mountain climber, trail boots, yellow windbreaker. No philosopher, I'm sure, no reader, no wit; not accustomed to writers, so much as to affluent fast-laners, a business major, maybe a geologist. Hang-glides. Surfs. "Ready? All set?" He waits at the platform, a railinged box center girder, where the bungee is attached overhead and gathered in coils to the side, and he holds the heavy clasp ready. He is my judge, my junior boss, smugly teaching the simplicities. "Face forward," he instructs. "Relax, go with it. Just do a swan dive." He hooks me up. "That's it, right to the edge. When you get to the bottom, I'll give you slack. Just reach around, undo the clasp. Okay?" I feel him check my harness, the bungee clasp. He pats my shoulder, like a parachutist's sergeant. "Let's do it!" He wants a good fall.

⸺

One! Two! Three! . . . Bungee! Your voice joins the amplified, big noise of his, as fuck it, the choice, you surrender: fall forward, as if to dive, pulling coils of the bungee after, so all becomes resistless drop, weight seeking earth like love, weight weightless, plummeting, dropping, nothing to catch, to grab, all loss and empty, wild, let be, let, plummeting, faster, instants and evers, like some years ago the slow motion of my bicycle as the motorcycle having seen me, pulled out anyway through the stop sign, that awareness past avoiding, happening, coming, coming, then the hit, the fact, and then the consequence, the hurtle, feeling rider and his cycle caving, feeling myself in mid-air and tumbling, feeling the drop and impact of the street, this is happening, bang, bang, my head bouncing on the pavement, here in middle of the road where cars are coming, bouncing like a basketball, and then stillness, lying still, the happening finished, consequence unknown, waiting to discover, am I hurt, how badly am I hurt, bungee like that, the plunge, the rush and surge of ground beneath, against the elastic tug, then pulled up, jerk, hard, and the reverse energy heaving me up, up, uncontrollable, and dropping again to the limit, the surge, the jerk, and up again, but not as far, writhing in mid air, shouting, and down, and jerk, and up not as far, not as far, and the elastic slowing, the up, down dying, fading, until I am lowered into the hardness of the inflated pillow beneath, my feet sinking into moonwalk, wading through the rubbery, chafing canvasy give of it, to the edge, where I reach around to unbuckle, and slide off the side to solid earth, wind blowing, normal sounds, and somewhere off there normal people watching, unexhilarated, inexperienced, pygmies as I stagger towards them. Done. I've done it.

—∞—

Did I jump or didn't I? Who cares? I have decided to start a new magazine called *Bungee*. Aside from attracting sports fanatics, I hope to attract those who understand the metaphor: isn't this life? Isn't this art? We live and trust in our safe suicides. We yield to sleep at night, or to sexual climax, like death, that unresilient and forever drop, but then, surprise, like the skydiver's opening chute, we have had the experience without the consequence. We are saved, as promised, this time. Or maybe not. Falling.

Gravity

I think of little deaths, a sneeze, an orgasm; how close such seizures are at once to vacancy and to the utter concentration of black holes, pure gravity. At once experience past will, past memory or thought; and an absence too, a non-experience. Comatose, the epileptic fit; no chance to dream. And yet like dreams, I hear reports of near-death experiences. My mother, after a worst of worsening episodes of heart failure, "They threw me back, like an undersized fish." Or on the talk shows, or in movies, survivors reporting, as if abducted by aliens. "I rose up out of my body, weightless, and was looking down at myself as the surgeons kept working on my open heart." Or before airplanes, let alone manned space flight, the poet's vision of Troilus slayn: "His lighte ghost ful blisfully is went / Up to the holownesse of the seventh sphere . . . And doun from thennes faste he gan advise / This litel spot of erthe, that with the sea embraced is." I think of weight, of burdens, of things we carry; of freedom birds, carrying us home. Of Walden Pond, the poet's fact; still waters I wade into this midlife summer's day, the sudden drop from shallow shelf to cliff-steep depths, buoyed up, treading and paddling; impulse, then, to plummet, deep breath, feet together pointing down, and arms outstretched, lifting to push down, again, again, the downward glide from surface, greenish light and body temperature, to cold, dark, and colder, and pressure's crush, one body's length, one fathom, two at most, blood's beat and thunder, nothing below, all depth and fathomless, and could go deeper, could stand more, but panicking and choosing to rise, as if below would be some point beyond return, past choice. The desperate rising then, the scramble, craving surface, air, as if beyond my reach, flutter kicks and climbing strokes, faster, nearer, out, and breaking into air, and light, gasping, sunlit world of other waders, parents, children, youths, and swimming in, first touch of bottom, standing, eyes and nose and mouth above the water, while checking on the shore, the languid eyes of strangers, oiled shoulders, tummies, and bikinied breasts. Then out, and down again, again, but each time rising, having touched in emptiness some point of dread.

—◦◦◦—

Years ago, my oldest brother visited me and my young family in Boston from his home in the Colorado Rockies. He flew cross country in a four-seater, single-engine, bi-plane, a 1939 Grumman Staggerwing, which had been built for long-distance flight, used for carrying mail, and later for submarine hunting during World War II; when I'd been married, he had flown the same plane to Florida, and had stood as my best man. He had rebuilt the plane himself, from motor to wing struts, and used it for his construction business. He loved to give us turns at flying it, or at least at holding the stick and steering crescent. That visit to Boston was my first turn, with my wife Connie and our four-year old Ruth in the back seat. I was accustomed to commercial jets, the rush and surge of take off, flattening me against my cushioned seat; the cumbersome lift, and climb and ground falling away, atilt. In the Staggerwing, I discovered the unnaturalness of flight, the violence in defying gravity with thrust. The huge single-propeller engine, with its exposed ring of carburetors, following on my brother's priming, as first, outside, he pulled full weight on the propeller, suddenly coughing to life, revving full, as inside we were buckled in and he managed the throttle. The roar, deafening, throatier than a diesel truck or fire engine. The alarm of our fragility, seated behind what seemed to be the world's largest and most powerful fan, which Jack throttled down for taxiing, then having been cleared on the radio for take-off, throttled up, let strain and shake, then brake off, let propel us, noise and power beyond imagining; until, rolling forward, ground speed gathering 30 to 50 to 65 mph, he pulled the stick back, and we lifted free, our climb abrupt and steep and the motor at its peak, churning, sawing and tunneling hugely into air. Later, once we had leveled off at our altitude, some seven or eight thousand feet, cleared with radio control, and above and below at different times, spotted and followed other small planes passing, Jack let me take the stick and steer. Go on, take it up to ten, he urged, and cleared it on the radio; just pull back, that's it, easy, feel it. Like swimming, free to head anywhere, it seemed, the vastness of choice, bank left, bank right, gently level. I'd grown accustomed to the motor's pitch, the roaring and vibrations, to shouting over the noise, to the boring fact of landscape below. I headed for the only mountain on the horizon, landmark for Framingham, some fifty miles distant. I was flying.

—◦◦◦—

The weightlessness of grace, Nureyev in ballet, Jordan in basketball. Defying gravity, floating, unnaturally and wonderfully free. But only through the costs of discipline, muscular strength and peak conditioning, distilling weight to power and purpose. The rise from anonymity to self, like that. From mud to stateliness and love, perhaps.

***

Another time, a worst year in our lives, July 4, 1985. I was struggling with the uncertainty of my infertility after two years of trying for a second child, and a gauntlet of treatments, this month a pregnancy maybe, this month, but the passing time and disappointment was taking a toll on Connie. We went into couples counseling. My closest friend, Richard Yates, who had moved to Boston, was having breakdowns, in and out of hospitals. My mother was living out her months of dying in her home outside Philadelphia. My bid for tenure at my only paid job was in political jeopardy on campus. My novel manuscript was repeatedly rejected.

Ruth was eight-years-old. She begged to go late to the annual carnival, a mile down the street, at the high school playing field. Connie was too tired to go, but I agreed finally. We set off alone, father and daughter, hoping to see fireworks. There was none at the field, but then we went on rides, two violent up-and-down and spin-around rides. The first was on rising and falling arms with rotating pods on the end, in one of which we sit, and it is fun at first, but as it speeds and the whiplash swoops and whirls have me on the edge of panic, and I'm waving to the operator kid to stop out of fear of my own blacking out, comes the swoosh! and I'm out of total control and god knows how many g's slamming your guts and heart and muscles all back against your body cavity, and then another, my god, another, and holding Ruth for fear of its effects on her, and her *I don't like this, daddy,* and then getting off, at long last, staggering, shaking, dizzy . . . then into fun house, then up on the Ferris wheel which was gentle, then one last ride, on what Ruth called bumper cars next to the whoosher whirl. We waited for a place on these, and the ride didn't look violent, but when we get in, it's the whole thing all over, same as the first ride, nightmare and torture on top of the muscle and organ memory of the first and we can't stop it, can't get off, fear being sick, fear blacking out again. When it's over, we stagger home nauseous, vowing never, never again. As for me, the rides remind me too much of the things being done and happening to us in our lives. I feel lost.

G's. Science fiction first. Nearly coincident with news of Sputnik, the 1958 movie, *From the Earth to the Moon*, impressed me with its nightmare images, as terrible to me then at age seventeen as images of skull-distorting birth, of astronauts (unlike Flash Gordon or Captain Video or any previous movie travelers into space), slammed into seats by rocket thrusts, their faces pulled down and back, screaming, lips pulled back, as if the flesh would split, eyes pulled back, blood streaking from mouths and noses, bodies crushed, all blacking out; then rockets quit; and one by one, the astronauts recover, faces back to normal, eyelids flutter, groans, bodies stir, cognizance, seats back upright. In the 1865 Jules Verne novel, which I had read at age thirteen, and on which the film was based, a projectile with three men inside is shot from earth towards the moon by a huge mortar. The film adds V2 footage and the image of a multi-finned rocket ship, but otherwise closely follows the archaic speculations of the novel. In Verne's prose, as the astronauts revive, they doubt that they are moving; they may still be "resting on the soil of Florida." Heat "produced by friction on the atmosphere" is the first clue they are in space. They unbolt window hatches, see stars, nearly collide with a meteorite, eventually sight the moon, then the earth: "that little thread; that silver crescent." The conditions of free-fall remain unanticipated either by book or by film.

An avid teen reader of paperback sci-fi, I was distracted and even offended by the scientific speculations of Arthur C. Clarke, whose spaceships weren't bullet-shaped or streamlined, but ugly and sprawling, and who imposed the rigor of physics on dreams of upward rocket flight. Instead of accelerating straight up, a moon rocket would have to angle into orbit, circle the earth, and using the earth's gravity for a slingshot effect, accelerate from orbit to an escape velocity of 24,245 mph. Interplanetary ships and space stations would be assembled in space, free of atmosphere and gravity. At the time, Clarke's insistence on debunking our conventional fantasies and updating them according to Einsteinian physics countered rather than captured my imagination.

Stanley Kubrick's 1968 film, *2001: A Space Odyssey*, was based on Clarke's speculations (Clarke co-authored the screenplay), as well as on discoveries from the space race. We had seen the film clips now of mice and chimps in space, floating, wired with sensors. From 1961, we had seen footage of twenty or more manned flights, showing man living and functioning in space. We'd seen instantaneous TV transmissions from orbit, heard the delay of crackly voices, seen pens and food packets floating out of reach, the astronauts' gymnastic somersaults. We'd seen space walks, astronauts suited with umbilicals. We'd seen the slightest touch propelling by reaction, like echoing sound.

Earthbound, Kubrick attempted vignettes of weightlessness, of Velcro-soled shoes, of a zero-gravity toilet, and of rotating space stations and rotating chambers that provided artificial gravity, with ups and downs. But the most haunting sequence, for me, was when space-suited Frank left his one-man service pod to glide, weightless, across to repair a communications antenna on the Jupiter ship; his abandoned pod, meanwhile, controlled by HAL, the psychotic central computer, moved to attack him from behind. Suddenly, from Dave's point of view inside the Jupiter ship, we saw Frank's struggling figure catapulted past the window, oxygen hoses cut, and cartwheeling, dwindling and slowly disappearing into infinite space.

A year later, July 20, 1969, we saw Apollo 11's manned moon landing in real time on television. Neil Armstrong, protected by a space suit, descended from the lunar module, pulled a cord, opening the lens of a TV camera, and reaching the surface, rasped, "One small step for man, one giant leap for mankind." Buzz Aldrin, who had been a teenage grease monkey with my brother Jack in high school, climbed down next. The two astronauts went bounding through the moon dust at one-sixth G, dreamlike, as if they wore seven league boots. They gave us photographs from a new perspective of the distant earth.

In recent years we've grown accustomed to watching, hearing, and reading about astronauts in orbiting space stations and space shuttles. Living in zero-g for weeks at a time, they tell us: "It's a very free and joyous feeling . . . You float. Floating is so extraordinary." Space shuttles don't have chairs. In zero-g, people go into a semi-sitting position and look as if they are sitting on invisible furniture. Body fluids move up toward the chest and head, making faces puff up and cheeks go higher, hands swell. Long hair needs to be held in place. Bones grow weaker; muscles shrink. Humans stretch in space, growing inches taller. Astronauts sleep on padded boards with an attached sleeping bag. Weightlessness, they say, makes you feel as if you have the softest imaginable pillow and mattress.

The weight of time, noses thickening, ears elongating, faces sagging. Shoulders stooped. Stomachs and breasts sagging, buttocks sagging. Forty, fifty, sixty, seventy years of weight, down pulling, down pulling, against our climb away, the force of steps, of lift. The nightly truce, of weight's surrender, lying flat (odd fact in 18th century, that Franklin, Jefferson, Washington and company slept sitting up).

As a college freshman, I memorized the tenets of quantum mechanics, without hope of understanding. Sir Isaac Newton: "All objects have a gravitational pull on one another." The strength of attraction, what we call "weight," is determined by the relative mass and distance between objects. The greater the mass, the greater the pull. Gravity bends beams of light. Gravity bends space itself. Collapsed stars create vortexes of gravity so intense that light cannot escape. Gravity is neither magnetism nor electricity. During my lifetime, we have built electromagnetic accelerators (I have wondered at the one at Stanford stretching for miles and miles), bombarded atoms and discovered smaller and smaller integers of matter, but gravity itself remains a mystery, like love.

Levity. Laughter. Levitation. Levitate. To rise. To make light of. Raised spirits. Risible. Comedy's lift, like a hot air balloon's. Resurrection. Erection.

The ship's hull ponderous, propped and cranked and craned, tonnage in dry-dock. Our strength is all gone into heaviness; that makes the weight.

A dream I remember from high school years is a dream of flying (my sister, on her own, also has dreamed of flying, she says). I practice by myself what everyone considers impossible. My arms are not feathered, but if I strain hard enough, I can compensate, for just an instant, for the lack of wing resistance by the furious flapping of my arms. I rise an inch, two inches, feel the unsteady suspension, then drop back down, exhausted. I keep practicing.

I tell my friends at school that I can fly, I can. Friends, bullies, girls, the disdainful and indifferent alike, all laugh. C'mon, no you can't.

Yes, I can. I'm telling you I can. Come on out to the football field and I'll show you.

Yeah, we gotta see this.

C'mon, Henry says he can fly. Gotta see this.

I'm ready in the end zone, facing them all crowded around the track. I start my routine, heart racing, knees loose, arms out. I smile at one friend, one face, Rudy, who is looking quizzical and worried. But then I get serious, lose him, lose myself. All their faces fall away, all sounds, cries, sneers, murmurs, gasps.

I concentrate, concentrate. Flap my arms, hands loose: up, down, up, down, harder, faster; up, down. It happens, finally! Just a bit. Lifting free, off heels, off toes. My feet have the familiar tingling.

Bear down. Eyes closed, clenched. Total effort, absolute, my arm sockets and shoulder muscles straining, searing, but I concentrate, up, until I'm utter body, free of body, lost in action, pure against all nature, inching up, laboring, as high as their knees now, their waists, Christ, as high as their heads! The work! But it is happening! Over their heads!

I am almost as high as the trees; almost, a little more, not quite. Higher, somehow, than I've ever thought, or meant to be. I am outside myself now, free of myself, at ease within my pain, marveling. There I am! Level with the third floor classrooms, gymnasium roof. I strain, but can't go higher. Can't last. Lapse, falter, my body thickens and grows ungainly, refusing to perform. I slow, struggling back. A little wobbly, side to side, afraid of dropping. Even with the crossbar on the goal posts, lower. My feet touch ground.

There! I look around proudly, hands propped on my knees, panting. I am drenched with sweat, coughing. My mind reels, eyes dazzle, pulse hammers. What do you think?

They look at me.

What "there"? When do you start? You haven't even left the ground.

Oh, yeah. Laughing. Some flying. What a jerk. What a loon. Did you see the creep? See his face?

They turn and leave in disgust.

All but Rudy. He crouches close. Dreams, he says. Anyone can dream. Me, I'm a rich dude. I'm a lead singer. His whisper grows maniacal.

Mercutio's dying wisecrack: "Ask for me tomorrow, and you shall find me a grave man."

The yearning of these words, tethered to vanishing.

Forces Of Nature: A Dream Retold

I was on a trip away from my family in Boston—my wife, my daughter, my son—to serve as a staff member for the Squaw Valley Community of Writers in the summer of 1993 in the California Sierras, near Lake Tahoe. Though I had been on trips before, trips of body and of mind, I had never been so distant from my family and my teaching job before. I was fifty-two. Back home at this time, close friends of my wife were living a family tragedy. Their youngest child, a boy the same age as my son, who was my son's best friend, had been fighting liver cancer for three years, and now the cancer had metastasized in his brain. I had just heard this news from my wife by phone. That same afternoon, the afternoon before my dream, I had been talking about my son to a young woman writer from Los Angeles who had been adopted and who was part-Korean and part-Jewish. Come evening, the hundred or so of us gathered to hear a talk by a dream expert, one Naomi Epel, whose hocus pocus talk about writing and dreams and the subconscious I thought silly. As I walked back to my staff cottage, I vowed not to dream. Of course I did dream. This dream. And yes, I did honor it on waking. I did write it down.

In my dream I am nine years younger and I don't live in Boston, but rather in a valley that's ringed by picturesque foothills and peaks and has been cultivated by damming a river, so that at one mouth of the valley there is an imposing concrete dam, not quite as imposing as the Hoover Dam, for instance, but imposing nevertheless. The dam has long spillways, a concrete span, floodgates, high-tension wires, and so forth, and behind the dam has risen a huge, recreational lake that stretches for twenty miles. The mountain valley is populated by privileged white families (including mine) and also by poor families of many races, which I am aware of as a fact, but not aware of as an uncomfortable one, any more than I am aware of the water gathered in the lake as an uncomfortable fact. Otherwise I am what I am in my waking life. A tenured college literature teacher, getting by. As in my waking life, my wife and I have two children, but in my dream they are younger. My birth daughter is eight years old, and my adopted Korean son is an infant, just as he was when he arrived in our home. Our decision to adopt followed several years of trying to have a second child of our own: years of trial centered on me, at my grief at being infertile, and on my reluctance to take on the responsibility of an additional child, but years, also, of mounting pressures from my wife.

In my dream, my daughter does not figure. Because of my privileged position in the valley, I hear that the dam is about to break, that the valley will be flooded. I hear this in time to gather my wife and son and drive to higher ground. So that when disaster comes, when the dam does in fact break and the tidal wave floods the valley, sweeping away all lives before it, we are safe. Afterward, we are able to return to our house to resume our lives. In my dream, the poor people, on the contrary, many of who are Korean, have lost everything, all of their children. They have had no warning. The water has descended upon them like a Biblical curse. Word spreads among these survivors that I have a son that is Korean. Not only do I carry on my privileged life in the face of catastrophe—my house modest yet comfortable, my grass green, my color television and lights beaming, my cupboard well stocked—but my son is one of theirs. This becomes a cause, reported by the media. There are slogans, placards, chants. I am horrified that our private lives have been transformed into images, symbols. The poor people organize and march on our house, surrounding it like the very waters we have escaped. They cry out for justice. Why should my son, one of theirs, remain with me? I try to explain, I am shouted down. They are pressing in on us, threatening to take my son from me. The dream, as dreams do, fills me with emotion, with guilt. My inability to explain. To reason with their calls for justice. To escape with our lives, and with my son. I am weeping, powerless, misunderstood, and futile. I wake. Wake to my life where there is no valley, no dam, no catastrophe. But where there is guilt, always. And where I will never, ever take the blessing of my son for granted.

Beautiful Flower

I. ON SELF-IMMOLATION

I have watched snuff films, the ultimate pornography; the idea of which is a verifiable, undeniable extremity, the viewer guilty of witness, if not of being an accessory after the fact. Increasingly graphic special effects have heightened our appetites for the literal. There is no faking a knife in the chest, not a real knife, a real chest. No faking a bullet. No faking the astonishment and terror of the victim. No faking strangulation and the death afterwards. Mean exasperation with the fake, strike through the mask. Faking of orgasm, yes. The male ejaculation on the female stomach for us all to see, we know that is real. But the female, who will ever know? And it matters, whether what we imagine and witness is real or is pretending.

The same, somehow, is true of mortal, self-sacrifice. I hate war. I hate the powers, beyond understanding almost, who propagate war. I could spend a lifetime, like Bertrand Russell's, expressing my hatred in words: but would you heed them? Would anyone?

Used enough to newsreels: the Buddhist monk in saffron, calmly cross-legged, hands on knees, as the flames sear and bloom, until finally, losing consciousness, he tilts and topples, consumed. How many in protest of the Vietnam War? But there, in Asia, on temple steps. Somehow alien, another world, another history, religion, character, culture. Human, but not us, not me. Maybe one or two monks here too, on monument steps, I can't recall. But do recall, from the news, a student's immolation on Amherst Common, the same Common where twenty-five years earlier, I had with drunken fraternity brothers, children of the 1950's, crowded in the city's Christmas Kresh, like a wise man, hiding from a police cruiser. *Ubi sunt*: Where are they, my friends, Tim Colvin (who later would die of a drug overdose in his adman's, swank Manhattan apartment), David Lahm (jazz composer and pianist), Dave Hamilton (teacher, essayist, editor), Jim Goldberg (technical writer, one-time Columbia University rioter and activist, who has never finished his thesis on Matthew Arnold). "Common," indeed, given supposed potential and privilege in common. At our twenty-fifth class reunion: doctors, lawyers, teachers, financiers. A carpenter or two. The self-disappointed failed to show.

What is a life's passion? I think of another classmate, Jon Rohde, working class background, regular guy, athlete, beer drinker, but a grind too, an uncompromising learner; married Candy from Mt. Holyoke just after graduation, went on to Harvard Medical, two daughters, dedicates himself for years in a research lab in Dhaka, East Pakistan, fighting cholera; relief work then in India; teaching medicine in rural Central Java; then to a post in Haiti in 1980, charged with "helping to develop"—he writes in our reunion book—"a nationwide rural health care delivery system . . . then, it all came unglued as Duvalier was deposed . . . Haiti, the nation of Job"; back to India as Advisor to UNICEF, USAID and other agencies working with child health.

Here is Evan Fraser, Amherst class of 1988, a sophomore, dreaming of a just society. Son of the Chairman of the English Department, University of Northern Florida. He came to Amherst on a merit scholarship. He wrote his high school English teacher, Rose Dufresne, that he sought with his life to express a brilliance that would stun the eye, so the image would linger. Five feet, six inches, 140 pounds, white male, reads the Town of Amherst Police report. No evidence of drug possession or use. Interviews with students, teachers, and neighbors determined that he was a "normal, young man," "decent," "earnest student," "good sense of humor." He lived in an apartment off campus, where other student renters saw him working hard, riding his motorcycle. He was survived by an older brother and sister. Mother died when he was fifteen. Father baffled. The message, the letter left for friends, society, the world: "I am Socrates, Jesus, Gandhi. Love one another."

Long run first, perhaps. Wonder at this world, this envelope. The shower, scalding, then cold. Skin glowing. Shaving. The layered, cotton clothing in eighty-degree heat. Save the Whales t-shirt. Heavy socks. The five-gallon can, heavy, sloshing. The rehearsals and viewings of news clips over and over. Saturate the grass first. Heavy can over head, after the clothes have been soaked. Sting in eyes, bitter on lips, fumes, cough breathing. Cloth heavy with wetness. Quick before anyone realizes or can interfere. Intensity of purpose, graceful, efficiency of movement. Like ablution. Flick the Bic.

It sears like hunger sears, like rape, like birth, like bursting bones, like impotence before the earthquake or the tidal wave, like cancer at its worst, like killing cramps, like migraine jaws, tightening, tightening. The pain is other, tangible, enemy and lover, engrossing, intimate. A corridor. A tunnel that I shoulder through, breathless and gasping.

But then sheer vision, faith.

II. ETERNE IN MUTIBILITY

Recorded lifetimes, stop-time photos, sped up after 90 years, so the faces morph like unfurling, then withering flowers, all in three minutes . . . The immolator, one of this study, needs to be slowed down in order to match the rhythm of the others; his twenty-two years ending in the stop frame, now, of two minutes, slow motioning his lighting of the bic, the flame itself like a bud, a flower unfurling, and then the bloom of fire slowly wrapping him around like a silken, bright robe, or even garlands blooming, something fragile, fragrant and soft, his face dissolving and melting, as all others melt at other speeds, within the liquidity, the pouring and the light.

An audience of fifty watches, ranging themselves in age from twenty-two to sixty, and evenly divided in gender, race, class, religion, and sexual orientation. After the fifty cases, result of a lifetime's experiment in film, the lights come up. Most in the audience are weeping, some are laughing, two, one fifty-two-year-old male, one twenty-six-year-old female, at extreme distances, up front and to the side, in back, are heedlessly masturbating. The rest are uneasily silent, denying and believing that they have seen anything yet, when will the show begin? They stare ahead stubbornly, expectantly, ignoring even the others as somehow rude, embarrassing, invisible.

III. A LECTURE ON LIEBENTOT

He stands before his fifteenth annual class in Shakespearian Tragedy. "Liebentot," he says to the thirteen faces, bright, young faces, college juniors, though sleepy and hung over this Tuesday, "dying for love. How do we understand this? Tristan and Isolde? Dido for Aeneas? Romeo for Juliet (the dope); Juliet for Romeo? Othello for Desdemona? Anthony for Cleopatra, and then a whole act later, Cleopatra, with the asp sucking its mistress asleep? 'O Anthony I come! Oh husband!' What is this? Jonestown?" And you, you Ms. Bright one, Ms. Mystery, YOU say: "Not Jonestown. Just proof. Proof of eternal devotion. Most lovers die one day at a time, like alcoholics stay sober. The silver, the golden anniversary. There's our proof, whatever they may think they mean themselves; they mean what they do. The deed in living, like those gison statues that Leonard Baskin did on the Smith College campus. Let attention be paid. Not kings and princes, memorialized for their nobility on burial caskets. But a steelworker, a miner . . . beer belly distended, naked, noble too in his self sacrifice, his daily endurance, his lifetime's act of love——" or perhaps, you sneer, "his failure of imagination." I wait and you go on. "One day at a time, like an alcoholic staying sober. Down all the days, adding up. A marriage, a career, a life's meaning. For the tragic characters, that's all sped up, is all. The same passion, less time." I pull a little rank: "Dying, you know, for folks in Shakespeare's time was a pun, based on the idea that every time you had an orgasm you took a day from the end of your life. The act of love, then, was a bargain, maybe a good one, maybe a bad, for intensity at the expense of longevity." YOU, you Ms. Bright, to be honest, you scare me. Maybe as much as Shakespeare scares those boys in back, the ones who, at Lear's entrance with Cordelia dead in his arms, start barking like dogs, "Howl! Howl! Arf! Bow-wow! Woof! Howl!" I tell them, "Guys, guys . . . you are giggling, wisecracking and whistling in the dark, like virgins in a whorehouse . . ."

IV. ONTOGENY RECAPITULATES PHYLOGENY?

"An animal in its individual development passes through a series of constructive stages like those in the evolutionary development of the race to which it belongs . . ." (Haeckel's biogenetic law, 1868).

Primordial soup. Thick and slab. Fire burn and cauldron bubble. Blake: "Eternity rolled wide apart/wide asunder rolling." Complex protein. Protozoa, four billion years ago. Sperm swarm, tail churn. Nature's germains. The single penetration, egg ignites. DNA. Chromosomes. Cells divide, divide. Germinal to embryonic. 3 billion years, future in the instant. Cambrian is gill arches. Placenta sea. My mother is a fish. Blake: "The globe of life blood trembled/ Branching out into roots/ Fibrous, writhing upon the winds." Now inner ear and neck, cartilages of larynx. Tail emerges, disappears. Zygote into embryo. Ordovician. 400 million years. Third moon, cartilage to bone. Fourth moon, heart forms; Fifth moon, ears, eyes, arms, and legs. Embryo to fetus. Mesozoic. Jurassic. 200 million years ago. Sixth moon, early primates. Skeleton visible. Sex organs distinct. Translucent skin. Eyelashes. Eyebrows. Body movements. Seventh moon, survival outside womb probable. Pleistocene. Homo erectus. Neanderthal. 100 thousand years ago. Holocene. Weight gains. Increased activity in kidneys, heart. Ninth moon, fetus to newborn. You. Me.

I ask you, now? The miracle, the life. The person out of the person, body from the body, flesh from flesh, crying we come forth. Time itself, apocalypse; ignition; Adam to atom; all existence in the flash.

V. NEW ENGLAND FALL, THIS YEAR

My fifty-sixth autumn, yet still, craning to peer through my windshield, then out my open driver's window, I stare with disbelief at the colors, the crimson glow, leaves lit by sunlight, against the deep blue of the sky.

VI. SOMETHING RESISTS

Something will not burn. King Nebuchadnezzar cast Shadrach, Meshach, and Abednego into the burning fiery furnace but this was God's showmanship, the clincher, preserving flesh from fire: "the hair of their heads was not singed, their mantles were not harmed, and no smell of fire had come upon them." Then there is purgatory, holy fires cleansing to essence. "I lean forward over my clasped hands and stare into the fire," says Dante, "thinking of human bodies I once saw burned, and once more see them there."

One dreams that faith itself preserves. To imagine burning is not to burn.

Wide-eyed

Young women in America will continue to look for love and excitement in places that are as dangerous as hell. I salute them for their optimism and their nerve.
—Kurt Vonnegut, from "There's a Maniac Loose Out There," *Life*, 7/25/69.

Unfortunately, in a father's overzealous desire to protect his little girl from risk and the discomfort of anxiety-provoking situations, he tells her that she is incapable, incompetent, and in need of help. His behavior sends a message that that is what he thinks of her, so she comes to believe it herself.
—Mickey Marone, *How To Father A Successful Daughter*, 1992.

I.

Neither my mother, nor my sister, nor possibly, my wife, felt that their fathers prayed for them. Nor have most of the important women friends in my life. What is a father's prayer? And why is it different for a daughter than for a son? Or is it?

My daughter, Ruth, is now a remarkable young woman of the Millennium.

I love her, and I fear for her well-being and pray for her future, but I have had to struggle with deep-seated instincts from my background in my regard for her. I was as a WASP manchild in the 1950's, a sexist bachelor in the 1970's, and a husband confronted with a wife's awakening during the women's movement in the 1980's, a time when divorce seemed epidemic in my generation. I have rallied, personally and culturally, to social progress in many ways and grown as a person in the process; but I have also, to be honest, often retreated to irony, casting a skeptical eyebrow. The Civil Rights Movement, resistance to the Vietnam War, the Sexual Revolution: all certainly bettered our world, but that was then. What quality of thinking now, I wonder, is involved in my personal efforts at recycling? Does returning empties amount to more than a gesture of morale, like my mother's saving bacon grease during World War II? Or take language: here I am politely vigilant about pronouns and gender (at a recent seder one of my wife's friends went laboriously through the Haggadah revising all sexist references to God), while grudgingly permissive about "it (or she or he) sucks" becoming acceptable usage for children. In my heart of hearts, the former seems to me humorless, the latter corrupt.

Thanks to my wife, Connie, my daughter's upbringing has been progressive. Connie has supported and advocated Ruth's full flowering as a woman and a person. Since 1983, Connie has taught at an independent K through six school devoted to progressive principles, and my daughter was one of the first graduates. For years, in cranky silence, I saw my wife's school as the Academy of Aunty Mame, whimsical and utopian in endeavor. I was preoccupied with my struggles as a writer and as a college teacher. I couldn't help patronizing my wife and her career, which seemed so opposed to mine.

During the process of adopting our second child, our son, David, Ruth combined with her mother to overcome my selfish fears about my ability to provide an adequate livelihood, fears postulated on my ambitions as a writer. In our application for the adoption, we characterized Ruth, at seven, in second grade, as "a happy, sensitive, unusually curious and creative child. She has a good sense of humor. She has wanted a brother or sister for a long time."

In describing myself, I wrote that "Pretty much I would be proud to bring my children up as well as I feel I was raised. I'd like to incorporate more of my mother into my fathering than I would my father, but as time passes I appreciate more his own practical insistence and the bulwark of his providing . . ."

Concerning our marriage, we wrote: "as Ruth grew to school age, Connie put her energies into volunteer political activities at first and more recently into earning accreditation as an elementary school teacher . . . The ordeal of infertility has strengthened our marriage, and has made us surer of each other and ourselves, of what each of us means and wants . . . We have a sound marriage, sound values, and a low-key, love-oriented life style (people first)."

Perhaps predictably the area of my greatest uncertainty and discomfort as Ruth has matured, and as the cultural mores of America have changed utterly, has been that of her sexuality. In reading recent feminist literature about fathering, I have been perhaps overly credulous, receptive to, and concerned about the charges of "distance." From Patricia Reis, for instance (*Daughters of Saturn*, 1995): "A father's inability to speak about certain things, especially his emotional realities, can later become a woman's silence." Also from Reis: "[The] internalized, vigilant father may also curtail a daughter's creative energies, especially if they are in conflict with his wishes or belief system." And from Victoria Secunda (*Women and Their Fathers*, 1992): "Fathers—not being female—compute a daughter's womanly body, not her immature emotions . . . Most fathers don't see the war within the daughter, her temptation both to retreat to Daddy's lap and protection and to push out of his embrace to that of beau and of the world beyond home . . . when a father gives his daughter an emotional visa to strike out on her own, he is always with her. Such a daughter has her encouraging, understanding daddy in her head, cheering her on—not simply as a woman, but as a whole, unique human being with unlimited possibilities."

II.

There I am, the fifty-five-year-old father, wide-eyed, heart racing at 5:02 am on the Sunday morning of Memorial Day weekend. Outside songbirds twitter and chirp. I am in bed, beside my wife, safe in our three-bedroom cape house in Watertown, Massachusetts, ten miles west of Boston. A noise has awakened me. A click. A familiar click. At 4:36 am I know what I have heard is the closing of the back door downstairs. That tell-tale whump. After a moment's listening, I hear the scrape of steps. This is no thief, no intruder. This is my nineteen-year-old daughter, Ruth, and her Hampshire College sidekick, Cassy, back from whatever adventure they had left for at 10:30 pm last night. I stare at the clock. I try to wake my wife. "It's 4:36, for chrissake. They've just come in!"

My wife remains intent on sleep.

Downstairs, water runs in the bathroom. For ten, fifteen, twenty minutes. What is going on? What could she, my daughter, have found in Boston or in Jamaica Plain? Or at salsa dance clubs, or in Greater Boston?

I am mindful of respect, of trust, but I already know too much.

I think of myself at nineteen or twenty, the summer after sophomore year. For me as a young man, an Amherst man, after all the deprivation of the hard school year, I had been out all night from my home in suburban Philadelphia, and I had come home drunk at dawn. I had come home and vomited in my family's downstairs lavatory, and the next day my mother had tactfully told me, here were my glasses, which she'd found in the toilet. How, my mother had wondered, had they gotten into the toilet? Had I been out with my old girlfriend, the Bad Influence, Brenda (home pregnant from Tulane)? Had I found a party of all-night booze and dancing at some suburban friend's house?

For my daughter, Ruth, now, I consider and fear the worst, while the poppa in me—the heart racing and troubled poppa of love and responsibility,

Conscience personified—churns over possibilities, discretions, indiscretions. I will talk to her tomorrow, after she wakes up in eight or ten or twelve hours, in the early afternoon. This isn't civilized, I will say. This isn't healthy. What are you trying to prove? This isn't hot-blooded youth; this is contempt for the whole normal world. This isn't partying in any sense but the defying of society, in this case the family you live with, us.

I can't get back to sleep. The daylight greatens. Distant crows or starlings now caww-cawww along with the susurrus of distant cars. Meaning not to disturb my wife, I get up and cross to my son's room, empty since eleven-year-old David is sleeping over at a friend's. I sit on David's bed (once Ruth's, as this room had been Ruth's, and later had been shared by Ruth with David, from the time David arrived from Korea as an infant). I look out the window at a deserted playground.

I imagine . . . yet stop: what *right* have I to imagine or to care? She is an adult. She has lived whatever private life she lives at college. She has held down her job clerking in a Northampton arts gallery. When she has overreached, the year before, and before, the instances have been those of what her mother calls "poor judgment." As Connie put it: "We are concerned about your having good judgment, for your safety."

A year and a half ago, Ruth had made an offhand statement to me, as the father, that she had an appointment at Harvard Health for an AIDS test. I had let that pass as worldly, until a few hours later, when it dawned on me, on the poppa in me—the poppa especially helpless and perplexed and guilty in the face of seeking to control or regulate her sex life among the predatory males that mirror his own worst dating years—that she was telling me she was having sex at college.

In such terms, I turn to my wife as Ruth's counterpart, the woman, the mother, the friend who projects her own overly sheltered girlhood and serves to champion Ruth's right to adventure, while also condemning her beforehand for provocative dressing (a charge that Ruth denies). My wife briefly and without further explanation confirmed the fact. I groaned.

Where do my responsibilities lie? I wonder. Again, now, this adult dawn, I go back and try to wake my wife. The water downstairs is still running—for what? To scour the taste of kisses or worse? To cover the sound of vomiting? A word or two passes between Ruth and Cassy. My wife mumbles, "No. I don't think there's a problem. Let me sleep." Which has always been her modus operandi.

Except for the bad times.

I remember December 16, 1994, two days before Ruth's seventeenth birthday. Ruth had just passed her driving test, and, newly licensed, had permission to take our station wagon, the newer of two used cars, to a party at a girl's house west of Boston, where she was sleeping over. The phone had rung shortly after 1 am, while I was still up writing at my desk in the basement and drinking vodka (an unhappy habit I have since quit). I did not answer my wall extension because my wife, who had finally gotten our son to sleep in Ruth's room, answered in the living room right above me. First I heard my wife's gasps and wails, then her calling down the basement stairs to me. That had been the police. The state police in Connecticut. Ruth had been in an accident. She was all right, but she'd broken her arm and the car was totaled. She was in a hospital in Rockville, Connecticut. When I got the gist of this, I shouted: "NONONONO!" and threw a coffee cup at the wall: dregs from it splattered everything, student papers, family pictures on my bulletin board, and the stains are still there to this day.

I was enraged, less at the prospect of physical harm to Ruth, than at her messing up. Her abuse of privilege. Her lie to us as a family. That in supposed innocence she was going to a sleepover, when in fact, or on impulse, she was driving to Connecticut to pick up an underage boyfriend she had known in summer camp, a boy fourteen, and to bring him to the sleepover, knowing that we, her parents, would never approve, let alone dream of such a thing in our philosophy.

At word of the accident, Connie never thought twice. She wailed and wept, but leapt to action. David was awake from the commotion, and Connie just dismissed the poppa raving and took David with a blanket and pillows and set off in our second car to go rescue Ruth and bring her home. I was left bereft, confused, guilty and worried. They arrived back later that morning, the three of them. Ruth with her arm in a sling. Connie glad to have her safe and alive. Police photos of the crumpled Taurus station wagon.

Temporarily, Ruth decided to stop driving, so that I worried and encouraged her to. The arm healed. Insurance on the book value allowed us almost overnight to buy a better car.

But the issue was her double life, much of which I trace to Rowe Camp in the Berkshires, an earlier way station into adult independence and license. My wife's friends had recommended it. They were social progressives and the parents of Jesse, the female Falstaff of Ruth's life since girlhood; where I have often felt cast as Conscience personified in Ruth's life, I feel Jesse personifies Id. In any case, Jesse was going, and the mother joked, to answer Connie's fears that the camp might be too conservative, that campers there, instead of burning crosses, burned question marks on the lawn. My wife championed the notion, and I went along with it.

Ruth, of course, had loved the camp, went back a second year as a camper, and a third and fourth as a counselor, age thirteen to sixteen. That first year Jesse had gone with her, but for Jesse the license had proven disastrous, I concluded, hearing of her sequel in drugs and truancy and runaway life in the Harvard Square underground, where a number of Rowe kids seem connected. Jesse did not go back.

The second year, Ruth found her first serious boyfriend, also named Jessie, by psychological happenstance. He was three years older, and after camp, Ruth wanted him to visit Boston and to stay overnight in our house, the way a girlfriend would. As Poppa, I had tried to object. I harked back to my family's standards. You don't bring temporary boys home (or if a boy, girls), especially at age sixteen. You don't waste your family's attention on learning experiences. My wife thinks, however, that this complicity with Ruth is healthy. She polarizes my misgivings—a pattern in our parenting. Ruth and Connie win, of course. Jessie boy arrives. Cooks vegetarian fare. Plays guitar and sings protest folk songs. Connie likes the boy. Myself, as Poppa, am civil with the boy, but guarded, and put off by the sentimentality and political activism. I am looking for irony. For intellectual edge, for questioning and alacrity. Also the boy does not appeal to me physically. Has a mealy, tubercular quality. He chats and entertains us all, especially David, whom he charms like an older brother. Bedtime approaches. Connie and Ruth make up the couch turned to double-bed-sized futon in the family room off the kitchen, where we've all been watching TV, and Jessie has lounged with his arm around Ruth. He "is not a virgin," Ruth has let Connie know, and Connie has told me.

They all set out for bed, goodnight, goodnight. Poppa, Connie, and David settle down upstairs, Ruth in her room, Jessie, after using the downstairs bathroom, snug in his bed in the family room. Connie, playing hostess, is the last one up. Lights out, upstairs and down, silence. Connie sinks into sleep, but The Poppa lies wide-awake, listening, too aware of myself at sixteen, too skeptical ever to believe Ruth's depiction of girls and boys at camp as living in some Peaceable Kingdom, transcending hormones. Was that a step, creaking? Yes, definitely. I try to wake Connie, unsuccessfully. Hear whispers, creaking. I am outraged. This isn't right. This is disrespectful. I can't ignore this, even if I wanted to. I have to go down. I have to let them know I know.

I don't sneak, but I don't call out either. Still not sure they are together. Just down the stairs, heart pounding, wearing t-shirt and sweatpants. Seeing light then, around corners, a glimpse through the kitchen into the family room; she is in Jessie's bed, they are making out. I don't want to see. I don't rage, but do say loudly, "Excuse me. With freedom goes responsibility! I just want you to hear that."

Ruth jumps up, flustered.

"I'm sorry, Daddy. We were just talking. We're going to bed now."

I don't wait for the final lights out, or her return to her room and shutting of her door, though all that happens as I turn angrily and retreat upstairs. Lie awake still, ever vigilant, no more creaks or whispers.

Still later, long after Jessie boy has become history (has gone to college in Florida, written and called, but gradually been replaced in Ruth's attentions by local boys), despite the Poppa's sense of becoming ludicrous, I will rehearse the principle: "not under my roof you don't"; don't flaunt your behavior, which you know instinctively upsets me, while you enjoy my hospitality and protection; and Ruth will counter with the ideology, supported now by intellect, reading and her peers: Only truth! Love me as I am!

⸺

6:04 am. Sounds again downstairs. More vomiting?

Was this some crazed orgy, I wonder, raving even as I allow for such thoughts to be irrational, unjust. If so, what? Have she and Cassy been loving physically with boys/men? If so, what sort? Dudes? Descendents of my bachelor pals? Drugs? What sort of parties would last from 11 pm to 4:30 am on Saturday night? What nightlife crowd in Boston's jazz or dance or nightclubs has she explored and found? The innocent version doesn't compute, the version she gives of hard dancing for hours which is no prelude to sex. The version which is not the ritual of oblivion, doped and drunk. (The summer before I have felt my worst fears confirmed by the unsolved au pair murder in Boston, where the top half of a twenty-year-old Swedish nanny was found in a dumpster and investigation had placed her late night dancing with a fast crowd at a club called Zanzibar.)

She provokes me, of course; provokes the foolish skeptic, the repressive Ego. This is my punishment for harboring suspicions and guilts.

As Dad, I helplessly project my own shadow self, a self denied and avoided by my wife, much as my own mother had supposedly avoided or hidden my father's alcoholism. The libertine Henry passion for extremes.

⸺

Three years ago, on her way to camp, she wrote me a note for my birthday:

"I hope you have a wonderful birthday, with lots of peace and quiet—
maybe I'll stay off the phone, or something. I really appreciate everything
you do for me . . . I also have a lot of respect for your integrity, as a writer, a
person, a father. You have a certain dignity which is difficult to emulate.
Perhaps we can spend some more time?"

Me? Dignity? With the backstage confusions and pathologies of my midlife
psyche? In my own notebook I am writing letters to myself about indignity.

<hr />

College at Hampshire, some three hours away (rather than at nearby Emerson,
where my faculty fringe benefit would let her go tuition free), has taken
some pressure off. She has her own roof there, her life. It is a family-financed
and supported progress into independence and responsibility. Ruth does
well academically, although now I am skeptical about her choice of courses,
primarily creative writing and courses in various Third World studies. She
seems sadly unfamiliar with literature by white males, living or dead. She
assumes that most of her liberal arts learning was covered by advanced
placement from high school. Cassy, the roommate, is her best friend, and
although Jesse remains her best friend at home, Ruth appears to me now to
be primarily under Cassy's influence. Cassy lives with her mother now in
Santa Fe and must badger her divorced father for money for college. Most
vacations Cassy comes to Boston with Ruth, so we never have time to visit
alone with Ruth, as family; the Poppa assumes this is deliberate, a kind of
buffer against intimacy. When visiting, of course, Cassy is restless, so they
must go out. They sleep late together behind Ruth's closed door; Cassy may
go off alone, briefly in the afternoon, but then after dinner they are showering,
trying on outfits, full of nervous energy, Cassy's platform shoes clomping
impatiently on the hardwood floors.

When Ruth is gone back to school I miss her. I hear, usually after the fact,
off-handedly, or as a foregone conclusion, about her impulsive trips from
college alone sometimes or with friends to Manhattan, say, or New Orleans.
Besides the salsa dancing, in which she has taken a course, her evident passion
is for jazz. Jazz clubs in Boston begin their sets late and run into wee hours.
Home without Cassy last spring and lacking local friends who share her
passion, she has taken to going out alone late to various clubs. I of course
object. See again, I think, her blindness to ways of the world, her lack of

suspicion and guard in "the cultural jungle of America" (as Robert Stone puts it); even when one night she takes me along. We sit cross-legged in a loft, listening to earnest young musicians, who play with eyes closed and faces twisted soulfully, reaching for an authority of experience that is still beyond them. The nightlife crowd is randy, high, and hip, some paired, most prowling, on the make. I think I recognize one of my students.

Our father and daughter sharing this past sophomore year has been primarily financial—the tuition bill, loans, our refinanced mortgage, contingencies about transferring to Emerson (free), worry about having any money for David's private middle and high schooling, let alone his college. I am again the practically concerned, world-fact rehearsing Dad (like my own father).

In regard to finances, she has demanded recently why I need a $500,000 life insurance policy with a $1440 premium due this month. I fume, the Poppa provoked and pulling rank:

"Because it is my place to protect you. People die."

And Connie huffs: "It's Walt Tolman, the financial advisor. My dad never had insurance and I turned out okay."

Me: "Your dad was a domestic disaster and besides you were a tough cookie."

Ruth: "I'm a tough cookie!"

Me: "No, you aren't; you haven't even had a taxable job in the world . . ."

This is unfair, inaccurate, and what are we shouting about really?

Everything else is between her mother and herself; and between her and her friends. During the school year, Connie calls long distance several times each week and has long, rambling, whispering conversations, girl to girl. I don't want to know Ruth's private life, perhaps, and haven't wanted to know, pretty much, from Rowe Camp onward.

"Did you know I had my heart broken this year?" she asks me suddenly, in another recent exchange.

"No," I say, "nobody said anything to me. You talk to your mother all the time, but it doesn't get to me."

Connie, listening to us, adds, "No, he doesn't know."

"I did," Ruth says. "I really loved this boy, but he cheated on me."

"Oh," I say, not pursuing it.

I want to respect her now at this adult distance.

—•◊◊◊•—

Am I a jerk? A stone-age patriarch unable to look past my father's saying? Or am I too permissive? Am I abdicating where in fact I owe? Am I too distant? Is her maverick nightlife an attempt to get a rise out of me, to challenge the distance? Am I sexist in the worst ways? Are those behaviors that I pride myself on in my own adventuring, my own bold explorations as a teenager coming to adulthood reserved in my instincts only for males? If my daughter were a son, how and why would I feel easier?

Yes, no, to such questions. These are the torments, the dialectic of best intentions and uncertainties.

—•◊◊◊•—

I feel awkward and reluctant to read her fiction in progress, however highly praised by teachers. I can and have read it, of course, at her insistence, especially when she is writing at the computer and in her excitement calls for me to see this paragraph or page. She is writing a novel more or less about Jesse girl, whom she calls Jorrie. In the section she shows me, both the narrator girl, based transparently on herself, and Jorrie, are intent on losing their respective virginities.

But then I am the cold professional, more exacting about artistic flaws than encouraging or proud. I would feel better about reading published work, I tell her, work that has signified publicly rather than privately. I don't want her to short-circuit art by using it as a way to communicate with me, the parent, as a private audience.

Is this felt by Ruth as a disapproval? I consider now that in writing she is in part competing with and taking on for herself my own ambition in the world; and in part communicating news of her private life and especially her adult sexuality to me (and in that sense, attempting to take her sexuality out of secrecy and asking for respect). I need to account for and examine my avoidance, especially since my own writing is confessional.

When my work is published, she is happy and, I hope, proud to read it, for this is my sharing, my human side. At the same time, I have warned her against reading accounts of my own coming of age or the follies and explorations of my bachelorhood as any kind of precedent.

—•◊◊◊•—

I do not go downstairs until 7:30, when the day has mounted in earnest; streets are busy, planes passing. Her door is closed. I open the front door and take in the newspaper. I mute my noises. I make my coffee, shower, dress.

She apologizes later that afternoon for waking me up. She and Cassy are up at last and showered, David is home, Connie cooking, life in full swing, all normal. Phone rings. Family bustle and chatter. I nod and grimace ruefully, "Right," I say.

There will be other wakings, I know.

III.

Such are this father's fevers. Vapors.

In present time, this summer's end, 1997, I apologize to Ruth, as she reads this writing; likewise, to Connie, who feels that discussing our daughter's personal life in print might be in itself a parental abuse. But a deeper form of trust, regard, and love is meant here.

Culturally Ruth's options, meaning path-trodden, recognized, supported, and progressive choices for women, are wider and more various and demand more free will than the options available for my mother in 1929 (when, having dropped out of college and begun work in commercial art and social work, she married at age twenty-three), for my sister in 1955 (when, pregnant, she dropped out of college and married at age twenty), for Connie in 1973 (when having finished college and begun teaching in Head Start, she married me at age twenty-four).

With such apparent liberty, I hope for Ruth that it may continue to prove the liberty of pastoral rather than of decadence, Arden rather than Vienna, folly rather than vice, and that it may lead, as it does in the Shakespeare comedies that I teach, to self-knowledge and to the union of ardor and intelligence.

Ironically, she, her mother, and I have enjoyed watching the series of recent Jane Austen movies together, not only as romantic comedies, but with some yearning, I think for a world of coherent manners, of measurable character and spiritual value linked to privilege and property; indeed, a racist, classist, patriarchal world to which the challenges and prospects of contemporary America stand in necessary contrast.

I pray that Ruth never feels "silenced" in Tillie Olsen's sense; never feels that her potential has been compromised by life and that, again, in Olsen's words, she "is a destroyed woman."

In terms of lovers and friends, also, and of the life partner that I hope she finds, may she have the luck and judgment to avoid the wasters, the self-defeaters, the thieves, the liars and pretenders.

May she resolve her own balance between ambition, love, and parenting. May she live whole and full, her inner life reconciled to the social roles that exemplify at least the fictions of our best. Our mutual support. Our pledge to futures. May she never lose her appetite for life, her joy, relish, and savor of living, sweet and sour.

May she inherit from her mother, and on my side, from my sister, what my sister inherited from my mother, a bravery of love, sheer love over betrayal, loss, and aging.

I have come to appreciate Ruth's commitments with deepening pride. Her love of her younger brother. Her natural gift for teaching children. Her counseling and loyalty to troubled friends. Her inquisitive and even contentious nature, aspiring to equal ground. Her questioning of authority. Her concerns for social justice. Her quick mind and good heart; her passion for experience; her omnivorous reading; her writing, acting, photography, and drawing. Her resourcefulness.

⸎

This mid-summer saw Ruth's boldest departure yet. She traveled alone to Tuscany, Italy, where she babysat for parents from Connie's school for one week, then spent another three weeks touring on her own, hostel to hostel, we thought, until on her return she told us stories of sleeping in parks. She furiously studied Italian from a travelers' textbook beforehand (building on her knowledge of Spanish and French). She called around for bargain airfares on her own. She obtained her passport. She packed one huge duffel bag. We spoke sporadically long distance while she was there, six hours ahead. She was able, she said, to have philosophical conversations in Italian with kids she met.

The family that had hired her returned home before she did and showed us photographs of her there, playing with their children: our Ruth, *there*, on cathedral steps. She herself took no photographs, but wrote in her journal and drew miniature pictures with art pencils. Her drawings were full of gaiety and color, celebrating people of all sorts. In her journal she wrote: "Here in Agropoli on a stone wall by a littered beach, trying to be inconspicuous so this old fellow pushing an accordion does not notice that I have been following his music for some time now. He has stopped to talk with a couple who are having a midnight picnic on a bench and I am lying here on this wall waiting for the music to start back up. Some regazzo comes by and tried to sweet-talk me and my halting Italian but I wish silence upon us and get it, stare past him at the water and savor silence: 'Lasciarme sola . . . Lasciarme avere questo momento sola.'"

Suddenly, I was proud of her adventure. I had never had one at her age to compare. I envied her the European experience. Envied her competence. I had forgotten my own pattern of departures from my family, and recognize now that Ruth's from her background, and from me, is part of that pattern too.

Daughter and father, both, are awake.

Of course, when it comes to her plan to take a leave from college next spring and study land reform in Guatemala . . .

Perhaps I have come far enough now, from jealousy and fear, to admit to my genuine curiosity. What will she see there? What will she experience? How will she grow?

My Dog Story

why should a dog, a cat, a horse have life,
and she have none at all? —Lear

My son at ten had had his share of grief.

His best friend, Gabe Farren, had been diagnosed with liver cancer. David never doubted that the powers of the adult world would cure Gabe. The sickness was curable, a passing ordeal. No one told Dave, or told Gabe, for that matter, differently. A liver transplant. Then remission, then more cancer. Then chemo, hair loss. Gabe was Gabe, boyish and plucky, Dave's pal triumphant. The fall of 1993, The Make-a-Wish Foundation sponsored Gabe's wish, an all expenses paid vacation at Disney World in Florida. Gabe asked that David as his pal could go with the family. They were driven to and met at the airport with a stretch limo. Two of every wished-for toy, primarily Power Rangers (the craze of the time), were shared, one for Gabe, one for Dave. On return, again in remission, Gabe visited our house once or twice, and then was bedridden, unable to get out. One last outing, Gabe's Mom and Connie took him and David to Boston's Chinatown where they got matching karate outfits, Chinese masks, and Nun Chucks, following on the Ninja Turtles' and Power Rangers' prowess in martial arts. I remember taking Dave to *Jurassic Park* at that time, Dad and Son, and being troubled by a pre-film feature on cancer research for children. Troubled that the shadow of Gabe's fate would trouble Dave, and squeamish myself about the impending tragedy and its impact on him.

By the fall of 1993, the doctors thought that they had eliminated all the cancer, but in the summer Gabe had several strokes and went back to the doctors. They told his family that the liver cancer had traveled to his brain, and that that was causing his strokes. Gabe then fought the cancer with radiation treatment for several weeks. The radiation made the tumors worse, so treatment was suspended and Gabe entered Home Hospice Care. Two months later, he died in his Watertown home at the age of eight, one month before his ninth birthday.

David was cheerful at Gabe's bedside in the Farren living room almost to the last, in trust and in denial. They watched television together. They watched violent R-rated films otherwise forbidden. All the rules of gunplay and movies and extravagant toys had been suspended and waived for Gabe, and David experienced and enjoyed the contact license. Dave went with Gabe to the hospital for radiation treatments and returned with his own gauze radiation mask, shaped to his features, like a life mask. Gabe's parents, Glenda and Pat, and Gabe's older sisters, Jesse (who was David's older sister's best friend) and Caitlin, treated David as family; and I confess I was sometimes jealous of the time and warmth they offered Dave, which I was at some lengths to equal.

My wife, Connie, whose friendship with Pat and Glenda encouraged the bond between Dave and Gabe, finally had to tell David that Gabe was dying. That he only had a few more days. She wanted Dave to go say goodbye to him. Dave broke down in grief and wailing and sobbing tears. No. No. No. No. I shudder inside now to remember. He was thrashing in Connie's arms. The two of them on his bed, and I was standing in the doorway, feeling helpless. "Oh Dave, I know!" Connie wailed with Dave. "I'm sorry!" And Dave: "Why didn't you tell me! I thought he'd be okay!"

When Gabe died, Dave and Connie took off school and work, while I could not, and went to the cremation ceremony. Connie later told me that everyone had sat around in a circle in front of the open coffin (which a woodworking friend of the family had made). That Gabe had been dressed in his karate outfit. That my son had never looked, but that he had asked Connie to put two of his favorite Power Ranger figures into the coffin. That different people had said things, read poems, whatever. That each person then had tightened one screw and then Pat and Glenda had pushed the coffin into the fire.

I tried some nights to lie with Dave and to talk about losing my mother. He would insist on company on his way to sleep, mother first, but if she were out, I was okay as a second best. I felt his grief as a test of lived, rather than of religious, consolation. I told him that I felt I was my mother now inside, that she was alive in my living. That that livingness was what I owed her. Still Dave wept. "But I'm just a kid. Imagine what it's like when you're just a kid!"

There was a public celebration of Gabe's life, an extraordinary event in our town where the tragedy for more than a year had been openly shared. The Hosmer School auditorium was filled with three or four hundred people, parents and children.

Someone donated bumper stickers, "LOVE IS THE ONLY SOLUTION" –DOROTHY DAY; IN MEMORY OF GABRIEL FARREN, which spread through greater Boston. Gabe's pictures, often with Dave, were everywhere in our house and his. Dave was mentioned in Gabe's obituary. Connie wrote about Gabe's death: "His battle with cancer and his death has altered my view of death and dying, and his life and death have changed my life."

Meanwhile David's surface reaction was not to think or talk about it. He felt listless, complaining that he was bored. He wanted to withdraw and watch TV. He wanted things, toys, a bike, always some new acquisition, wild and loyal consumer that he was. He didn't want to go to school. He didn't want to go to bed, ever, and pushed the issue as late as midnight. He didn't want to get up once he had gone to sleep.

As for me, I felt my own grief for the death, grief for the parents, and real regard for the way they had all lived the loss so far—braver and better people than I, I felt. But they were not my friends. They were my wife's friends. I was reluctant, as was David, to go to a fifth-month memorial for Gabe at the Farrens', a pot luck dinner, family and friends, including a folk singer who had sung "Puff, The Magic Dragon," at the public celebration. The folk singer had written a song about Gabe's dying that was partly the occasion of this gathering. David was careening around the familiar house. Chat, chat, eat, eat. Then Glenda's sister set up a screen and slides, and there were pictures of Gabe from the fall ceremony. From Glenda's pregnancy through Gabe's last days in the wheelchair. Dave was nervous, glancing around for directions, not crying. Connie was openly weeping. Then the singer sang his song, the refrain of which was Gabe's line from real life, "Who will lie down next to me heaven?"

I didn't know what to say or feel.

Less than a year later, we heard that Gabe's Dad, Pat, at fifty-one, whom Dave called "my second father," had a malignant brain tumor. While undergoing chemotherapy and radiation treatment, Pat openly shared his struggle with a healing circle, which my wife regularly attended: "thus began a series of healing circles, that, while fairly common among some feminists and in communities of caring for persons with AIDS, seemed culturally distant from many of us," Pat himself wrote. "Our gatherings have been remarkably successful on a number of levels . . . while the healing had been intended for our family, a sense of mutual caring had spread easily, as acquaintances deepened and friendships were renewed."

Pat lost his battle with brain cancer three years later on September 17, 1998; four years after his son had died.

During Pat's struggle, while Connie visited regularly, Dave and I only visited for special occasions, which marked Pat's decline, Thanksgiving dinners, Christmas exchanges of presents. Pat was always loving with Dave, but Dave felt clearly overwhelmed—subdued, typically; closed down—both by Pat's decline and by the reminders of Gabe and his own role now as a reminder to Pat and Glenda of the life that Gabe might have lived.

Almost immediately after Gabe's death, Dave had begun seeking out new friends to fill the void and to prove that Gabe was not his only companion or refuge in life. He sought out larger boys, as Gabe had been larger, who in some sense might serve as protectors at the Atrium School and on the playground.

Before long, Alex Lawrence became his best pal, from nice parents in a big house, much bigger and more luxurious than ours, in Weston. Alex had a dog. A Portuguese water dog.

Jonathan Valetin, a Watertown friend who had known Gabe from play-group days on, but who had never been best friends with him, also had a dog. Gabe himself had had a dog, an unruly, high-jumping mutt named Zoe.

Phillipe, another friend from Atrium, did not have a dog, but his father had run a pet shop in Brazil and knew everything about dogs.

David for years had been begging for a dog, and Connie and I had put him off. One Christmas we gave him a stuffed beagle named Freckles, which he slept with. Connie promised him later, when he was older, we would in fact get a dog. But I kept arguing reason. No. No. I who myself as a boy had had my dogs. Me, the dog person. I was afraid we had too small a house and yard and too little time at home to care for a dog, but I was caste as the work-distracted, nay-saying heavy and overruled.

David and Connie talked unilaterally. The dog had been promised. Connie told Ruth, attending Hampshire College then, worldly, and at home for the summer working in the Belmont Book Store, that Dave needed something to replace her when she was away at college (the equation of older sister to dog made Ruth angry, says Ruth now). Phillippe's father lent us a CD ROM for the computer, which served to match the buyer's preferences with different breeds. Oddly, our preferences (short-haired, small, good with children, etc.) kept coming up with Boston terriers, which we thought were ugly, preferring beagles. Connie went through the Sunday paper want ads with David, and the search became an adventure. When I was off at summer school, teaching, they went on an expedition to Worcester with Phillipe, who was proprietary about our search. As I heard the story, Connie drove David and Phillipe out to this farm that had advertised dogs and Phillipe was attacked by a Doberman that took a chunk of flesh off his right calf. Not only did they find no dog, but they brought home Phillipe, after emergency care and rabies shots, with stitches, bandages, and hobbling on crutches. The Doberman's mistress had been apologetic and solicitous; Connie was distraught; Phillipe and his parents took it as an accident of life, and chose not to be litigious. But for weeks later, Phillipe was still on crutches, healing.

That had doused the hopes for a dog, I figured; at least for a while.

But then one day, with no warning other than that they had gone someplace to look—I had just returned from a week away as a staff member at a California writers' conference—the car pulled in, voices. Connie entered first, with the kind of promissory, apologetic smirk I knew meant she had bought something without consulting me. "We have a dog," she said. "Wait until you see her. She's so *cute*! She's in the car!"

"You didn't."

"Come on, you'll love her—Shhh, David needed this."

"Dad! Dad! We have a dog!" Dave was shouting outside.

I went out just as they rounded the corner, David as excited as I had ever seen him with the beagle pup in his arms, big smile; and Ruth behind him with dog stuff, leash, blanket, food dish, bag of Kibbles 'n Bits.

"Hey, Pup," I said. "Hey, hello. Welcome to the Henrys." Classic beagle, white flash starting above and between the eyes and wrapping around snout, black nose, and neck and chest, soft tan over the rest, big brown eyes, silky beagle ears, black and tan patches on her back, white tipped tail, shoulders, haunches, legs, and belly all white. She licked my hands.

The future in the instant, I thought; just as I had watching Ruth's birth, that first sight, first eyes open, waking to the world; and again, just as I had at David's arrival as a seven-month-old from Korea—though we had treasured his photograph for over a month—as the adoption service greeters filed down a long staircase at the airport's international terminal, each with a bundle in arms, we spotted our greeter, and rushed over, eight-year-old Ruth, thirty-seven-year-old Connie, forty-five-year-old me; and there, awake and wide-eyed, David was handed into Connie's arms.

After Connie's misadventures with the wants ads, Ruth had told her boss, the bookstore owner, about our dog search. The owner had told Ruth about a place nearby offering free beagle pups that had been used for medical experiments. Ruth, then, had called Connie and David, and all three had set out for the laboratory, which had a score of pups, all of them healthy, all with breeding and inoculation records, all one-year-old. Ours immediately stole their hearts, the smallest of the litter. If the pups couldn't be placed by a certain time, they would be put to sleep. None had names, but blue tattooed numbers, instead, inside the right ear. Ours was A3049.

On the ride home, they had decided on the name Sassy, Ruth's suggestion, which somehow fit the pup's jaunty and flirtatious nature. Subdued at first, within a day, Sassy was yapping at everything. Though David loved to play and cuddle with Sassy, after a few first proud neighborhood walks, and after reluctantly helping to clean up her poop and wet newspapers, he balked at the responsibility and she really became Connie's charge, Connie's pride, even. If Sassy went out for walks enough, we thought, her housebreaking would be easier. Connie would rise at dawn to take her for walks on her retractable leash down the street to Gore Place, a cloistered park with wood walks and fields. They would be gone for half an hour or more. Connie discovered a small society of neighborhood dog people, also out early walking their dogs, and would chat with them. By local ordinance you had to take a plastic bag with you to pick up the messes. Connie would also slip doggy treats in her pockets, hoping to train Sassy with rewards, "Good *girl*, good doggy, Sassy," each time Sassy did her business outside.

Treats didn't work and walks didn't work, including walks late each night before bed. Loud, rolled-up newspaper spanks; open hand butt spanks, or sharp snout snaps with fingers and harsh voice rebukes for bad behavior; and petting, cuddling, and syrupy praise for good: these didn't work. Pushing her nose in puddled urine and snarling "*bad*," and then picking her up and pushing her down on the dry newspaper spread out and in changed tone insisting, "this is *good*," didn't work. If anything, over time, Sassy trained us to accept and make the best of her nature that we could, though we never stopped trying, as if in this regard her Pavlovian conditioning was slow, but somehow gradual.

We could never let her off her leash outside, or she would run off heedless of our calls and chasing after her, heedless of traffic, heedless of lacking identification or license, heedless of randy male dogs and pregnancy (the vets told us she must be spayed before she could be licensed, and that she could not be spayed while she was in heat, so we kept talking about it, but given our uncertainty about her cycles and our distraction by greater emergencies in life, we never got around to it). We tried to limit her drinking at home, because a drink surely led to pee someplace other than on newspaper. We had to block her access to the house with baby gates left over from David and Ruth, which we then had to step over ourselves, back and forth. Times she slipped through she headed straight for the bathroom toilet to drink her fill. Likewise, outside, in rain, or rain puddles, she would strain to drink, often on a walk where she failed to deliver. She was a little dog, puppy-size though full grown. No more than fourteen pounds. Her messes were small and easy enough to clean up. It was her pee that stank, stained, corroded floors and threatened rugs and furniture.

We tried putting Sassy out in our backyard, which might work for ten or fifteen minutes before she started barking, either to come in, or at another dog or birds or squirrels. For the first two years, we kept a rope strung diagonally some fifteen yards from the first post of our stockade fence, which closed in the back from our driveway and the street, to the trunk of a weeping willow on the property line with our young neighbors, Lisa and Ron. We put an eye clamp with a swivel on the rope and attached a light chain, which gave Sassy another ten yards reach in all directions, as the clamp slid freely along the rope. Of course she would wrap the chain around and around the tree trunk and howl and yap until we came to untangle her. In time, however, our neighbors, who were tolerant otherwise (they themselves had a docile, well trained Rottweiler named Precious in their backyard), finally complained that she was crapping habitually around the willow tree, which we failed to clean up, and that they were tired of having to step around it. I moved the rope end from the tree to a diagonal from another point of our fence, away from their yard, where now Sassy got her chain tangled up regularly in bushes.

Children loved Sassy on the playground. Sometimes Dave and I would take her on the length of her chain with its clip and reclip the chain to the fence as we shot baskets on the tarmac court. Small children would gather around her. Sometimes with a parent or two. After a while they knew her name, "Hi, Sassy. . . . Oh, she licked me!"

She was cute and loving. A cuddler, fawning. She was a life. A spirit, even. The responsibility was indeed like having another child, another infant. All our love for each other was somehow vested in her well-being, and love for her bespoke love for each other. She was the inferior, younger sibling David didn't have. In that sense, David's dog craving was also a craving to be more grown up and powerful than at least one other member of the family.

Sassy snapshots: stretching in the morning, or after a nap, butt high, front paws flat out, eyes rolled up.

On hot days, beagle sprawl, on a throw rug in front of the refrigerator, or outside in the shaded grass: back legs spread out, rather than tucked, tummy flat to the ground.

She could almost walk on her hind legs. And we would take her front paws and dance her around and around.

Dinner or night walks were David's chore, with me at first, then for a while alone, at least around the playground. When we walked together, Dave would let me take the leash, because little dog or not, Sassy would strain ahead, feet digging in, neck stretched out and gasping from the collar, and once or twice she had yanked the leash from his hands.

I liked to take her to an unused industrial parking lot, overgrown with weeds, behind the lumberyard across the far side of the playground. I liked it because we didn't have to clean up her messes there. Sassy loved it because so many other owners took their dogs there, dogs that left smells, and because nearly every visit we scared up wild rabbits. She would be sniffing and suddenly a rabbit would dart off zigzagging. And then her belling beagle cry: *OrrrrrrRooooo*! Total outcry: *Mine! Quarry! Let me at it! Don't you see it! Quarry!* A bark of protest at the leash, front legs up and pawing, or at my ass-over-tea-kettle lumbering run trying to catch the rabbit as she tugged. A bark of primal yearning. I used to think of the rabbit or rabbits stopping out of reach to watch us, the eager beagle and the panting human alone or with his son stumbling through puddles or snow or just stopping winded. I imagined them jeering at us. Slapping their rabbit haunches in glee and rolling on the ground in laughter. I came to think they actually baited us, lying in wait. A great night, a record night, might be five rabbits. Most nights at least one; poor nights none, all for naught. There were many close calls, but I had no idea what Sassy would do if she ever actually caught a rabbit and I doubt that Sassy did, either. Many times in the arc lights, I would see a rabbit frozen before she did. I would whisper excitedly, "Sassy, look; no, over *there*." I would have to throw a stone, so the rabbit darted away through a fence before she saw it, too late, and then she would all but fret and dither.

While we were watching TV on the family room couch, she would curl up next to us. We would pet and pet her, her silky ears, and when she slept, her curled-up body radiated heat.

Perhaps for several days in a row she would pee on the newspapers we set out, and we would think, aha, she is learning. Dave begged to sleep with her. Sometimes on the futon, sometimes in his own bed, like a privilege. But inevitably, after once or twice without problems, she would pee on his special quilt and we would have to wash everything, quilt, sheets, pillowcases.

When I pulled the car into the driveway, I would hear her excited bark, see her paws on the windowsill, see her leaping as I reached to open the back door. She was always excited to see us, each of us, any of us.

Now and then she slipped out from the baby gate and chairs blocking the kitchen doors. We would be sleeping late at night or in the morning, and here comes this scratchy clip of her nails full tilt galloping up the stairs, leaping like triumph onto the bed, onto me, and making for my face, to lick.

Her love was glad and unconditional, this dog love, at a time in my life when the stresses of parenting, family love, and work were making me feel that my own love was never good enough. I could please no one enough.

The Atrium School, David's elementary school, ended with sixth grade. Connie taught there, and Ruth had graduated there too, and it was only a few blocks from our house. All Dave's friends were in his class, including girls now, and they would all be splitting up for seventh grade in different private schools. It was a progressive school, to which Connie had given and would continue to give her heart and working life. David's new school would be Beaver Country Day, an awkward twenty-minute commute to Chestnut Hill, near Boston College (we viewed Watertown's Public Schools as unsuitable; we couldn't afford a move to Newton, a better district; and though the extra expense for Beaver was a sacrifice, we would manage to manage somehow). The new rigor for David, twelve now turning thirteen, in getting up early, the challenge of the new setting, the academics, the discipline, afternoon sports, and making new friends: all left him little time to play with or care for Sassy.

Increasingly, she became my dog, my responsibility.

Even though she was like a greyhound when she got loose and tore off streaking, she was not a running dog. She was a hound. When I tried to take her jogging on her leash, she would stop at every pole, tree, bush or other protuberance a male dog had marked, sniffing away. The more we tried, however, the longer the stretches when she would trot along with me, and sometimes it was fun to have her company. But then after three or four miles she would lag. One run I actually had to carry her home the final mile.

I loved the sense on those runs that I was serving her, serving the family, as well as serving myself. I took joy from her great and evident relish. *Oh boy, boss. I love this out here! Oh man, smell this. Who's that?*

Our closest communion, however, other than petting, was the nighttime rabbit walks. Dave had stopped coming with us, except sometimes riding along on his bike. We had our favorite routes and haunts. In addition to the parking lot, in addition to Gore Place, we explored a bicycle path that had just been completed along the Charles River, where inevitably we would meet other dogs on leashes or solitary walkers or joggers, who always smiled or maybe stopped to pet her, "Oh, she's cute. How old is she?" All seasons, all weathers. They were slow, meditative walks in interactive company for me. If we were running, I might let her drink the river, where she would wade in deeper, drinking, and even swim a little on her leash, her eye on ducks.

For Connie, however, increasingly Sassy had become a bane, a force against a house already difficult enough to keep orderly and presentable, and against any sort of life that felt sane.

Her pee and her claws were causing wear and tear on the parquet floor; she had chewed the arm of the prized futon; she had clawed portions of the backdoor lintel and the windowsill where she leapt to see us. We lived with barricades and newspaper spread in the kitchen and family room. She couldn't travel in cars for more than five minutes without throwing up. Trips were a problem, when we all had to be gone for more than six hours, we would come home to a wild dog, jumping as high as our faces for yipping licks. Her shit would be scattered all over, paper torn, puddles of pee. If she had gotten run of the house, there would be shit on my mother's special rug in our living room, or pee on the loveseats, or later we would discover the wetness of pee on our upstairs quilt. She couldn't resist garbage, whether in the house or outside in the trashcans, if we were careless enough to put them in reach of her chain.

Connie's frustration was honored by her friends, even Glenda, whose own dog, Zoe, was a chore; by Ruth; and by her mother: *It's okay to feel that way. It's okay. You shouldn't have to live that way.* On the phone her mother, from Manhattan, would say, "Don't tell me you still have that dog. Get rid of that dog."

We tried to joke, bad-mouthing Sassy for being dumb, for being a crapper, yapper.

You get what you paid for, we lamented. We had gotten a yard sale dog, a dog from an experiment that had been brought up in a cage for over a year, and never spayed or housebroken. We had gotten a beagle, a breed that has its stubborn traits. By contrast, Alex Lawrence's Portuguese water dog was a rare breed and had cost hundreds of dollars.

Out of David's hearing, Connie and Ruth joked about looking for a no-fault way out. If she got hit by a car when she ran away, for instance. If she ran away and never came back. We did in fact come home one morning to find her gone, her chain broken. We split up in different directions. Check the lumberyard, check Gore Place, check the river, check two streets over with dogs in the backyard. No Sassy. She would have to come back to us on her own, if she did. We were driving home from an errand in the afternoon, when David spotted her with kids on the back stoop of a row house.

"That's our dog," we told the kids, who had found her with her broken strand of chain on the playground and been playing with her since.

David joined in the bad-mouthing. But when Ruth or Connie or I talked half seriously about not being able to keep Sassy, about his never cleaning up her messes or walking her regularly, as he promised, about us all being gone from home so much, about perhaps one of Ruth's friends taking her, David had nothing to say, no suggestions, no protest. He seemed preoccupied with other things, his friends, sleepovers, TV. Although Ruth had left for college, she kept her bedroom on the first floor. David's room was across from ours upstairs. While he went to sleep, he still liked one of us to lie down with him. Sometimes we would read to him or tell stories. Otherwise these were talking times.

Then Connie told me she had contacted Buddy Dog Humane Society at Glenda's suggestion. We would have to take Sassy there, some fifteen miles west, in Sudbury, for an interview. If they accepted her, they would guarantee to place her with another family. They did not put dogs to sleep.

Assuming she had already at least planted this idea with David, that night when I was lying down with him, I told him that Connie was serious. That we'd been talking about taking Sassy to Buddy Dog, and now she'd called and made an appointment for Friday. That I was sad about it.

Dave broke down and begged me to intervene.

"This is no surprise, son. You know we're not here enough to watch Sassy. It's not your fault. It's not Mommy's. We just aren't the right family for a dog right now. We're all too busy. You don't even play with her anymore."

"No, no, please. Please. Dad, please. Don't let them take her." He was sobbing.

"I didn't realize how important she was to you, Dave. Listen. Dave. I promise. I'll do everything I can, okay? I'll do my best. I'll do anything I can so we can keep her. That's my promise."

Next day, Connie asked: "Why did you tell him? I hadn't had a chance to talk to him first. I was going to. I wanted to break it to him my way."

"I thought you had told him. I thought you guys had talked. And this was all in the open."

Reluctantly, Connie agreed to keep Sassy for one more year. David would be older. Another friend, Sam Vanderpol, got a dog, an expensive, hairy dog.

I tried. I did the walks, the cleaning up. I tried to discipline Sassy. To pay attention. To correct a lot of the bad behavior I thought was more out of Sassy's being left alone, than simple stupidity. Things got better, or I thought they did.

Then Sassy would revert, an escape, messes in the living room, our inside garbage can ravaged, spilled, bag rippled open. And I would admonish, "Don't you see you are ruining your chances, Sassy? Don't you get it? I know you are trying, but you have to try harder."

My own nurturing instincts had cut in, which I was also trying to model for David. You took the good with the bad. The cute loving warm cuddly or the exuberant world-lover along with the perversely stupid, the sheer inability to control her urges where she clearly understood we wanted her to. In some primitive way I missed the infancy of my children. What else could explain those nights when Sassy would yap incessantly at two, three and four am? I would be the one to get up and stumble downstairs to tell her be quiet. She would be berserk. Over rabbits underneath the floor. A roving dog or raccoon outside, though nothing I could see or hear. One night I got up and spanked her, stinging her butt and snout, *No, no, no barking! Go to sleep.* Picked her up and forcibly put her on the couch. *Stay there.* Half an hour and I had to do the same thing again. When I came down for the third time before dawn, frustrated and sleepless myself now—I had to teach in the morning, a full workday—and while she leapt crazily all over me, barking like emergency and wouldn't quit, I actually in exasperation kicked her hard—yelp!—and hurt my bare toe (a confession that sickens me even now). "Oh, Sassy, Sassy, hey c'mere! I'm sorry! Here, come here!" I ended up holding her on the couch all night, so she couldn't struggle, hand on snout so she couldn't bark, until she quieted, her breathing slowed to mine, and we went to sleep together. All for the sake of the household, including her.

I had my loneliness, too. Running alone. Working at my basement desk alone. I missed Ruth at college. David was with friends or at school. Connie was at school or at meetings. I had Sassy. Though her housebreaking muddle made her a liability anywhere, my basement rug, for instance, as long as I kept her near my chair on a leash, she would watch me or sleep. I talked to her. I enjoyed her company in the car, too, and tried to get her sea legs by keeping her in my lap as I drove, my body absorbing the shifts and unsteadiness for her. She would balance all four paws on my legs, ears pinned back by the steaming wind.

Still the tensions in our lives worsened.

Though David rarely saw him, Pat Farren was visibly declining through this time. Connie still attended the healing circles, though Pat could no longer speak, and on his good days, he could sit only for ten or fifteen minutes before he had to go lie down. His death and funeral were to come in September.

By June 1998, we heard that Hazel, too, was seriously ill. She was diagnosed with pancreatic cancer, and over the summer underwent surgery, then chemo.

At seventy-five, she lived alone in her East Side apartment, and her children took turns visiting, Connie from Boston, Lonne from Miami, Raymond from Washington, D.C., Danny from Chicago. There seemed, from stage to stage, to be medical hope; a different doctor, different options, different regimens. Connie lived each hope and each reversal. Ruth, who at seven had shared in my mother's dying, now as a young woman of twenty-one, shared in Hazel's last months as often as she could. Lonne's daughter, Jana, lived in New York and was often with Hazel as well.

Loving Hazel, as Nana, as mother-in-law, David and I, in different degrees, also felt intimidated by Connie's grief. The maelstrom of it was Connie's, rather than ours, but it took her away from us, even when she returned from her stays in New York.

Over Thanksgiving, David and I visited Hazel for my last time, joining Connie and Ruth there (work would prevent me from attending the bar mitzvah for Danny's fifth and youngest child in Chicago in December, which Hazel, miraculously, managed to attend, along with all the rest of the family). We left Sassy in the family room, well barricaded, ample newspaper on the floor, two dishes of Kibbles 'n Bits and one of water; we put chairs upside down on the futon, so she couldn't sleep or pee on it. As we backed the car out of the driveway, her face was at the window, yelping, then down, then she was jumping; and we heard her yelps well down the street. Glenda and her daughter Caitlin had promised they would stop by to check on her.

David had fought the obligation of the visit all along, and once we got there, he clung to what normality he could, TV, movies, his CD player, earphones on. Hazel was in her window bed, in her combined bedroom and study—she could no longer come out to the living room to visit and eat with us—and Connie had to harangue him whisperingly to go in and take Hazel soup.

I worried about how closed down David was, insisting on life as usual. I took him out of the pressure of the apartment for an afternoon in the nearby Metropolitan Museum of Art, where we wandered into the Egyptian wing, and he was troubled by the mummies, "all those dead people," so we went to the exhibit of medieval armor and weapons instead, where he was especially taken by the life-sized Samurai.

I wanted to ask him (but thought better of it, keeping silent): "Son, what do you think of all this, your Nana's dying? Is it a big inconvenience, or a sacred, gradual goodbye? How do you imagine my turn or your mom's? You must have such a tenuous sense of attachment compared to what I had at age thirteen. So much difference for you, David, which has to have its bearing on your different cast into life. You must survive. Somewhere deep inside you must be feeling that instinct. Birth parents are tenuous. Loved ones are tenuous. Parents, grandparents, childhood friends."

I treasure now my own goodbye to Hazel, and our last kiss, her shining eyes. And my attempt to tell her that her life was a success of love, if not of career, since she had fed on the dream in her later years of writing and seeing a Broadway musical produced; and short of that goal, none of her accomplishments satisfied her, however much they impressed us all. Her workaday independence as a theatrical accountant; the handholds and footholds of projects that had brought her from Miami to Manhattan in the first place; praise from Broadway somebodies for her talents as a songwriter; showcases for two musicals and all the haggling and conniving behind them. The big deals always just around the corner. The feverish, optimistic phone calls to Connie about imminent success. She had come now to accept the finality of her career dream, and to relish the affirmation of family. She had four adult children, married (not divorced) themselves, the parents of two Weinstein's (Lonne), five Sherbill's (Dan), two Sherbill's (Raymond), two Henry's (Connie). Lonne was an interior designer/sculptor. Danny was a rabbi. Raymond was a lawyer. Connie was a teacher and artist. They were not shattered or deracinated. They were not self-destructive. They were all generally thriving and close as family. She had led a full, brave life.

Towards the end, Connie was just back home from five days with her mother. It was 7:35 am and we were leaving for school and work. I heard her sobbing in the shower, loud, heaving gasps and sobs. I was at a loss, and feeling her soul's plaint: that we don't make enough clamor about lives in this disposable, convenience-minded society of ours. We celebrate entertainers but don't care about them as people. And people we do and should care about, we let go by quietly day by day and never celebrate, until maybe they die, and then we have a celebration of the life. Then turn to our affairs, even in families, even in friendships.

Hazel was dying clearly. Before the last week in New York at her deathbed, Connie called Buddy Dog again to schedule an interview, which I kept denying, hoping one day at a time that it would go away.

Still, I felt we owed this to Connie. She herself was overstressed to the point of physical risk, suffered migraines, and had collapsed at the Chicago bar mitzvah in front of Ruth, who had been scared, and who had bent over her thinking she was dead or dying, and had wept and beat the floor with her fists (Ruth's words now), then had rushed to get David in the room next door, scaring him. Connie had been rushed to an emergency room and diagnosed with atrial fibrillation. When they called from the hospital, Connie herself was scared, as was I, when Ruth put her on the line. She would have more tests when she got home. "We have to get Mommy to slow down," Ruth insisted.

Now added to the question of Sassy was our fear for Connie's health.

While Connie was called back to New York—Hazel was in "pre-death restlessness"—and David was at school, the Buddy Dog people called. We made an appointment. I checked directions and a map, gathered up Sassy and we headed off. Sassy thought we must be driving somewhere for fun, maybe to the disused tennis court a few blocks away, which was closed in if you latched the doors at either end, and where we could unsnap her leash and let her run free. We got lost. We were late. I stopped at a gas station in Sudbury and called Sassy eager on her leash. It was farther down the road still, another three miles. A statue of a boy and dog outside, sign, parking lot, modest one-story building. We pulled in and Sassy was playful, straining to go walk, squatting to pee, smelling dog smells. We went in for our interview. A lady just coming out with a basset hound on a leash. Sassy all alert, friendly. The kid at the desk, Tom, with whom I had spoken on the phone, and who had been waiting for us, ready to close, looked her over, asked how old she was, why I was giving her up, did she have papers, shots. Gave me a two-page questionnaire to take home. In back, we heard muffled barking. Another helper, a girl, petted Sassy, while Tom showed me through the door to a kennel with cages of barking dogs, both sides. Volunteers came to walk them twice a day, he explained. They were full up.

I told Tom that we were worried about leaving town at any moment, probably this weekend, for Hazel's funeral, and that we had no place to board Sassy. He said the best they could do was to put her on their waiting list. They would call as soon as they had space. They'd have to have her immediately then, with the questionnaire and a check for the $100 relinquishment fee. She needed to be spayed and the vet worked Mondays. They would put her up for adoption for a certain time, for up to two placements. If she were brought back a second time, they would return her to us.

"Oh, she's so cute, we'll have no trouble placing her right away," the girl said. The older woman, who had come back in with the basset hound, commented smilingly that everyone wanted beagles. Sassy and I drove home.

When David came home from school that night, I lay with him on his new bed, in his bedroom downstairs now. He was in his first week back, while my vacation, on college schedule, would continue for two more weeks. He knew already that Connie had called Buddy Dog, and had taken in my news that they had called, and that I had actually gone there today with Sassy. I thought he was taking it well, as a hard, best thing, and I had wanted to make him part of the process, to have him help fill out the questionnaire. The detailed questions were heartbreaking: "How old is your dog? How long have you had your dog? Why are you giving up your dog? Where does your dog like to be petted best? What is your dog's favorite toy? What is your dog's favorite activity? What problems does your dog have, e.g. barking (the more specific information you give, the better our chances of a permanent placement)? Is your dog housebroken? Paper-trained? Not housebroken at all?" I had written that Sassy liked her ears stroked and scratching under her collar. Dave corrected me, urgent to be accurate:

"She loves to have her tummy scratched." His eyes were tearing up.

"Honey, really. I went there. I saw it. I liked the people. They love dogs. I wouldn't even think of putting her there if I didn't think she would be happy there."

"No! I've seen it there. We looked there with Philippe. They have wooden board walks between cages filled with dogs barking and howling!"

Suddenly he was weeping and gasping his heart cries, even worse than the year before. "I don't have any choice! You and Mommy are doing it anyway! What can I do?"

"Honey, I know it's tough. It's tough for me. I love Sassy. I've done my best, like I promised you I would. But we just can't give her the kind of life she needs. It's no life for her here like this, locked up in the family room alone all day, no one to play with. She needs a big yard. She needs children."

"Dad, she's never known anywhere else. She doesn't know what's happening. She's taken from the only world she knows, us, our yard and house, for three years, and suddenly we vanish. She's in some cage in some crazy place. She won't eat, she'll howl and bark. I want to see her with her adoptive family. I have to see them."

"Okay," I humored him. "Maybe they'll let us do that. I don't know. We'll have to ask, okay?"

Adoption grief, I was thinking; Gabe and Pat grief; sister-gone-from-home grief; Hazel grief, fear-of-losing-Connie grief: all primal and unspoken emotion for him. For Dave the idea was Sassy's powerlessness, like his own, and maybe, I thought and felt, he was also projecting the idea of adoption as the denial of unconditional love. Before vacation we had put in a call to his school psychologist, who had then called back and talked to me in Connie's absence, advising that we get Dave to a grief counselor as soon as possible.

School was a struggle. Dave spoke of being bored. He had no positive goals. He threw periodic tantrums at home.

Later that night, I called Connie. This wasn't the time to add to David's grief. "I'm not trying to keep Sassy because I love the dog," I tried to explain. "It's because I love David. We have to get him to a grief counselor first. He has to feel that he is part of this. You didn't hear the school psychologist."

To my surprise she understood readily. With Hazel's dying, this wasn't the time. It was too much for David to handle. We would put off Sassy for still another while, until this was all over.

Buddy Dog called two days later, as if they were making an exception for us. A space had just opened up and they could take Sassy immediately. I told them no, I appreciated it, but we had decided to wait a little longer. They said that they would call back in a few more weeks.

Hazel died in her apartment that Friday, Shabbat, with her children around her, Connie there for the last breath. From the tearing of garments, wailing laments, to prayers and blessings, they followed the orthodox Jewish rituals, directed by Danny. Together, they wrapped her body. The funeral and shiva were in Miami. The body was shipped. Connie and Ruth flew from New York. David and I flew separately from Boston, with Glenda Alderman and her oldest daughter Jesse on the same plane. Her younger daughter, Caitlin, had stayed home and was keeping Sassy, along with Zoe, for three days. Thinking of my own family and the mannerly emptiness of our Presbyterian funerals, I envied the rituals that connected my wife to her family and to the Jewish community centuries old. We traveled in procession after a service to a distant cemetery, where each of the children and grandchildren shoveled dirt into the grave, including my son, my daughter, and I remember each scrape of the shovel and each scattering of earth as it fell on the casket liner. Later, we sat shiva in Lonnie's high-rise apartment, overlooking Biscayne Bay, ritually visited by relatives and friends from the Miami community where Hazel had settled, married, then divorced, where the children's father, Joe had died, and where the children had grown up.

Connie would stay on for the ritual week, and Dave with her, skipping school. Ruth, after another day, was leaving in a different direction, for her planned vacation in Puerto Rico.

I came back to Boston on the same flight with Jesse and Glenda. We picked up my car outside the airport in heavy snow and crept home, heater blowing, windshield wipers batting, to rescue Caitlin from Sassy, whom we knew from phone calls had been an ordeal. Caitlin actually was gone with Sassy when we arrived, out walking in the snow, and when they came in, Sassy went wild with reunion, barking her joyous squeal, licking, jumping, writhing and squirming as I held her. "It wasn't so bad," Caitlin said, as I apologized and thanked her. But a week later, after Connie had returned, the tolerant and dog-loving Glenda told her: "This is it. Now we are even." Never again, rolling her eyes. Apparently Sassy had howled the whole time there, escaped and peed and crapped in house. Never again. Never with this dog.

Back from the week sitting shiva, Connie re-embraced her life, her work, her friends, us. She would weep uncontrollably, but she had set herself to fare forward with new determination.

She was on her hands and knees, cleaning the parquet floor furiously. "Try to understand. I can't see why this dog is alive and my mother is not. I can't call her on the phone. And I come home and this dog is in my face. I know it's not rational."

"Try to understand," Connie said again. "What if you came home and found one of Ruth's friends, someone you can't stand, was living in this room. Every morning you got up, and there he was in your face!"

Finally, the time had come, I decided.

Dave was with Connie for another New York trip. There had been several trips since the death, to meet with Ruth back from Puerto Rico, to meet with Jana, to stay over in the apartment and to sort through and dismantle Hazel's belongings, clothes, furniture, paintings, books. It was spring break for their two schools, not mine (our vacations never coincided). The Buddy Dog people had called back once already and I had put them off. Now they called again. They only had so many spaces.

We had been talking openly about Buddy Dog for long enough. We'd even looked at their website, where their mission stated, "Once accepted in Buddy Dog's adoption program, an animal will be cared for until a suitable home can be found," and they posted pictures and descriptions of available dogs: "Keesha . . . Shepherd/Mastiff Mix, 3.5 years, female . . . Keesha was raised with kids, is good with cats and ok with other dogs . . . She loves car rides and fishing . . . Her family has moved and can no longer take care of her; Norman, Labrador Mix, two and a half years, Male, etc. . . . ." I felt that I would spare Dave and Connie now by acting alone. I would do this for them, this hard thing, because I loved Sassy most, and because it was a ceremony for me. I made the appointment for noon.

Sassy jumped down from the futon, excited to see the leash, and waiting while I fastened the clip. I had the completed questionnaire in my pocket, with my checkbook. Again, we started off, midday early spring, a clear, bright day, and this time I knew my way, windows open. The mission was dire, I thought, our last ride together. Through traffic, past fields, this was happening, now, now, now, the simple enactment, with her hind paws braced on my legs as always, front paws on the steering wheel with my hands. *Oh boy, boss. Oh boy. Look at the world. I love this, boss.* Again, we arrived. I don't know if Sassy even dimly recognized the building, but again she went with me, eager, trusting, and curious on her leash, as if for a visit.

Tom was on duty inside. He had me sit at a desk, with Sassy at my side, patient as I petted her head. He was businesslike. Took my dog profile. Had me sign the relinquishment form and write my check.

"I love her a lot," I said, smiling balefully. "This isn't easy, understand?"

Everything in order, I handed him the leash.

"She'll go fast," he said. "We'll have her spayed on Monday. We'll call if there's any problem."

"Can I hug her goodbye?"

"No. We don't allow that," he said, holding up his hand. She was their dog now.

"Okay, kiddo, good life," I said, looking my last look. He tugged and led her bewildered through the inside door, a chorus of barks audible as the door opened and closed.

I drove home. When I told Connie on the phone, she was taken aback. "I thought you'd wait," she said. "Why did you do it? I don't know if this is good."

"It had to be done," I said. "They called and it was now or never. I had to get it over with."

For the next three days I checked their website, the list of dogs. Connie and Dave had returned to a dogless house. Dave seemed okay. On the fourth day, March 29, there she was: "Sassy . . . 3y, f.sp. beagle . . . To look at her, you'd never realize that this tiny beagle is full-grown. She was just spayed this week." The picture, in color, a distended top-view Polaroid, showed the most lost and forlorn Sassy I had ever seen, droop tailed, thin, ears limp, even circles under her eyes and her eyes pleading, reflecting the flash. I kept checking it from my computer at school. Obsessively I showed the screen to students and colleagues. "That's my dog," I said. "We had to put her up for adoption. Did you ever see a creature more forlorn?" I printed out the page, and showed Connie at home, but thought better of showing David.

Then after two more days, she vanished from the website. No listing, no picture. She'd found a family, I told David.

"How do you know?"

"They put this up on Wednesday." I showed him the printout. "Now it's gone. That means they've placed her. She'll be loved. I hope it's someplace with a big yard and kids."

Dave-style, he didn't say much more. Sometimes we'd be out driving and see a dog on a leash, sometimes even a beagle, sniffing, while an impatient owner tugged and tried to make it follow.

"Can we get another dog?" he asked once or twice, wistfully.

"I don't see how, Dave. Jeez, we can barely take care of each other."

Like a protest, perhaps a rebuke, old photographs of Sassy started appearing prominently on his desk and taped to his wall, along with the gallery of sports action posters and pictures, basketball, football, a picture or two of Ruth, and later still, the posters of Britney Spears.

At fourteen, his periodic tantrums escalated, scaring him as much as they scared us, and followed by contrite calms. Slammed and locked into his room, music blasting. They were heartbroken times for all of us. The issue, as best we understood it, other than physical fatigue or hunger, was Dave's aversion to responsibilities–homework, getting ready for school, household chores—as opposed to escape and self-indulgence.

He was popular at school, too much so, according to teachers who complained about his socializing during class. He loved sports. He had dates, parties out, overnights, which were really TV binges followed by sleeping until mid-afternoon. He loved his computer, the Internet, electronics, his radio, his CDs, DVDs, all forms of power and control without effort: on, off, channel surf, loud. He was sensitive and soulful in his relationships. "I can tell my friends more things than I can tell you!" he shouted at us in one outburst. "You don't know anything about me!" He loved sitcoms and standup comedy as subversive. He loved the Simpson's. And things, things, things, expensive, replaceable, disposable things. We were in the full swing of adolescent life. Ruth had an apartment with friends across town, keeping her adult distance.

For Dave, I was proud to be in the audience last spring, a year after Sassy's departure, for his interdisciplinary presentation at Beaver, the primary moment of his completing eighth grade. His topic, with Connie's prodding and blessing, was "The Legalizing of Marijuana for Medicinal Purposes." In front of friends, teachers, peers, and us, his parents, he gave his rehearsed talk, along with visual aids on a monitor and VCR. He opened with a statement of his losses of his best friend to cancer; of his best friend's father, who had been his second father, likewise; and most recently, of his grandmother. Their photographs were flashed and held up on the large screen monitor as he spoke: Gabe and him fishing; Pat holding up fingers in a victory sign; Hazel with her head kerchiefed surrounded by her family at the December bar mitzvah. Beside me in the audience, Connie started weeping. The connection to marijuana was that of these loved people, only his grandmother had had the side effects of chemotherapy eased by marijuana, which Connie had acquired at the oncologist's suggestion, even though it meant breaking the law, and had made into tea for Hazel to sip. He wished that Gabe and Pat, also, might have had this benefit; and he felt that marijuana should be legalized so that others suffering from cancer, from AIDS, and from multiple sclerosis, could have their time left made more livable.

This, I thought, heartily applauding, was the first time he had found voice for his human losses. And perhaps for that hardest loss of all, the end of childhood.

I still have my reunion dreams, life being what it is. The accidental recognition in some park, Walden Pond, perhaps, or Lake Cochituate. I've gone there on an impulse for a weekend walk, the foliage turned all yellows and crimson, air brisk. I'm approaching on a path. Suddenly, that joyous beagle cry, like the frantic cry pursuing rabbits, but for me. In slow motion. The startled master, a ten-year-old girl, perhaps, a woman, a man; the little dog jerking free, the leash trailing behind. I know her instantly. I stoop, hold out my arms and take the squirming, licking lunge of her mid-bound, all fourteen pounds. Sassy! She'll love me always. She'll never forget.

This has to stand for all grief, all love, the vocabulary for more than a dog.

Visiting Bill Knott

Bill Knott has been my colleague for over fifteen years. We have shared students. We have moved from one office building to another, and most recently to the Ansin Building, a downtown Boston high-rise, where our offices are side by side, and often I hear Bill through the wall, cursing to himself, rearranging his stacks of books, or sometimes shouting at a student.

Bill's various offices resemble the trashcan of Sesame Street's Oscar the Grouch. They are legendary caves of a mind dwelling, spider-like, in a web of seeming confusion and disarray. Soda pop cans. Trash. Orange peels. Books everywhere, stacked on the desk, stacked on the floor, stacked and spilling off of shelves. There is a desk chair, and there is a reading chair, usually jammed in a corner, with cushions.

During my years as chairperson, hence my quasi-official position at the time as Bill's boss, he came to me with a private, personal distress. He had fleas, he explained. His office had fleas. He had gotten them from petting the resident dog and mascot in Cambridge's only all-poetry bookstore, The Grolier. His apartment had fleas. He had had to fumigate. He had to scrub his office rug now with flea soap, and was worried about health hazards in terms of the building's closed-air circulation.

In a recent memoir, poet Charles Simic writes about first meeting Bill as a young man in a Chicago rooming house in the early 1960's: ". . . we had to wade through an ankle deep layer of empty Pepsi bottles to advance into the room. Bill was a large man in a dirty white T-shirt; one lens of his glasses was wrapped with masking tape, presumably broken. The furnishings were a bed with a stained mattress, a large poster of Monica Vitti, a refrigerator with an old TV set on it, and a couple of chairs and a table with piles of books on them. Bob sat on the bed, and I was given a chair after Bill swept some books onto the floor . . . Bill had read everything: we spoke of Rene Char, and Bill quoted Char from Memory . . ."

Though I love and have learned from Bill's startling and musical poems, we have rarely socialized over the years. In a 1977 interview with James

Randall, the man who managed to hire both of us at Emerson, Bill says, "I'm kind of cold fish, aloof and distant, and I know that has a lot to do with the orphanage and being isolated [he spent much of his adolescence in an orphanage] . . . and I'm shy and find it hard to speak to people." But he goes on to say, "I'm not a 'loner,' if being that implies it's *my* choice to be alone. I'm alone because no one wants me around—they reject me—so 'rejectee' is more apt than 'loner.'" He has devoted literary friends, and he has girlfriends, but has no children and has never married.

Our first meeting was when I was selling the Randall-edited issue of *Ploughshares*, not only featuring Randall's interview, a critical appreciation of Knott by Thomas Lux, and new Knott poems, but also a cover monotype portrait of Bill by artist Michael Mazur. I was manning the *Ploughshares* table among acres of the commercial glitz and clamor of The Boston Book Festival, when a stoop-shouldered man in glasses hovered around our display and fingered a copy of the new issue. "Hey, wait a minute," I said, looking at Mazur's portrait and then at the man, "aren't you Bill Knott? Isn't that you?" And flustered, he replied, "No, no, I don't know him. I'm not him. I don't know what you're talking about," and walked away. Later I went to a reading by poets featured at the festival, where, himself indeed, he read to an audience of mostly empty chairs and called the people there boneheads, if I recall.

He is in the audience, faithfully, at practically every local poetry or prose reading I have attended, always as far back and in a corner as he can get, hand to chin.

Over the years his students have flourished. He Xeroxes poems for them maniacally and buys and gives them poetry books, sympathizing with their penury. During the obligatory evaluations of institutional rank and tenure, where teachers must all but strip and show battle wounds in the marketplace, the student evaluations, letters and testimonies have characterized him as one of the outstanding teachers in the field, at Emerson and elsewhere. "Very intelligent, great sense of humor, direct and honest to the point of cruelty . . . absolutely devoted to his art and his devotion is contagious . . . opened my mind . . . best professor I've ever had," various students have commented. "He demands students to read conflicting or provocative critical arguments," I myself reported for an official review, "and that these arguments differ from his own opinions or practice as a poet indicates a generous and professional catholicity directed at informing and developing each student's individual talent, rather than cultivating disciples." Ten feet of wall outside his door is papered with publication acceptances for past and present students.

He came to my house in 1993 for a dinner with James Laughlin and Mary Karr, before a benefit reading in Cambridge for *Ploughshares*. I felt self-conscious about my own domestic family life, as I had on other occasions with Richard Yates visiting from Yates's own Spartan writing life. Here we were in my three-bedroom suburban cape, in my living room, furnished formally with vestiges from my dead mother's house: stuffed pink couches, wing-backed chairs, a fireplace and mirror, a mahogany counterpane, a turquoise rug with a regency design, a thickly framed imitation Renaissance painting. Here was my wife, Connie, gracious, welcoming and at ease, serving salad and pasta and some chicken concoction we all found delicious, eating off plates on our knees. Here my daughter, Ruth, in her sophomore year of high school, shyly greeting everyone; here my son, David, in third grade. Bill has brought a two-handled paper shopping bag, from which he brings books, his own books, each copy hand-made from Xeroxed typescript, with a unique drawing in pen and ink and tempura. He has made fifty copies to be given away for free at the reading, *Excerpts from the Diary of [deleted]*, and offers us each our choice.

<hr />

One of my favorite Bill Knott poems:

RIGOR VITUS

I walk
On human stilts.
To my right lower leg a man is locked rigid
To the left a woman, lifelessly strapped.

I have to heave them up,
Heft them out and but they're so heavy heavy as head
Seems all my strength
Just take the begin step

All my past to broach a future. And on top of that
They're not even dead,
Those ole hypocrites.
They perk up when they want to, they please and pleasure themselves.

It's terrible. The one consolation:
When they make love,
To someone who's far or close enough away appears it appears then
Like I'm dancing.

⸺

I have this dream. I am invited to visit, a new apartment. It is my first encounter with Bill's private, at-home life, a social gesture on both our parts. I ring or knock. Bill calls to me to come in. I recognize his voice. But as I open the door and step into a foyer, I am in total darkness. No Bill. No light. I am puzzled. Have the fuses just blown? *Did* I hear Bill? Or is this the wrong apartment, somehow? I call out a couple of times, no answer. I start to grope my way forward and into what seems to be a parlor. "Bill?" Suddenly a light, a flashlight, shines on me and I see a figure, matronish. "I'm looking for Bill Knott. Is he here? Isn't this his apartment?" The woman demands: "Who are you? What are you doing here?" At the same time, out of the darkness, a small yappy dog starts to attack my pant leg, and I try to dissuade it and pet it at the same time. I think I hear Bill's voice, down the hall in the opposite direction. This is a trick, a test even, I sense. The woman and her light have vanished. The dog has vanished. I'm more and more convinced that Bill is somehow playing a game, that he is in some room down the hall. I grope my way to a closed door. *Bill?* I hear his "Okay, okay, come on in!" And, just as I thought, he is there. Lights on. In a bookish, furnished room. He is a sorcerer, I have decided, who can make things appear and disappear just by imagining them. "Where's the dog?" I ask. "What dog?" "The little dog," I say, and just at the moment, "There," he says, and as I reach to pet what is a complicitous and friendly creature, it is a very *big* dog, a mastiff, under my petting hand. "That's a big dog," I say, laughing. There is more of it, his entertaining my conventional expectations with witty surprises, puns, images, conjured from emptiness. We laugh and laugh, inside the delight of invention, wit, and imagination. His magic, my appreciation.

Improvisational

The hall was clogged with bodies; none of them hers, but who could be sure?
—Leonard Michaels

The hall was clogged with bodies; none of them hers, but who could be sure? This had all been a terrible mistake and none of it her doing. Higher powers were at fault, and surely higher powers had no business asking her to solve the problem.

She had been at that Internal Revenue Service desk, in the lobby of the John Fitzgerald Kennedy Building, Boston, Massachusetts, early in the afternoon of April 14, dutifully attempting, as a good citizen, good mother, good single parent, good employee, and loyal, practicing Catholic that she was and always had been, to have her long form 1040 completed with the help of the IRS itself. W-2 forms, receipts, medical bills, bank statements and cancelled checks; everything was ready and neatly organized in an accordion file within her capacious straw purse. They had x-rayed the purse as she stepped through the metal detector, just inside the lobby doors. She had had to take four different busses to get here, all the way from West Somerville. She had waited in a line that had had to shuffle and stand for five, ten, thirty minutes, while some baggy pants young so and so, an overbearing, indignant young man, white, but unable to speak English, fought with the clerk behind the desk. Similar lines snaked towards other clerks, other desks. She was forty-two years old and in good health. She worked two different jobs, meter maid for the City of Somerville from 7 am to 3 pm every day but Sunday; then from 6 pm to midnight every night except Wednesdays, she folded laundry and oversaw the Davis Square Laundromat. Oh, there was more, much more to her living. Lives depended on her. And as she waited, she was lost in thought of these lives: five year old Jamie, with his bad cough; his eight-year-old sister, Wanda Jane, whose birthday was this weekend. Thinking of the rent. Thinking of her own father, bedridden in the home. Standing there feet aching and more and more uncomfortable with her soul's and body's suspension, when the bomb— it was a bomb—bloomed everywhere. When she felt massive force crushing her at once, all over, lifting and rending and then like being pulled inside out, like a rubber glove stripped off the hand, the dry part, pale, inverse, she was herself, substantial, essential and certain, and not in line at all, but hovering, like smoke, but concentrated, like a nebula in space. And judgment surrounded her. Not condemning judgment. Not praising or loving or welcoming. But indignant and self-perplexed judgment. What was she doing here? No words, but the question. The knowing. Not her. This is not her death. This is absent-minded omniscience. This is impossible. And then again, the inside-out, implosion. And the hall was clogged with bodies; none of them hers, but who could be sure?

Bodies sundered, shredded, torn. Shreds without bodies. Wetness, stink, and smear. The shower of sprinklers, pouring. Bone. Debris of glass. Caster from a chair. Paper, plastic. Landfill detritus, rubble and dust and guttering fires. And starting in heaps, heaps like those filling trenches in concentration camps, yet worse, heaps of dismemberment: would be some part intact and recognizable. Two shoes, red pumps, neatly side by side, as if the feet left to climb into bed. The gory hand. The torso, male, shirt torn. A search, desperate, obliged like a punishment, through lifelessness ripped past shape or meaning. And if she'd vaporized? If in that instant, her solid flesh had melted and dissolved? Or if this unfamiliar leg, round, raw and marbled as a mutton, but perhaps, were hers? Would she recognize her parts and how? How to identify your own disfigurement? Where the scar? Where the bit of clothing?

And if she did, as she felt bidden and all her passion craved; if she found this part, forearm or hand, or skull pan like a melon rind, or that; and if she searched and searched, and gathered all. Or if there, under X, Y, Z, intact she lay, whole, unmarked, as if in sleep. A sleep deserved. A sleep denied by all her love and effort to bless life, to give, to serve, praise the Lord, and make him holy. If there. Her. What then?

Was she to rise? Eyelids flutter. Pain flood in. Her gasp for breath, her cry. Was she to complete some answer like a harmony? The one whole flesh, reviving. Among so many bodies and so many parts. Like judgment day. All the broken and diseased, the aged, the maimed. The poor, the rich, the takers and deceivers. The righteous. The millions from the trenches.

"Your life's a miracle!" the fireman said, g's of amazement, like a rocket's thrust, stretching his beefy face.

Like that, as if. Her refund due.

Arias

My wife is singing an aria of love, Puccini at the least, top of her soul's lungs, all night, all morning. She is singing for our daughter, just turned twenty-two, whose birthday we celebrated at dinner out last night and who is visiting from her apartment across Boston at 1 pm today, Sunday, to exhibit her paintings for sale to friends at our home in Watertown. The proceeds will support her trip to Cuba in a few weeks, where she hopes to explore the culture, write, and look for opportunities to teach English.

My wife loves Ruth with all the passion of her own life at fifty, her own joy of art and dreams of painting more than she herself has been given to; and her own sense of mortality too as a woman, and the passion of her grief in relinquishing her dreams of body and of youth.

She sings, my wife, not by singing, but by cleaning, painting, rearranging our small house. Several young artists on Ruth's street in Jamaica Plain had proclaimed a neighborhood open house several months before, and having sold a few paintings then, Ruth was inspired to stage her own show out of our house. She had invitations printed and sent them out to everyone of her and our acquaintance.

Our family room, off the kitchen, entered by our backdoor, is the designated art gallery. Out goes the television, TV stand, table, and the bookcases; the futon couch moves from one wall to the other. The rattan rug is cleaned and turned. Thump busy. Sweep. Mop. Scrub. A fury of commotion. Curtains are washed. A bathroom rug is washed, throwing the washing machine off balance so it bangs all night.

My son, fourteen, and his overnight friend, have retreated from 10 pm last night on with the moved television and VCR behind the closed door of my son's room, off the kitchen in another direction, first floor. They are watching VCR movies. They will persist until 4am or later, DVD on my son's computer, Play Station. Three movies. Four movies.

They are each on Christmas/ Chanukah/ Winter Solstice/ Kwanza vacations at last—my son from his private school eighth grade; my wife

129

from the private elementary school where she teaches (and where both our children have graduated); my daughter from her job teaching ESL. But I am not on vacation, yet. Thursday, at final class meetings for each of my three courses, I have collected term papers. It is a seasonal convulsion now, on the brink of vacation, to concentrate with surgical care on grading the papers and then computing final grades, which are due Monday.

I think of Robert Frost's apple picking: "there were ten thousand fruit to touch, / Cherish in hand, lift down, and not let fall." I want silence. I want gratitude and deference as I labor in my basement study for my family, but also for the standards and profession I believe in and my responsibility to each student. I pride myself on being the polar opposite of the caricatured professor who grades by throwing unread papers haphazardly on the stairs. I am counting the hours and stamina left before my deadline Monday morning. After two days steady reading, I have finished twenty-six undergraduate essays on Shakespeare's tragedies, averaging ten pages each, correcting sentence-by-sentence, idea-by-idea and writing lengthy comments to justify the grade. I have turned now to the stack of graduate literature seminar term papers. At 1:30 am, I am still working hard, but I have to quit and head for bed. My wife says go on, it is one of those nights. The kitchen is all bric-a-brac. She is cleaning the stove.

I head on to our upstairs bedroom, bone tired. Try to sleep. Washing machine bangs. TV sounds rise and fall. But mostly the energy of her bustle, the crackle of doing, muted but wild and manic, keeps me awake. I head for a couch in the basement where it is quieter and sleep in bursts with wakings all night until 9am—wake to the same bangings, clunks, stomps, rattles, clinks, scrapes.

Groggy, I risk emerging for a cup of instant coffee. We say good morning. I say she is going wild. She says it is an estrogen imbalance. She has insomnia and sudden energy. She has just repainted the entire kitchen. The family room is transformed.

I go back to my basement study. Concentrate on and comment on two more twenty-page student essays summing up thirteen weeks of shared discussion of classic American short stories. I write sincere comments, moved by the quality of criticism and intellect in these students. But my head rings from lack of sleep. The mania continues upstairs. Showtime for my daughter's exhibit is 1 pm. Will I go down the street and buy our daughter some flowers?

I say no at first. I am in my own crisis. I can't intrude on my wife's cleaning even to make lunch. I can't concentrate—the unabating emergency upstairs is too much. I am exasperated and feeling wronged in my way, and knowing that feeling wronged isn't fair. We are at cross-purposes. God, I love my daughter too—my way. But this isn't my way. This is my wife's. No one warned me our night would be without sleep and the house cleaned and rearranged as if lives depended on it.

I need to get out. I take my papers with me.

Where am I going? Connie asks. Will I be back by 1 pm for the event? "Gene is coming," C. yells. Gene is the gynecologist father of one of David's pals from his private school. He lives by delivering babies and is often sleepless, yet he manages to be a wholehearted family man to wife, son, daughter, dog, and family friends. C. is close friends with Lauren, the mom, and has been cultivating the friendship, couple to couple. I reply, "I am in my own crisis here!" I need support, encouragement and appreciation, not rivalry.

I don't know where I am going. It is Sunday, so the town library is closed. We rent space in a storage facility about a mile down the street, a small unit with a window, where I have a desk and chair among heaped boxes and family overflow, but the facility doesn't open until noon on Sundays. Until it opens, I figure I can wait in the parking lot and work in the car, if I have to. Anything is better than this.

On my way there I see that the florist shop is open in the mall, so I do go in, buy the flowers, then turn back home, pull in the driveway, and motor still running, hurry in and out, just leaving them inside the back door with the ungracious shout, "If these aren't good enough, I don't want to hear about it!" Then I exit before any possible words or retort. Back into the car—again I pull into the mall and stop at D'Angelos for a $4 veggie sub. As I wait gritty-eyed for my sub, I stare absently and resentfully at a Christmas tree lot across the street. This is a holiday weekend. The bustle in traffic on the streets and in the mall lot is the bustle of the last weekend before Christmas. Look at those weekenders, that Dad and son buying a tree. Look at those vacationing and out readying for their family holiday. We don't have a tree yet. I've done no shopping. The pressure and stress of my teaching responsibility preempts me and I resent it. I am trying to budget my time, all to serve, to offer, to sacrifice for, and I am made to feel stingy and selfish. I take my sub and drive to sit in the vacant but sun-warmed industrial parking lot outside the storage facility. Fifteen minutes until it opens. I am at peace. Eating. Shut my eyes.

Ungracious. I apologize: my wife, my daughter.

Love is sorting these things out. Paying attention. Listen, listen, listen to the purity of my wife's life singing! Sheer ardor!

I'll be there, of course. 1 pm. I'll manage.

-∞∞∞-

I do manage. I work in the storage unit for forty minutes, two more essays. Then I head home, our driveway blocked with cars, one of which I recognize as Gene's and Lauren's. I park on the street. I see the crowd in our windows and enter the back door to a scene of mostly familiar faces.

Louise and Alan. Barney. Gene, indeed, engrossed with framed paintings displayed on corner table and with the vase of daisies I had gotten. We shake hands hello. Twenty or thirty people. Nancy Lubin. Ruth's friends Jesse, Cassy, her boyfriend in and out. Plates of fruit and cheese and crackers circulating. Soft drinks in cups. Music playing. And Ruth in the center of it, bandana, leather vest, slacks. Hello Daddy, hug, buss. People are studying the paintings hung on our walls, and others displayed laid out flat or propped up. They are writing checks and Ruth is busy keeping accounts, taking commissions. Most of the work I have never seen, though I do recognize the mode and subjects from earlier pieces. Some are Guatemala scenes, from her nine months there (on leave from Hampshire College, where she concentrated on Third World studies). Others are of her impoverished Jamaica Plain neighborhood. They are collages, with shapes and colors cut from gift papers. Some are painted. Some incorporate painting and collage. Her art celebrates the vitality of rural village life and of her crowded city neighborhood, and is the felt opposite to the art of loneliness and disconnection I love in say Hopper or Wyeth. She sings of people people, the folk, families, and of underclass solidarity. Her human figures are faceless, but they are dancing, romancing, fighting, tending children, hanging laundry, drawing water from a well beneath a canopy of stars. The colors are joyful, brazen, earthy. In the midst of hardship, there is joy.

-∞∞∞-

When Ruth tallies her checks, she discovers that she has grossed $3000, a figure that astonishes, though we live for service rather than for money in our lives. It is more than enough to finance her Cuba trip. She has sold nearly everything she displayed and has also gotten hefty commissions. For months to follow we will visit friends for dinner, say, and there will hang a Ruth Henry in a place of pride.

I turn my grades in Monday, on time, along with the stacks of papers. Three days before Christmas, David, Ruth and I go get the tree.

Besmirched

Along came inkjet printers, standard fare now, and I bought a new Lexmark Z22 for my seventeen-year-old son, David, to go with his computer, so he wouldn't need to use the old, even cheaper Canon BJC-250 that went with my computer in the basement study. The reason that inkjet printers are cheap (under $100) is that their ink cartridges are exorbitant (over $38) and quickly run dry. Of course, you can refill the ink cartridges from different inking kits. I had refilled my black cartridge some four or five times from one kit I bought for $30. It came with a little screw hook, which you twist, into a pinhole on a plug near the top of the cartridge. Then you twist and pull and the plug comes out. Inside is all sponge. The trick is to take an accordion-like cylinder of ink with its needle spout, insert the needle through the fill hole deep into the sponge and squeeze the accordion slowly so the ink goes in. You keep going until a bubble comes up in the fill hole and that's how you know it is full. You pull the needle out, reinsert the plug. Voila! A new, full cartridge for $10 at most. Of course, after five refills, I got lazy. I bought new cartridges too.

I bought David two color cartridges and two black ones for the Lexmark over time, wincing at the ink's costing more than the printer itself. Then in Walgreen's, I saw a new brand of refill kit that purported to be easy, mess free, and able to refill all brands of inkjet cartridges, both mine and David's. It cost only $26. Sold! I stashed it away, pending emergency.

So yesterday, David called out to me from upstairs. He was trying to print out homework and his cartridge was out of ink. Could he use my printer? Alas, my printer was dry also. "Okay, wait," I said, "give me your cartridge." He did, although he was annoyed that he would have to wait. "Just give me a few minutes," I said, showing him the refill kit. His girlfriend was over and he went back up to be with her.

I took the new kit into my basement lavatory – mostly white, with sink, mirror over the sink, tub with white shower curtain, toilet, overhead florescent light. Said kit has an instruction book with pages for refilling every possible brand of cartridge. I find the Lexmark Z22.

In the kit are four little bottles of ink, three black and one pink. There is a plastic hypodermic with an attachable needle three inches long. There is a screw eye for boring a hole if you can't get the cartridge plug out (I can't). This is better than the accordion, I think. Less mess, safer. I place each item along with the cartridge on the flat rim of the porcelain sink.

I am wearing glasses. My favorite, baggy tan shirt and a sleeveless fleece vest because we keep the heat down to save money. A good pair of tan slacks. My good Nike running shoes.

Did I mention that this was a snow day? The blizzard of '03, resulting in clear skies and thirty inches of snow. The night before Dave had defied our cautions, dug one of our cars out of our driveway and gone sledding with pals in nearby Newton, then stayed overnight. This morning I shoveled the whole driveway by myself, the exercise making up for my daily trip to the gym, which was surely closed along with my college, my wife's school, and Dave's school. Shovel, shovel. Family service, creating a cleared space for him when he came home. Which he did that afternoon. With his girl friend. He had been doing his homework with her when the printer problems started. I had been correcting papers in my study.

So here I am, trying to help. Resourceful Dad. Meanwhile my wife is busy cooking them dinner and they are eating.

Directions: remove plug or drill hole. I hold the cartridge in my left hand and firmly twist the screw eye, boring a hole through the side of the plug. Open black ink bottle. Attach needle to syringe; the metal cup at the top end of the needle fits snugly over the plastic nipple of the syringe. Draw 20ml of ink into syringe. Insert needle into drilled hole until the needle hits inside the cartridge wall. Done. Carefully, slowly, I depress the syringe, saturating the interior sponge with ink, and then withdraw the needle.

Done. Well, almost. That was just a little bit, not 20ml. So I try again. The needle is in, touches the wall. I depress the plunger. This is easy, smart. I've used half the syringe; I push a little more, the cartridge held steady to the basin with my left hand, the syringe in my right, between forefinger and middle finger, thumb pushing.

WHOOSH! A geyser of ink in all directions, everywhere. Like a cartoon bomb exploding in Elmer Fudd's face, the ink had splattered on my glasses, on my face, on my hands, on my shirt, my vest, my pants. Ink was on the mirror and all over the basin; all over the white, faux tile walls. All over the toilet, the shower curtain, the carpet underfoot. As I had compressed the syringe's plunger and jammed the needle itself against the cartridge wall, the sleeve of the needle had been forced off the syringe nub and nearly all the ink had exploded out and up.

"Help!" I shouted, inanely. "Help!"

I had no idea what to do. Black, black ink, perhaps indelible. In the spotted mirror I saw my face, blackened as if for combat. Ink smeared and splattered on the lenses of my glasses. Swatches of black over both my cheeks and chin. Ink over my hands and on my wrists and arms. Ink splattered on my shirt up both arms, on my slacks; and the toe of my left running shoe, totally black.

They were preoccupied upstairs in the kitchen, chattering and eating. No one answered me, so I shouted louder, "Help!" I went across to the bottom of the stairs. At a loss for words, I wanted to be seen.

"What is it? Dee?" Connie appeared at the top of the stairs, took one look at me and said, "Oh, no. I don't want to know." She turned and I heard her telling them that I needed help; I was all covered with ink.

The black badge of courage, I was feeling. I was ludicrous, but only in the cause of serving Dave. I grabbed a fresh roll of paper towels from a shelf near the stairs. This was grave. This was major. My clothes and the bathroom were ruined. Who knows if I could get the ink off my face? How could I go into teach the next day looking like a Dalmatian? I looked at myself in the spotted mirror, then took off my glasses and tried running water on the lenses. The ink diluted and with the water spread, creating a black pool in the sink, but I kept wetting and rubbing the lenses until they came clean. When I tried to wipe individual splash marks off the wall, the sink, or the mirror, the ink smeared, making it worse. I tried washing my hands in hot water with soap, but the stains wouldn't come off. I got a paper sack, sat it open on the floor, and carefully put each inkbottle into it, along with the syringe, the needle, the instruction book and the ink cartridges.

Dave came down, sent by Connie: "Oh, jeez!"

"Nothing anyone can do," I said, tearing off more paper towels, working on the porcelain. "Go on, I'm all right." He went back up, and I imagined him announcing: "You gotta see it. There's ink all over everything. He was refilling the cartridge and something must have slipped. He's okay. He says he can handle it."

I started undressing. Wiped off the toe of my shoe with a wet paper towel as much as I could, shoes off, socks; I wanted to get the vest, my shirt and slacks into the wash before the ink dried. I took them over to the laundry room, stuffed them into the washing machine, added detergent; then hurried back to start a shower, first laying down paper towels over the splattered carpet so I wouldn't track more ink. In the shower, I scrubbed my hands, wrists and face with a soapy washcloth, again and again. After hard scrubbing, my hands were clean, except for under and around the nails. Then my face, as hard as I could, more soap, harder. I turned off the water, stepped out, toweled dry, checked the mirror. My face was sore and chaffed from the rubbing, but the black was gone. (Later my face would become as sore as if sunburned and I would gingerly treat it with ointment.) After dressing in clean clothes, I went to start the washing machine. Then I had another idea.

I would at least finish filling Dave's cartridge. This time I would kneel, leaning over the rim of the tub and performing the operation inside, on the floor of the tub. I lifted the inkbottle, syringe, needle, and cartridge out of the bag and placed them on the rubber mat inside the tub. Fit the needle firmly onto the syringe nub, drew 20ml of ink from the bottle, slid the needle into the cartridge, slowly depressed the plunger: Spurt! Again the needle slipped, but this time the ink only went into the tub and onto my hands. I put everything back in the bag and ran the shower to wash the ink away; again scrubbed my hands with the cloth until they burned. Okay, okay. This had to work. I saw the problem now. Design flaw, I thought. I put on plastic gloves from a hair dye box. Then I lined up ink, syringe with needle and cartridge again on the mat. I drew the 20ml of ink–from a second bottle, since I had emptied the first—inserted the needle and firmly held the joint of syringe and needle with my left hand, while I held the syringe itself between my right forefinger and middle finger and pressed the plunger with my thumb. All the ink went in, no mess. Inspired, having filled Dave's cartridge, I filled two for my printer as well. Not a hitch! But here was all this mess, my ruined clothes, the catastrophic splatter on the walls: all because the needle wasn't designed to screw or clip on to the syringe, and could easily slip off, and because the instructions had said nothing about holding the needle on while emptying the syringe. I should sue!

In any case, I yelled upstairs for Dave. Instead of him, his girl friend came to the top of the stairs and I said, "Here, the cartridge is fixed. It should print now." She gave me a commiserating look, but also laughed, and turned to give the cartridge to Dave.

Downstairs, I fit my own refilled cartridge in my printer and: yes! It worked! Then I went back to deal with the bathroom. I spent another full hour–my own schoolwork postponed—dabbing every splatter spot. My first attempts with a wet paper towel just led to smears, but then I got the knack. A fresh towel, a flicking motion on the splatter, and it would come up without smearing. When there was a smear, I needed more wet towels, wiping and wiping. I went through a full roll, filling the wastebasket. I got up all the ink eventually. Splatters on the tub, splatters on the sink pedestal, splatters on the toilet and over three walls. However, I couldn't scrub the carpet without smearing ink more deeply into the fibers, so I left them, hoping that daily use would wear them away. After two hot washes, my vest came out clean, but the tan shirt and tan slacks kept their splatter stains. I would only wear them around the house from now on; I would live with my stained Nike shoe as well. I did buy a new white shower curtain for $5.95 and threw out the stained one.

I had no way to explain the trouble and fuss. When Dave had stopped down again, in the midst of my cleaning, he had said, "Who cares about that bathroom? No one wants to use it anyway." He never thanked me for the cartridge filled. Connie sympathized with my fury at the kit's manufacturer; and she was glad that I'd managed to clean up the mess. But the folly was my own.

I had hoped that my son would understand that I'd done this for love. I had also been trying to teach him lessons in economy and perseverance. For years, I had been waging a losing battle against his consumerism. I tried buying economy-size Coke (he would drink half then leave the rest to go flat). I tried buying hamburger patties ready to cook, along with rolls and cheese, to save on the $5 trips to McDonald's, but he still insisted on fast food. In clothes I wore utilitarian fashions and shoes that would last. I turned off lights. I turned off the TV if no one was watching it. I shut windows when our heat was on. I tried filling the washing machine before doing a wash, in order to save water. I took him to a distant Reebok outlet, trying to save 40% on overpriced running shoes. I repaired appliances. I became a Home Depot handyman, installing a storm door, a lighting fixture, a light switch. I wore his cast-off shirts and slacks when they went out of fashion.

Of course the lesson that David learned this time was not the one I meant to teach: whatever the cost, convenience in the long run is a bargain.

Two weeks later, he had more homework to print out. He never had gotten his printer to work, he announced (perhaps having said nothing earlier in order to spare my feelings). He showed me that when he tried to print with the refilled cartridge, the page came out blank. "Why don't you just go *buy* a cartridge?" he suggested.

That's what I did, finally. In fact I bought a two-pack, ten percent off.

Gym Jerks

A jerk is that hirsute, slouchy, 175 pound, thirty-five-something man, black, scraggly beard, black hair and bald spot, hairy back, neck, arms, undershirt, baggy shorts, tennis sneakers, who lets us all know how furiously he is working out, gasping loudly with effort on the exercise bike, then whistling to himself, as if he were alone, the way he must sing in the shower. A trim red-headed woman, whom I know from an overheard conversation between her and another girl the other day on the stair climber, is twenty-eight, unmarried, Irish, and if not a barmaid, then a regular at local pubs, is intensely biking in her Nike warm-ups near him to the left, a *Redbook* magazine open on her console, and she glances at him in the mirror as he whistles, grunts and makes his other noises, then glances directly at him a couple of times. "Whatsa matter, don't you like it?" he asks loudly, pointedly to her. Keeps on, all the more loudly. She catches my eye, reddens and grimaces. "You got a problem?" he demands again. I'm tempted to intrude as I continue to step in my row of stair-climbing machines behind and facing their row of exercise bikes and then the row of treadmills along the mirrored wall opposite. I think this is his way of coming on to the woman, and of breaking the pretense of silence; or perhaps of revenging himself on the pretense. She is reading his contact as harassment. I don't intrude, but we all three continue, the man whistling and grunting louder than ever, as if he's won a point; the girl grimly ignoring him and absorbed now in her reading and biking; and me intent again on my stair climbing and pondering the unwritten mores of gyms.

＊＊＊

When I first saw this gym, Superfitness, in Watertown, near the Arsenal Mall, I was fifty-five and had been living the lifestyle of a would-be marathon runner for seven years, had trained at fifty to seventy-mile weeks somehow, spending two and three hours on runs around the Charles River bike path. The total loop from my house into Boston and back was twenty-five miles.

Winters were the challenge, once snow closed the paths. Running on plowed roads with slush and traffic was desperate. Even then I would go over to Heartbreak Hill, where Commonwealth Avenue was plowed and had an access road, out of the traffic. I ran in temperatures under ten degrees. From January on, the training intensified, with the Boston Marathon coming in the third week of April. I finished five Boston Marathons as a bandit, never as a qualifying runner for my age group.

Only jerks, I believed then, joined gyms. Not real athletes. Just cosmetic wannabes. All that useless muscle. Lifters. Boxers. Martial artists. Hard bodies. Real runners ran their distances on land. But then each of the past two Januaries I had gotten walking pneumonia that lingered and not only spoiled my training, but threatened my teaching. It was time to train inside, at least for the worst of the snow and frigid weather. I would keep fit through the winter for the next Boston Marathon. This was my dream.

I rationalized the membership fee of $149 per year with the idea that my running shoes would last longer. Instead of four pairs a year at $70 per, I would need only two.

The layout, as the salesperson routinely explains, constantly showing around prospects, includes two floors. To the right, as you enter and check in at the desk, is the "cardio club"—in its first stage of evolution, when I joined originally, it featured five or six sky walker machines (arms and legs swinging against resistance for low impact) off on one side, along with a row of abdominal exercising machines (sit and bend, sit and swing left to right, lie down for sit-ups and crunches) and then perhaps a long space, perhaps one hundred feet or more, with treadmills facing both walls, which were all mirrors, and two rows of exercise bikes facing each other in the middle. New equipment came and went every six months or so, upgraded treadmills; different varieties of exercise bikes; stair climbers; two rowing machines. Off in another area were various weight machines, arranged in stations, each machine specializing in a different exercise and muscle group. Straight ahead as you entered between these two areas, were the entrance to "the women's area"—a private room with a variety of exercise and weight machines—and the women's locker room and showers, and down a corridor, the entrance of the men's locker room and showers. Upstairs, also, beyond the weight machines was a for-pay, staffed childcare room, for parents to park infants and young children while they worked out. Down the stairs, just to the left of the women's room, you would be shown some 10,000 square feet of free weight benches and machines, and then to your right, the "Aerobic Studio," a carpeted room with windows on the back wall and mirrors otherwise all the way around. A tan carpet strip around the perimeter purported to be a track for jogging, one circuit equaling one sixteenth of a mile.

Over the sound system the same popular music station plays throughout the building, so that hearing the songs later, while food shopping, say, becomes synonymous to me with working out.

Smugly the proprietor (Paul Secon) struts around, needing some conditioning himself. His hard body wife (Sally Fisher) leads an aerobic group. His object is to get the maximum number of memberships to keep the equipment occupied to capacity as many hours per day as he can.

⸙

Clothes, I judged, made the jerk, with at one extreme the worn undershirt and Bermuda shorts, say, for men, dress socks, and sneakers; and at the other the perky fool, soft bodied, all duded out in the most expensive Gortex warm-up suit and $125 Nikes. Me, well, I was stylish to be utilitarian, of course. The same outfits as my street running in summer, only all year around. Tee shirts earned from marathons and 10Ks. An Emerson College tee shirt maybe. Gortex running shorts, dark blue.

For a while, to augment tread milling, I tried to jog in the basement aerobic area. One day I think I ran forty-eight laps for my three miles. Round and round. And there was one other male jogger close to my age going in the opposite direction, both of us avoiding eye contact as we passed each time— a real runner, I wondered, or a dilettante jerk? I decided the latter, from his slow shuffle. Another day, an aerobic class was in full swing. The leader babe wore a headset with mic, barking over the loud speakers along with hugely amplified, driving music. "A one and two and three and four. Give me more now." Twenty or thirty women—no males—stepped up, stepped down on special boards they had to unstack and stack back neatly afterwards. Clapped their hands. Kicked left, kicked right. I figured I had my right to run (was I a jerk?)—I was paying for the right—so around and around I went, trying not to be self-conscious, intent on my own workout. "Okay, girls!" the leader shouted as their workout ended, "give me a lap! Go chase him!"

Proud of my own fitness and ambition as a runner, I had my eye out for other runners, who, like me, had been driven in by the weather off the streets. I felt some shame too that I had made this concession, and I was looking here for kindred company, much as when, hitting my wall in a race, I would commiserate with other walkers. None of the trainers or staff were runners. All appeared to be lifters, even competitive lifters, heavy, thick-necked, with bulging thighs, bulging shoulders, chests, and biceps, like football players without a team.

I can imagine the franchise managers' seminars on business retreats. I'm sure there is a manual for the fitness industry about the importance of fantasy, voyeurism and exhibitionism in maximizing levels of membership and usage. I suspect from time to time, the hiring of professional shills is advised.

Of course, the need for the women's-only area suggests that many women want freedom from the male gaze, the male example, or the male object as they work out—enough women to justify the square footage and the equipment. Feeling vulnerable and shy about their bodies, at least in front of men, they want to focus on athletics.

Downstairs, the acres of free weights and weight equipment are beyond the strength of most women, and for a while it seemed the exclusive province of men who could lift their own weight, four by four lifters with their tattoos and broad leather midriff support belts. But increasingly the rank and file, including women, has infiltrated it. In order to make the gym pay, the owner must have reasoned, you have to guide ordinary people into the benefits of body building, as a golf pro might guide duffers into the higher skills of golf.

Here is a jerk who gets dressed up to come to the gym and then self-consciously does sit-ups on the red carpeting, or practices suspect routines in front of the mirrored walls—not the clearly disciplined warm-up routines of karate or kung fu, which several regulars practice; but truly inane arm flutters and waggles and kicks: a workout she or he could do at home. Why here, except for the theater of appropriate surroundings?

And here, just as aimless, is a thirty-something guy, who lies down and apparently naps on the crunch machine where I crisply do my one-hundred crunches; he gives no sign of exercising for three, four, five minutes, until I have to go break the surface. "Excuse me, are you using this? I'd like to use it when you are done." And the reply, defensive and annoyed: "Yes, I am using this." I apologize, supposing now this to be his exhausted breather between sets, afraid that I have been pushy. He starts up again, pulling at seventy pounds I now see, twice the weight I use.

Later the same guy just sits and gazes, as if on the john, in one of the crunch chairs.

Then there are the cell phone jerks—that guy over there, for instance, hunched in a mirrored corner and having a fifteen-minute chat instead of working out.

The vain and the wishful annoy me. The seventy-pound weakling dreaming of Charles Atlas; the 270-pounder dreaming of Barbie Doll. The old man leering over youth. The pampered rich girl with a bead in her nostrils going through four different trainers, while the friend or sister who comes with her works out alone; and then at home, I imagine, this girl must eat junk food like a pig, because she appears actually to be gaining weight.

On the other hand, I admire the fitness dwarf, who is odd, but not a jerk. Imagine being a dwarf in Watertown, of all places. Imagine the moxie of swaggering into this arena of big people, intent on muscle and power. The bravado. Why not? Dwarfs have muscles. If six-foot-six lifters weighing 220 can lumber on the treadmill, if fatties can waddle, then why not a dwarf, churning his short legs, while the jogger beside him makes two or three of his strides with each single stride? Effort and seriousness compel due regard.

I admire the friendless, dogged, uncommunicative red-headed mesomorph I call "Rusty" to myself. He is short and by nature hefty. He speaks to no one, makes no contact whatsoever. Late twenties perhaps. He always brings a towel, which he folds over the bar of the treadmill, and uses to wipe the sweat from his face and neck. He slogs along for thirty minutes, an hour, sometimes longer, until his tee shirt is soaked and his hair matted. Dedicated, doggedly punishing himself. Never really losing weight, but keeping to his level of endurance.

I admire the fifty-year old woman who works out like a mother in childbirth. She pedals a sit-down machine with levers back and forth to work her arms. Straw-like gray hair, wet and matted with sweat to her scalp; face reddened with effort. Every day. Also, a younger woman, who must have weighed 250 pounds. She is 5-6, pleasant face, straight back hair; she talks to regulars regularly, as she works out on the walk-stepping machines. In sweatpants, working out, her buttocks and thighs are massive, each butt cheek bulging like a sack of grain, but all muscle now, not flab, her calves and ankles as thick as my thighs.

God knows who these people are with street clothes on, with social identities. There is a pretense of disposable wealth. New Lexus outside, say, new Corolla. There are also off-duty mail people here, men and women. I see twins come in, women, both in their postal slacks and blouses. I see postal slacks hanging in the men's locker room. Opening an unlocked locker for my use, I am startled to see with folded slacks, shoes and shirt, a pair of handcuffs in a holster.

Sometimes there are people I do know, by surprise. Three women friends of my wife. A rowing fanatic and former graduate student of mine, a part-time stand up comedy teacher I hired, and then one day an overweight young man who calls "Dr. Henry!" and I recognize as a student from last semester's Shakespeare Tragedy course.

⸺

Over my five years of membership, the gym appears to be prospering. There have been stages of new investment. First some twenty or thirty new treadmills, honoring the demand of more runner refugees like myself as well as of more arm-swinging walkers. Then also in the cardio area, more sophisticated exercise bikes with arm levers for upper body workouts. The second big change was a franchised juice bar, as if presumably upscale members had been longing to socialize on a break. After much hammering and sawing, this materialized as a glassed-in 15x15 cubicle on the first floor back by the water fountain. The third change was to move all the abs exercise equipment down to the windowed front of the "Aerobic Studio," facing away from the open expanse where classes still were held.

Also within the past year or so, personal trainers on staff (for a fee per hour, some percentage of which must go to the owner) have been multiplying. One in particular, a young ex-Marine named Roman, has been introducing some bizarre regimens to his clients. Actually I noticed the regimens before I realized he was their source. Duck walks around the workout room flanked all-round with mirrors, downstairs. People rolling on exercise balls of various diameters. People down on one knee and one arm, the other leg stretched out and arm stretched out, like a pointer dog.

Lights were dim one afternoon and a curtain hung over half the room, incense choking the air. Now he was running a class in yoga.

A different trainer, a new one and the first runner, had a whole group upstairs faithfully following his regimen to loudly blaring music of different sprints on the exercise bikes, followed by thirty minutes on the treadmills.

I have my vanity, to be sure. What is this midlife gut suddenly? What am I doing differently? Why can't I make it go away? Where is my stamina? It dawns on me finally, that I am eating and guzzling Gatorade in the same quantities as when I ran seventy miles per week, while now I'm doing maybe twenty on the treadmill. My weight has peaked at 185, up from 170.

One day I stop the man who used to run in the basement with me. I congratulate him. "How did you lose your gut? I see you, you're really looking great. I don't know how to get rid of this." I slap my own gut.

He tells me, "Use the abs machines in the basement. The bend-over machine. The crunches. The lateral machine, swing left, swing right. It takes a lot of work, a long time. Six months maybe. Do fifty or one hundred on each machine, every day. You drink beer?"

From then on, he salutes me from time to time, as we work out same time of day on the same machines. "How's it going? Keep at it."

I have never questioned the investment of time. One hour five days out of seven. I look forward to the workouts and to the sweet ache afterwards. My gut has toughened. At fifty-nine, I can run 10K races still, but completing marathons is a foregone dream.

Old people in the gym, I ruminated, definitely were jerks. They should know better. The gym is not meant for physical therapy.

But there he is; there she is. In this theater and palace of ruddy fitness. This hall of self-regarding mirrors. This leveling zone. There: seventy, if a day. What a joke. A geriatric jerk. And there, another. Pathetic.

Except, as I confess to my son, who tells me I will be seventy when he turns twenty-six—age, unlike other differences, is destiny. There with god's grace will and shall go I. *If* I am lucky. *If* I'm half as plucky too as that treadmill walking, gut sagging, ass sagging, arms stiffly swinging, white-haired and balding old jerk.

Returnables

Most of the fifty treadmills in my suburban gym face mirrors or TV consoles or both, but my two favorites face floor-to-ceiling windows. As I pound away my four miles on schedule each day, I can watch clouds drift or birds on the phone wires or sometimes an airplane or—predictably enough that they no longer surprise me—the elderly Asian couple pushing shopping carts brimming with bags full of returnable bottles and cans. They look Vietnamese to my ignorant eye. Both are bent. Both wear wide-brimmed, upside-down bowl-like hats, loose, pajama-like trousers and tops, and sneakers. The man pushes his cart first, followed by the woman. They look like pictures of Vietnamese peasants in the textbooks and newsreels. Their carts full, they pass my gym nearly every day at 3 pm, heading from Arsenal Street down the two miles of side street towards Mt. Auburn Street. On several occasions, other times of day, morning or evening, when family errands have taken me down Mt. Auburn, I have recognized them on the sidewalk, one cart followed by the other, heading towards Watertown Square. I imagine them working every day like farmers, dawn to dusk, harvesting returnable bottles and cans from public trash barrels in parks and along the river.

Two years ago, I tried to interest my teen-aged son in collecting the returnable bottles and cans from our home and taking them to the recycling machines at the local supermarket. Each can or bottle is worth five cents. He wasn't enthusiastic, but we collected bags full several times. The machines spit nickels, dimes and quarters as we thrust in each can, and as the inner workings read the bar code, shredded and compacted the can, or shattered the bottle. Forty cans for two dollars. I gave my son the change and he went to buy treats with it in the grocery store, including a chilled bottle of Coke. But soon he tired of the trouble, as did I. Before long we were putting out our refundables for curbside recycle collection. One morning, on our way to school, we were surprised to see a man pull up beside our recycling bins in a pickup truck and rapidly sort through for the returnables, which he tossed into the truck bed. He was working our neighborhood, bin by bin.

My son and I tried to imagine what numbers would make such systematic scavenging worth a person's time. The truck man got perhaps ten returnables from us. He would need one hundred to earn five dollars. His truck bed could hold perhaps one thousand bottles and cans. If he collected and redeemed that many in two hours, one neighbor's bin after another (assuming our neighbors were as lazy as we were about returning cans) he would make fifty dollars, or twenty-five dollars an hour. Nor was the redemption all that simple. The supermarket machines filled up quickly with scrap and couldn't accommodate more until a clerk came to open and empty them. Liquor stores would only redeem the brand of bottles and cans that they sold. If there was a central redemption center nearby, I was unaware of it, but even so brands would need to be sorted.

Last summer my son worked his first part-time job at a bakery for minimum wage. $6.50 per hour. He would need to collect and redeem 130 cans per hour to do as well, and where would he find them? Where did the Vietnamese couple find them? They had no truck or car.

Surely they were refugees. Later, when I tried a computer search at home for "Southeast Asian Refugees," I decided that they probably weren't Vietnamese at all; they were probably Cambodian. The Vietnamese exodus had followed on the fall of Saigon in 1975. Hundreds of thousands of so-called Boat People had fled, casting themselves upon the waters of the world, clinging together for strength. In small wooden boats, they headed for Southern Thailand, where if they survived the voyage and attacks by pirates, they were herded into asylum camps, and waited for months, sometimes years for flights to Hong Kong, and from there to Japan and to refugee centers elsewhere. By mid-1977, most boat people made for Malaysia, and ended up in the Philippines, Brunei and East Malaysian States. In the mid-1980's, the communists agreed to an Orderly Departure Program, allowing people to leave for humanitarian reasons. The U.S. Congress also reduced entry restrictions, admitting former political prisoners and their families.

The Khmer Rouge killed more than one million Cambodians between 1975 and 1979, and after Vietnam invaded Cambodia in 1978, survivors fled to Thai camps, where they spent from one to six years, and where, at best, they were given orientation and language instruction to prepare them for life in another country. In 1989, an international conference in Geneva formulated a Comprehensive Plan of Action, whereby economic refugees would be screened from those with humanitarian or political claims and would be sent back to their home country. Refugee groups already in the U.S. fought this process and raised money to help people in the camps gain refugee status. This went on until 1996, when the screening process ended, and the last refugees in Thai camps returned home or settled in Thailand, and 2,500 were accepted into the U.S. With new unrest in Cambodia, however, still more recent refugees entered Thai border camps.

In any case, these grandparents, as I imagined them, were recent arrivals to Boston. Perhaps their son and his wife had settled here first, aided by the grandparents' savings, and then had sent for them. They lived, perhaps, five or six miles across the river in a three-bedroom Waltham walk-up. The son and wife had learned some English, but the grandparents knew only Khmer. The church relief organization had helped both son and wife to find jobs, long hours as cooks. They had two daughters, eleven and eight, and a son four, born just after the grandparents arrived. The grandparents kept the house. They cleaned, they washed laundry by hand and hung it out on the back porch; they cooked. They watched the color TV that their son had found on a curb, the constant jibber-jabber of English, the puzzling and inane commercials. The church relief people suggested healers, but otherwise there was no health plan and the notion of hospitals was terrifying. Three times they had had to take the boy to a clinic in Wellesley. They had no truck or car. The mother and father each had bicycles. The girls went to school from eight until three. The grandson stayed in the apartment with them, or they would take him out for walks or to the nearby playground. The grandmother, surrounded by English she could not understand, would take buses into Boston's Chinatown, an all-day trip, to shop for fresh poultry, meat, fruits and vegetables, while at home the grandfather watched the boy, sewed clothes, and did laundry. The father and mother were tired when they got home. There were fights over time in the single bathroom with its stall shower. The girls learned English in school and practiced together, mocking the parents, translating for them. The parents knew they must learn more themselves, for better jobs, so they took turns at a night class run by the church. The church was the center of what social life the grandparents had. Altogether, twenty Cambodian families belonged to the church and they met regularly afterwards for lunch.

The idea of collecting bottles and cans had been the grandmother's.

Three days a week they traded care of the boy with neighbors; the other days they looked after four more children in exchange. The grandfather read and smoked and complained about their lives here, nostalgic for their farm back home, as if the terror and the killings were forgotten. Although their rightful place had been stolen from them by history, now they had this new chance. They were among the fortunate. But without English, aged and unskilled, they had no hope of finding work. Son read papers daily, looking up advertisements. But at church, with other old men and women, everyone said the same. No laundry, no cooking, no gardening, no sales, no clerking, no bagging even in the supermarket. What could they do without English or any understanding of this world? The mother and father earned barely enough to pay the rent and buy food. Their savings were wiped out. They owed money to the hospital.

⎯⧓⎯

In their own house, the children wanted soft drinks, Coca Cola, Pepsi, Sprite and the girls would buy cans from vending machines for $1.25, while half gallon plastic bottles cost only $.89 on sale. Tea or water was not good enough. Juices were no good, only soft drinks. But when the grandmother saw that each empty bottle or can was worth money, she insisted they keep them in a box. After those first redemptions at the local supermarket, she saw each can as money. She saw cans thrown in the gutter, or in the playground trash.

These rich Americans. She saw them. She saw their children. Careless.

When she dragged the grandfather out one day, carrying trash bags, they searched and collected in the neighborhood until both bags were full, but when they brought the bulging bags to the market, two workers shooed them away. She couldn't understand the words, but she grasped that the redemption machines were full. Another worker was cleaning them, overflowing with plastic and metal confetti. They didn't want so many cans at once.

⎯⧓⎯

In the yellow pages, her granddaughter looked up "recycling," then "redemption centers–bottles and cans". The nearest was on in Waltham, on Elm Street, off River Street, the one the store man had told her. She got a map and walked there by herself, first, perhaps a mile from their apartment, and discovered it around back and underneath a big landscaping and concrete company. There were men and women with shopping carts and there were empty carts and there was one old man with his whole old car filled with bottles and cans. Inside was a counter and five or six young Asian women working, one of whom looked Cambodian. There were cartons everywhere and conveyor belts. The place smelled of stale beer and the air was filled with the clink of bottles. She spoke to the girl and the girl replied in Khmer, explaining the rules. Yes, anyone could bring bottles and cans here, as many as they could. They paid cash, five or ten cents each, depending on the deposit. They were open six days a week, 8 am until 6 pm.

The grandfather complained. Why, why do we do this? She answered, because we can help. Do you see these cans everywhere? They are worth money, understand old man. It's easy work, even for you. We don't want to be a burden. We need to help the family. You can't just sit there all day long watching the TV and dreaming dreams. Do you have a better idea? Come with me. And grumbling, he did. He felt some act of dignity as they rose early. They asked for help from no one. They took plastic trash bags and collected cans even on their way to the supermarket parking lot, where empty shopping carts waited, and they borrowed one, which the old man pushed. They would search everywhere. In the weeds at parks. At each public trash receptacle. At dumpsters behind restaurants and bars. The old man had sharp eyes. Sometimes a windfall: a carton of empty beer bottles on the curb. Sometimes they walked blocks and blocks without a single find, pushing the cart. They ranged farther and farther, through Nonantum, through Watertown, five, ten, fifteen miles in good weather. They hardly ever spoke. When the cart was full, they would head back to Waltham along a stretch of river path to Elm Street and the redemption center.

She grasped that first $20 bill as if it were love itself, fiercely, proudly. The grandfather would want to take it or to stop on the way home for a beer, but she stuffed it deep in her pocket, alert for any lurking teenagers or possible robbers, who might have watched them, who would know: two old people, so easy to terrorize. They went directly home, pushing the cart. She made him promise. This was money not for escape, but for their keep and for the children. This day's labor and tomorrow's, trading strength, trading time, good weather or bad, hot or cold: the aching steps, the toil and sacrifice, the steady harvesting.

Scavengers who had trucks or cars would be wide ranging, stopping for the obvious park and school trash barrels, the dumpsters and the alleyways. But she earned her territory on foot, and gradually expanded it by steady, systematic searching. "Enough for today," the old man would whine, but she wouldn't quit unless her cart was full, or they had run out of time.

Daily passing homeless people along the river, she wondered why they would rather beg than work. They only wanted money for their drugs or drink. They had young bodies. They had English.

Up twice as early, ranging twice as far, she and the grandfather could fill two carts before the redemption center closed. $150 was their best week so far. The exercise was healthy for their bodies.

Some days were bad. They barely found fifty cans. They started too late. Or the MDC or town trash collectors had emptied the barrels. Or someone else had winnowed out all the redeemables first. Hot weather was best. Sunday and Monday mornings were best. Some days were so good that both their carts were overfull while they were still six miles from home. As they pushed their loads carefully, slowly, they passed enough cans in gutters, enough full public barrels to easily fill two more carts, and they could only pray that tomorrow, when they returned, the cans would still be there for the taking.

"You are our steady. You are our regular," the girl at the redemption center said in Khmer, smiling always and giving her special attention. "478 cans today. That's a big haul! $23.90!" The girl counted out two tens, three ones and coins.

—∞∞∞—

"Why are you doing this, mother?" her son asked. She had been sick for three days and now insisted on going out, with or without the grandfather. Or: "Let us have your money for the rent this month." At first she'd meant to earn her and the grandfather's keep, and to help out however they could, but now she insisted: *No, this is for your son.* She had her dream, not of the past, like the grandfather, a dream of their old ways, their country, their village, their friends, their cousins, neighbors and family members long since dead or lost; but of the future. This land, this America, would be for her grandchildren, for the granddaughters, who would marry; and for the grandson, who would go to college. In her locked metal box, high on a shelf, she had $2000 now. When she and the grandfather were alone, she would take it down, unlock and count it. "For college." She asked a friend at the church about banks, how to keep it there, safe from robbers, but safe from family too.

❧

Past regarding us with irony, past humor, they trudge daily past the factory-like gym. So many rich cars. So many people. Paying money to trudge also.

❧

In this culture of selfishness, I wonder if we have lost the sense of direction and collective emergency such a family has. I wonder as I treadmill alone, strengthening my body not for work, but for fitness at best, for longevity perhaps, and for vanity for sure. I wonder, as I chafe against my nine months of college teaching each year, the committee work, the numbers of students.

❧

My daughter Ruth, aged twenty-four, leaves in three weeks for a year in Bogotá, Colombia, to study on a Fulbright. My wife and I are proud of her dedication and her resourcefulness but we are also scared. Having majored in Latin American Studies and Writing in college, then having grown as an artist, Ruth feels compelled to witness political and historical atrocity. She wants her art to create a bridge between the oppressed and the privileged. During college she spent a year in Guatemala and witnessed mass graves. Now she is venturing into a Colombia unsettled by generations of violence and war between drug lords, FARC guerillas, paramilitaries, and a conservative government. Kidnappings are commonplace.

Over the summer I tried to tell Ruth the best that my education could offer. That you cannot suffer for or intercede in all global suffering. That you had to let hands go. I quoted George Eliot's passage from *Middlemarch*: "If we had a keen vision and feeling of all ordinary human life, it would be like hearing the grass grow and the squirrel's heart beat, and we should die of that roar which lies on the other side of silence."

Imagination of course is obligated to heed, and in heeding to sunder self;
to live at once aware and powerless, except in the living, like representatives
or heirs.

Rescue

My wife and grown daughter had decided we should have a family outing to the beach. I agreed, reluctantly, having teaching work to catch up with that weekend. Our son, Dave at fifteen, was all the more reluctant. Ruth, twenty-two, had her apartment with friends across Boston. She was visiting us at home in Watertown before leaving for one of her trips. She tried charming Dave in his room, where he was playing a computer game, but somehow the charm attempt resulted in a fight. He refused to go. Then I announced that I was going, and just as we were leaving the house, he grumpily agreed to come along. We all went, car loaded with cooler with drinks and sandwiches, towels, Frisbee, books, sunglasses, portable CD player, portable radio.

The objective was a beach that Ruth had taken David to several times with her older friends. Dave enjoyed it there. I worried about public access and where to park, but they said not to worry, they knew the tricks. White Horse Beach, Williston. Through unfamiliar routes and traffic, we found our way there, an hour from home. Off a crowded, local street, we pulled into a private parking lot. "Everybody parks here. Don't worry," Ruth assured me. Given the heat, I felt lucky to find a space in the shade. We climbed out, unloaded—me carrying the cooler and towels, Connie with her bag, Ruth with towels, Dave with the radio–and headed for the beach, which I couldn't see yet. Ruth led the way, plodding through hot sand, then up wooden steps and out of sight. Connie and David followed, with me trailing after. What were these crowded beach cottages, practically window to window? We seemed to be trespassing. TV noises. Leaving the board path, I followed through sand on past open screened windows, turned a corner between cottages, and there was the ocean front, a coarse, kelp-strewn beach, perhaps some thirty yards sloping to the surf, with scattered bathers settled on towels, blankets, and beach chairs. Ruth was already staking territory that I thought might belong to the nearest cottage. A man and woman were watching from aluminum loungers in the sand nearby, shaded by its porch. The breeze flapped

Ruth's beach towel. Connie helped her to spread it and anchor the corners. We settled down, *en famille*.

The sun was hot and burning, but the breeze was brisk and the water too cold for swimming. I'm not a fan of beaches. Other than my jogging, if that (depending on how flat the beach), there is nothing to do. I can't concentrate on reading in bright sunlight and a high breeze. Ruth and David enjoyed showing their bodies off and attempted a Frisbee catch at first, then quit and tried the water. Connie was happy just to bask. I peeled off my windbreaker, shirt, and sandals and headed after my children. Dave was waist deep in the surf shouting and howling. Ruth had gone under and tried a few crawl strokes, then stood and waded back, hugging herself and shaking her head. Of course I thought it was just a matter of getting wet as always, take the plunge and before long my body would adjust. But this was numbing cold, biting. Waves rose and broke against my thighs. To my right, Dave turned and waded back then ran to follow Ruth. No one was braving this water, so I retreated too. I had counted only three maybe four bathers. Two teenagers far out, maybe fifty yards, swimming, playing with a raft. Another one or two figures wading. All up and down the beach, hardly anyone was in the water.

I picked my way back to our blanket and towels. The people in loungers right behind us seemed to pay no mind. A man stood with them talking on a cell phone. I was hunkered down. Ruth and David were teasing each other, chattering over David's music; Connie was trying to interest them in food, sandwiches, cans of soda, apples from the cooler. Then we settled into languid idleness. Connie was sleeping. Ruth was with David on a larger towel, drying her hair.

Against the wind, the vista of slate ocean, the breakers, my eyes followed one or two sailboats far off shore and one motorboat that came in nearer and kept cutting back and forth, slapping the waves, a low, open outboard, with a pilot and two passengers. Joy riding kids, I assumed.

A call for help!

A swimmer, a boy, was in trouble, waving and shouting. He was in deep water out beyond the breaking surf, a good fifty yards from shore. He'd paddled out too far, then lost a raft or tube and couldn't get back. He was drowning! People jumped up and stood waving and shouting. Help him! Do something! No one did anything but shout. He kept waving. He was too far out and the water was too cold. There was no hope of reaching him. There were no rescue boats, no Bay Watch guards with floats. I sat motionless, gripped in the fatality. This was not my human moment, except to be helpless and to witness. There was nothing I could do, nothing that would help. The boy would drown. We would have lived the guilt of helplessly watching.

But Ruth was up. She was running to the surf.

I yelled after her, "Ruth!"

Like a bird I remember caught in my sister's teenage room—a robin that had blundered in through a screen-less sash and that flew, frantic, wings beating into windowpanes—now Ruth flew and beat herself against impossibility.

"Come back. Ruth! You can't do anything!" I stood and ran after her, afraid that she would run headlong into the surf.

At water's edge, wind in our faces, she was determined to go: "Daddy, get away!"

I was poised to grab and wrestle her back.

But suddenly the motorboat that had been heading out veered and came rushing back. They had seen! They would save the boy. The man with the cell phone, the man who stood behind us, up by Connie, David and our towels, had called the pilot of the motorboat, who also had a cell phone. They all must be family. We watched, relieved, as the boat slowed and reached the swimmer, then idled. They hauled him safely aboard. They wrapped a towel around his shoulders. Then they eased the boat towards shallow water, where they helped the boy out and he came wading to shore, a shivering ten or eleven year old, skinny, red haired, trying to act like nothing special had happened, waving back at the boat as they reversed and headed to deeper water. His mom came running with a blanket, joined by the man with the cell phone. That was that.

Once Ruth was certain that the boat was saving the boy, we had trudged back to our towels, where Connie and Dave stood watching. We let it pass between us as another incident at the beach. Everybody did, including the kid himself apparently. Everybody went back to basking, especially Ruth and Connie, adamant for this family time, and for the sun.

But what if the boy had drowned? What would be the aftermath between Ruth and me, I wondered? What if I had stopped her? Or what if I hadn't and she had rushed ahead, swum ten or fifteen yards, then floundered, numb in the cold? I would have followed as far as I could. To keep her in sight. To be close enough to rescue her.

Innocents Abroad

I. Overloon War Museum

We are tourists, the summer of 1991, my wife Connie and I, on our first (and so far our only) trip outside America. We have come to Holland for the second annual Ploughshares International Fiction Writing Seminar, held at a fifty-five room, double-moated medieval castle in Castle Well, near Venlo, on Holland's border with Germany, which was also the site of one of the bloodiest tank battles during the Battle of the Bulge in 1944, a battle recreated in the film *A Bridge Too Far*. This entire region had been razed, except for the castle, which had served as a Nazi hospital. The nearby villages have all been rebuilt in the late 1940s and early 1950s, prim brick houses, like the smart little pig built, window boxes, little flags, gardens, no squalor anywhere.

Emerson College had bought the castle in 1986, and during the winters used it as the base for a junior year abroad. As our novelist-in-residence, James Carroll had organized the fiction conference there the year before, along with his novelist wife, Alexandra Marshall, and short story writer, Pamela Painter, and her husband, the writer and editor, Robie Macauley. Carroll had guest-edited an issue of *Ploughshares*, and originally we had planned on relating this conference to the magazine as well as to the Writing Program. I had been invited over from Boston to talk about *Ploughshares* and how to publish in literary magazines, and as program chairman, to familiarize myself not only with the conference and the Castle, but also to visit the new headquarters for our European programs in Maastricht, and to discuss developing a graduate writing program there.

For Connie and me it was a job-paid, one-week junket abroad. We were anxious, exhilarated and smitten. Our fourteen-year-old daughter was working as a counselor at a summer camp and our six-year-old son was staying with family friends, and it was our first time vacationing and traveling alone together. I had just turned fifty. We had flown into Brussels, caught a train, straining to make little bits of sense of overheard conversations in

German, Dutch, and French, and if you disallow anxiety as an event, reached Maastricht, somewhat reminiscent of Worcester, Massachusetts, but with cafes and cathedrals.

We stayed in an Emerson-rented condo for a few days of meetings, a lot of different beers, and four cathedrals (my cloddish response: boy, it must have taken an Age of Faith to put up one of these! . . . sort of like JFK's getting us to the moon—a whole society's effort—and then I thought of Henry Ford's "the man who builds a factory builds a cathedral, and the people who work there, worship there"). One morning when I went jogging, I followed streets into a park, and then followed paths through the park, and recognized what I realized were World War II concrete bunkers and pill boxes; still farther, emerging onto another road, I came to the actual German border, with guards, a guardhouse, and a weighted lift gate across the road, just like ones in the movies.

My Maastricht meetings finished, we took another train, with changes to Venlo, where miraculously we were met by an Emerson van, driven by a kid from Boston who had married one of my ex-students. He drove us through bucolia to Castle Well, and the chateau. Double moat, with black swans. Courtyard. Because the rooms were filled with staff and conferees, we were put up at an Inn perhaps a mile away. From there I went running at dawn, learning the terrain by foot. First to the Castle, where I surprised Jim Carroll going for an early walk. We had been filled in on the war history the night before. 25,000 men had died here, Jim had told me, and the streams had run red with blood. Now, at dawn, as we walked, with mists rolling off the cultivated fields and rabbits darting, I tried to imagine this as a place of combat, that copse of trees ahead as a machine gun nest, the panic here, as in so many films, of a patrol, walking on both sides of the road, fearing mines, fearing ambush.

Happenstance that I grew up playing on another battleground, Valley Forge State Park, though as a boy I never really thought of it as more than a movie set and playground for imagination. My friend John Barnett and I were conditioned in the mode of western movies and serials, and somewhat, as boys of the 1940s, by the glamour of WWII militarism and its echoes in Cub Scouting and later in Boy Scouting. Across the hundreds of manicured acres of Valley Forge were scattered earthen forts on higher ground and our favorite was Ft. Washington, a rectangular earthwork where we would lie against the inner walls and shoot our western cap guns or toy rifles over the top. The battery of Revolutionary War cannons alongside the fort was somehow disappointing, even after seeing films with casts of thousands, such as *War and Peace*. We would try pretending, but the pyramids of cannonballs soldered together and painted black nearby, and the cold, frozen iron of the cannons themselves, with their high-spoked wheels, aimed out over the Brandywine Valley, somehow seemed too specialized and antique for our fantasies. We wanted Indians, at least, or at most, Corregidor, as in the Movietone newsreels. The log cabins scattered around the park, which you could walk into and through wire mesh gaze at displays of cots, clay pipes, flint, candlesticks, and cookware, all relating to the winter bivouac of Washington's troops (where I learned later in school, hundreds froze to death or died of disease), seemed to us equally beside the point. The Battle of Germantown remains to me even today as quaint and remote as the Battle of Concord/Lexington, which is reenacted by costumed volunteers each July 4 just miles from where I live and which I have only seen on the 6 pm news.

At noon that day, as a break from the conference, the staff had planned an expedition in a touring bus to something called the Overloon National War and Resistance Museum, some ten miles away. Other staffers had already been there, but Lexa Marshall was going again and she particularly urged Connie and me to come along. The bus was air conditioned, and we set off chatting and all but singing camp songs, lugging our cameras on neck straps, some with lunch-bags, purses, hats. Again, we travel through bucolia, open fields, copses, dirt road, gorgeous summer weather. We pull into a parking lot. We're there. "You'll like this," Lexa says. "It's very moving, especially the holocaust exhibit." I feel Connie, who is Jewish (to my own fall-away Presbyterian), go suddenly solemn and tense.

The parking lot is surrounded by thick, vernal woods, and at the start of a beaten dirt path is a memorial stone, which reads (in Dutch, then translated to English): "Linger a moment, visitor, and consider that the ground upon which you are standing, once was one of the most contested sectors of the battlefield of Overloon. In bitter man-to-man fights many young men, having escaped death on the battlefields of Nettuno and Normandy, found their final resting place under these trees."

We wander the muggy woods path, redolent of sunlight and pine, filled with scampering squirrels, birds chirping, breeze heavy in boughs, sunlight dapples and blazes, and are surprised, station by station, turning by turning, by an imposing British tank (put out of action by a direct hit at the rear during the final attack at Overloon), a French tank, a midget submarine, an American 155 mm field gun, a British carrier, a Sherman tank, a German 75 mm anti-tank gun, a Russian tank, and on and on, including three huge, complete aircraft, a Messerschmitt with its rusted Nazi insignia, a British

Spitfire and an American B-25 bomber, each surrounded bizarrely by trees, as if lowered from above by helicopter. "In order to avoid damages and accidents, one is not allowed to clamber on [exhibits] . . . Leaders of youth-groups are entreated to point this out to their pupils," reads the printed guide. World War II is in my childhood's memory and has been told and retold throughout my adult life in novels and in film. There is the temptation, as at Valley Forge, to see this Panther tank, this machine gun, this V1 flying bomb, this half-track, as toys, as playground marvels, realer than movie images, realer than words, yet not in themselves objects of terror or experience.

Having followed the path around past some fifty such exhibits, we arrive finally at the entrance to the War Museum itself, a low, landscaped modern building resembling a one-floor high school. Just inside the entrance, through thick, double glass doors, we are in the Arms Hall, where there are uniforms and side arms and manikins in glass cases. German soldiers. French. Dutch. American. British. The uniforms are faded. Some with bullet holes and blood-stained.

Progressively down the corridors, there is an attempt with exhibits to tell the story of World War II from Holland's perspective. As the group of us begin milling and browsing, suddenly a guide appears and gathers us for a formal tour. He is in his forties, perhaps, somewhat resembling the actor Mel Gibson. Well kempt, his English accented. This is his job. He is Dutch. He tries to explain his personal motivation for being here, speaking to us as writers from America.

He was a six-year-old boy at the end of the war, he tells us. His grandfather had been a farmer, and, at risk of death, had hidden a Jewish family with a boy near his own age. They had been in the loft of the barn when the Gestapo came to search and had not been found. Nearly every Dutch family, he said, had their own Anne Frank story to tell. The war was real to him because of this memory, even though he had been too young to understand at the time. Why was his grandfather risking all their lives for these strangers? He himself had only glimpsed their faces once, perhaps, ordinary strangers in the barn. He had been ordered to carry a soup kettle, accompanying his mother. He remembers his terror at the German soldiers, searching his room. What he had not understood then, he grew to understand later. He now wants others to understand, others who have had no personal contact at all with the war.

He leads us from exhibit to exhibit, giving an informal narrative, sometimes answering questions, or pausing to explain or lend greater dimension to a specific item or station of the tour. The first hall depicts the period between the wars, the Weimar Republic, the rise of the Nazis in

Germany and fascism in Italy, the Civil War in Spain. Mostly there are yellowed photographs from the 1930s, newspapers, art deco posters. Mostly it is flat and boring, at least to any reader of William Shirer's *Rise and Fall of the Third Reich* or even of a high school history book. The next hall deals with the war in Holland, the invasion and then the occupation by the Germans. More posters and photographs. The next with the first year of the occupation; the next with the Dutch Resistance, with alcoves branching off dedicated to the war in Russia and to the Dutch Indies (I am impressed here by a scale model of a Japanese concentration camp, because my older brother-in-law, Hans, had been imprisoned from the ages of ten to fifteen in one in Indonesia, along with his mother and Dutch diplomat father; and when he had left my sister, just five years ago, my sister had told me that in leaving her and their three children for a younger woman, he had had "concentration camp eyes"). We turn a corner then, as if to the inner circle of the Inferno, to exhibits dealing with the Nazi persecution of resistance fighters, the persecution of the Jews, and the concentration and extermination camps. Our guide stops in front of an oversized steel coffin, its hinged lid open, and tells, spontaneously it seems, and just for us, this story.

"We had just acquired the box, this box. It had been used by the Gestapo for water torture. It is all metal, like a coffin. The victim was stuffed inside, then the Gestapo sat on the lid and the box was slowly filled with water, here at this valve. Before the man drowned the torturers would open the lid, allowing him to gasp for air. If he still refused to talk, they would shut the lid again, over and over, until the victim talked or was drowned. . . . I was leading around a group just like yourselves shortly after we had just opened the exhibit. I had recently started here myself. Not the first, but one of the very first groups. As we turned the corner and came towards this box, we found an elderly man had climbed inside. He refused to get out. He was holding the sides and rocking and tearing at his hair. 'I want to die! I must die!' he was sobbing in Dutch. He was a lean, grizzled man, seventy perhaps, looked like an engineer or a teacher, a man of learning rather than a laborer. Casual slacks, sports shirt, sleeves rolled, casual and prosperous, on holiday. Scholarly perhaps. We had no idea how he had gotten there. A family man. A burgher on holiday. A grandfather. In 1945, he might have been twenty. We begged him please to get out. 'You may not touch the exhibits, no! Please! Here, let us help you!'

"And him: 'No! No! No! Don't touch me! I must die!' Guards came to help me. Three, four of us. We still could not make him let go. He gripped the sides with all his strength. 'I must die! I must die!'

"I asked him, 'What is it? Please let us help you. You can't stay here, sir. You need help. Come, sir!'

"And he: 'No!' Weeping, red face, rigid, raging at us.

"I was afraid the old man would have a heart attack. It took very long. Medics arrived. Police. In bits, gasps, cries, we got his story. . . .

"'*This* box. This very box, I know it,' the old man told me, brokenly, gasping. 'I was *in* it, understand. This very box. They put me in this. Twenty good men shot and thrown over the cliff. I told. Twenty good men!' We let him go on, and he grew calmer, sobbing still, dropping his head in silence, finally, and going slack, a sour smell of sweat and fear about him.

"'Here, come on now. That was long ago, my friend, long, long ago. Here you must get out now,' I urged him. He let us lift him. Let us support him.

"'Sorry, I'm an old man,' he muttered. 'I'm so sorry. I know this is wrong. A man can't help himself. I have lived a good life. I have five grandchildren, you understand? Three grown children. I am retired teacher. I am sorry to impose. So embarrassed. This museum. Such memories!' We led him to the door. 'I'm fine now. Fine. I'm Fine. Thank you. Sorry to make this display. I must go home. I must go home.' The police had come and we told them, no trouble, it's all over, all okay.

"That man still haunts me. What choice? What life?"

We shook our heads, listening, peering thoughtfully at the coffin-like artifact. Imagining the scene. The old man, the young guide. The older guide's telling now. Was this spontaneous? I believed him. I tried to imagine the terror. The guards perhaps torturing, blows to the face, broken teeth, bleeding mouth, ripped ear.

The young man pushed, wrestled, locked inside that death box. Pistol muzzle in his face; lid closing, clamped.

What gasp for air? No! I don't! Please! What panic, cold, dark, still; then suddenly cold water pouring from behind your head, a gush, as in a bathtub. My imagination now, not prurience. Not a horror movie. Feel it. Be it. Let me out, out, please! Pushing on the lid, the lid immovable, the total dark; kicking in panic, splashing, twisting, heaving with a naked shoulder, pushing with all your might. Steady gush and pour of water, cold, rising, box soon half, then more than half-full; rising.

Muffled, the human voices, curses in German. Tell us. Die namen, jetz. Spricht du! Spricht ober draubst, draubst, draubst, ja—hands banging back in sarcastic reply—draubst du, dumbkopf!

Kicking, kicking, batting with flat palms, hammering with fists. Straining up against the lid, away from the rising, the cold, the surging, the total dark. Time! Time!

No mistake. You know the names they want, you know the families. You have grown up with them. Dieter, Wilhelm, Thomas, Bruno, Hans, Stephan, Dolph. You don't even like them all. You have joined the meetings.

You have been caught, by accident? Betrayed? Who has informed, and given your name? What brought soldiers to your door? What word? What slip? What carelessness? Your daughter cringing; wife protesting, pleading: why him? He has done nothing! Nothing! We are loyal! Her voice as plaintive as a love cry: Alfred! Alfred!

They still have time. They know and choose their risks. They are resistance fighters. There is a world for them yet of time, of chance, of justice in their fates. But yours is set, here, now. The breaths left counting, heartbeats.

What choice is choice?

That last, last breath, involuntary, gasping in water, more water?

Or: the gulp of air, lid lifted, light's blaze, heart racing.

The voice isn't yours. You have no control over what it gasps, chokes, sobs. Involuntary as vomit, it rises and spills from you, your body's cry.

Dieter Wiltsheim, yes, grocer. The leader. Thomas Stegmann, postman. Say it. Who else? Die namen!

Priest. Father Droste. Peter Droste.

Druggist.

(Almost proud of detail, proud of so many names, how many you can offer now, at last, so valuable.)

Dentist.

Printer.

Carpenter.

Electrician.

Clerk.

Tailor.

Garage Mechanic.

Plumber.

(I think of my own life's neighbors, and ludicrously, of my wife's political action group, mostly women, The Watertown Citizens for Environmental Safety, their names, their lives; I think of Lilian Hellman refusing to testify at the McCarthy hearings, "I refuse to cut my conscience to the fashion of the times"; I think of my own cultural dissidence in founding *Ploughshares*; I think of art's imperative, life's compromise . . .)

What instinct of soul refuses body? What desperation? No real choice. Die here, now, at killers' hands; or ransom life by sentencing others to die, and live on then yourself as one of the living dead, in the hollow motions of a citizen and family man. Life will be your sentence and punishment.

The concentration camp survivor—my brother in law—riven with survival. The torturer, the war criminal, the banal, good German, living his postwar life, or perhaps in Buenos Aries, or in Scarsdale: the changed name, changed country. The sleepwalk of normality, the putting behind, the distance, day by day. The marriage. The children. The parenting. The teaching job. The students.

Forty-five years from that twenty-year old (twenty!), Alfred, the man who didn't drown, who was perhaps sent on to prison or a camp instead, his secret never revealed, has lived in a reconstructed Europe, in Holland, in those Levittown houses, through the Cold War, in the industrial economy of the Common Market, with his own generation of survivors, and with new generations—their children grown, their grandchildren growing; generations disbelieving or tired of the old stories, rejecting the horrors, the cautions. He was a science teacher, perhaps, in high school. Following the space race, physics, the new math, computers, genetic engineering, nuclear power. One day, retired, perhaps aware that he has cancer, only months to live, he comes to visit the museum, a tourist like the others. But then there is the box. The very box. The past itself is vomit. He spews and gasps his own name, pleading to strangers for his soul's life.

⁂

The guide moves on; and we follow. Some of us murmur, some give muted groans, but mostly we view in silence, as we pass from one mural-sized enlargement to another of photographs taken by the Nazis themselves. How, why, I wonder, could such pictures be taken? In pride, in sadistic pleasure; in numb devotion to the process of recording itself? Connie has found my hand, and now her grip tightens.

Looking and not looking: we see the worst, and then worse than the worst. The starving and diseased. The unknown victim, who once had personality and name, bearded, hands behind his neck, moments before he was shot. Over and over, the victims' abject eyes, shining with appeal to us, the just spectators somewhere, someday; while in comradely ease, their killers taunt, joke and pose. The yellow stars. The boxcars, jammed, hands reaching. The gas chamber showers at Auschwitz, accommodating two thousand people at a time. The corpses heaped. The skin lampshades ("skins of concentration camp prisoners, especially executed for this ghoulish purpose," writes William Shirer, "made, it was found, excellent lamp shades . . . Tattooed skins appear to have been the most sought after"). The industrial ovens from Krupps, like a bakery. Mountains of eyeglasses. Mountains of shoes. My mind and heart cringe. One whole alcove displays photographs and descriptions of medical experiments. They are familiar icons, all, over-familiar. The children deformed. The prisoner in striped uniform, hanging dead in harness, from a high-altitude simulation. Another held down in a tank of ice water, while an SS officer sits on the rim, timing the man's death from exposure. Was it Stanley Kramer's 1961 film, *Judgment at Nuremburg*, I had seen, with Spencer Tracy as the judge? Or a documentary in high school?

But one large photo I had never seen before: a tiled infirmary, white-coated doctor at work, flanked by a second doctor, a nurse, and two SS officers in black uniforms, and on the operating table, a man strapped down, eyes rolling, the top of his skull missing, his brains hanging out.

Six million. Three million. Ten million. One. Many.

The final exhibit is dedicated to the Normandy landings, the Allied advance, the liberation of the southern Netherlands, a scale model of the Overloon battle, the Battle of the Bulge, the German surrender, the liberation of the Netherlands.

Our guide wishes us farewell, like an intimate, one who has bared his unguarded self, shakes hands, *thank you, yes, you are a good group, it is a privilege, please come again*; we can see the cost to him and the relief, like an actor at curtain call. He must go, he says. He has another group.

On our way out, he tells us, we must visit the chapel of contemplation.

We crowd in. Connie and I linger, as others leave. Connie, who has let go my hand, bows her head in silent prayer. I see a barbed wire altar, behind which stands an eternal flame flanked by a cross and a Star of David.

The Museum, I think, is dedicated to turning memory to imagination, as Tim O'Brien, my friend and the Vietnam War writer, would say. In his story, "How to Tell a True War Story," O'Brien writes: "There is no rectitude whatsoever. There is no virtue. . . . you can tell a true war story by its absolute and uncompromising allegiance to obscenity and evil." The Museum strains towards the sacred by contemplating the profane.

II. Bruges: The Groeninge Museum

On our second day at the Castle, I joined Jim Carroll and Pam Painter in a three-way discussion of a conferee's story, in which a young girl visits a kinky married couple, each of whom tries to have sex with her. At story's end the girl is both doubtful about her own desires and disillusioned about adults and love, if I remember rightly. Pam wanted the writer to explore the girl's character more; Jim saw the ending as symbolizing "the end of America." In my own way, I agreed with Pam, as did the author, who said she would work on it more: "I'm curious now myself about what she will do next. I want to find out."

Meanwhile Connie had set off on her own for a day visit to Amsterdam and the Anne Frank house, and managed to return safely in time for dinner and my goodbye reading that night. I read from my just completed "documentary novel" in manuscript—a true family story, based on ten years of probing my personal history and my family's, in an effort to imagine my father's alcoholism, and to view his commitment to marriage and family as parallel to mine. Where my older brothers and sister had been teenagers during the worst of his drinking, I had only known him in my growing up as a recovering alcoholic, who claimed brain damage, sought renewal in material income and in the unscarred lives of his children, whose destinies, one by one, he would rehearse with satisfaction in his final years. The book's ending, which Connie herself had not read yet, described first my father's, then eight years later my mother's, death, and my love for Connie. I felt privileged to perform; and reaffirmed now, as Connie wept at the account of my mother's dying as she had wept in life.

We socialized until late at the Castle; then next morning we said goodbyes and left for Venlo and the train to Bruges, in Belgium, where we would stay two nights before a last overnight in Brussels and the flight home.

In Bruges, again, cafes, cathedrals. Narrow cobbled streets. Canals with arched bridges and canal boats for tourists. Lace for sale everywhere, as the signal, local pride. We were missing our children, but did manage to hear their voices on a transatlantic phone call, carefully allowing for the six-hour difference, our six o'clock, their noon. We were also aware of these being our last days in Europe.

The next morning, we set out to sightsee, though we are small spenders. Lunch in a cafe, a beer or two (we actually found a beer called DeWitt). A tour in one of the twelve-seat canal boats seemed too extravagant. We looked for the museums. We followed our Bruges street map. We found some ancient plinths in a circle, dating from 550 A.D., and some other tourists took our picture there. We bought some lace. We entered a huge cathedral—the Church of Our Lady (13th-15th century)—the vastest so far, and a hundred yards away, on an altar as spacious as a Broadway stage, a wedding was taking place. The atmosphere was cooler here than outside, but still musty and humid, and the stone pillars, floor and walls were stained from industrial smog. On either side were ornate alcoves, chapels, the size of churches themselves. The arched roof, gold inlay, beams, frescoes, ornate chandeliers, drew up and absorbed our eyes, like an architectural symphony. I thought of Jim Carroll again, practicing Catholic, former priest, and the connection in time and spirit that all this grandeur and art must have for him. But for us— even for Connie, the college art history major—the sameness of the religious paintings was numbing. Or perhaps we were simply overloaded, unable to focus. St. Whosis, read one plaque, St. Whatsis, another. There was a cordoned-off alcove with Michelangelo's white marble sculpture of Virgin and Child (1501-1505).

We left by a side entrance and crossed into the Hospital of St. John and the Hans Memling Museum. I don't recall either the art or the history here arresting us. There were a few Memling portraits and religious paintings, "The Last Judgment," "The Adoration of the Magi." Connie, however, insisted on yet another stop. Map in hand she led me down crowded blocks, a turning or two, searching for the Groeninge Museum, which is really supposed to be good, she says. There it was, unimposing, a round sign hanging out.

This was better, we both felt. The inside was intimate, and nearly deserted. White walled, small rooms, lit by skylights, polished hardwood floors. The paintings, primarily by Flemish Primitives, were immediately familiar from reproductions, but without the halftones, smaller in some cases, and larger in others than in my expectation. I marveled at their richness of texture and color: Bosch, Pieter Breugel (and family), Jan Van Eyck. I tried to photograph them in natural light (flash devices were forbidden for some reason). And then I came upon an enormous diptych, which had Connie transfixed as well.

Panel one showed a red-robed, bareheaded judge in full estate on his throne, bejeweled, surrounded by citizens and with a favorite pet dog at his feet, very bushy with a jeweled collar. Some sort of bailiff has taken his left arm, and the judge stares at a stern, bearded figure with a crown, robed in ermine, who stands in front of him, pointing or counting with the fingers of one hand on the open palm of the other. To the left of the ermined figure is a soldier, whose helmet reflects buildings and sky.

Panel two shows a man being flayed alive—the same judge, we realize—tied naked to a table, in conscious agony. His red robe and clothes are in a heap under the table. His shoes lay cast aside, awry. Above the victim, in painting's center, stands the ermined and crowned figure, supervising, and flanked by a solemn retinue. Four separate flayers work intently, while a fifth pulls the left arm taut by its rope. One flayer each slices each upper arm, another has just started cutting down the breast bone, and the busiest, knife in mouth, strips skin like a leotard from the left ankle to above the knee, exposing the red meat of muscle, vein, and tendon. They are workers, diligent experts at their task. Far in the background, we recognize the same throne and enclosed porch as in the first panel, with another robed figure now occupying its seat, and more distantly watching. As a surprise touch, there is the same dog too, tied to a table leg beneath its master, but the dog has been shaved and is as naked as a dog can be, except for the hairy head.

I didn't understand the story at first. Neither of us had heard of the artist, Gerard David (1460-1523). The title read: "The Judgment of Cambyses." I recalled that Shakespeare's Falstaff promises to play Prince Hal's father "in King Cambyses' vein." Who the hell is Cambyses? I assumed at first that he was the victim deposed and flayed, probably for an abuse of power, but as we read the museum notes, it seems the victim is one Sisamnes, a corrupt Persian judge. Cambyses is a Persian tyrant from the Sixth century, B.C., who, according to Herodotus, "cut Sisamnes' throat and flayed off all his skin because he had been bribed to give an unjust judgment. Then he cut leather strips of the skin which had been torn away and with these he covered the seat upon which Sisamnes had sat to give judgment. After doing this, Cambyses appointed the son of this slain and flayed Sisamnes to be judge in his place, admonishing him to keep in mind the nature of the throne on which he was sitting." David's two huge panels had been commissioned by Bruges city authorities in 1498 as a justice scene for the Town Hall.

Sisamnes as portrayed by David clearly is in agony as sober sadists vivisect him. There is something Christlike about his naked body, and the impact of the scene is not one of punishment so much as of persecution. Various modern commentators have found the subject "gory," "gruesome," "the execution is represented in a callous and brutal way," "the execution of the guilty judge is observed with pedantic accuracy like a surgical operation." I think of the Roman soldiers on Golgotha; of zealous and self-righteous Nazi Storm Troopers; and of the Nuremburg Trials' futile search for justice.

I can only view the diptych through my memory of the black and white, magnified Nazi photographs, especially those of the freezing experiments and of the brain surgery. Both photographs and paintings are graphic representations of the unthinkable: the photographs documentary, from experience within my lifetime; the paintings imagined, portraying for Renaissance culture a pagan story from over one thousand years ago. "About suffering they were never wrong," writes W.H. Auden about the old masters. What seems mythic in the paintings is made literal by the Nazis, by photography, by living memory.

I have a vertigo horror of Europe. I want to get back to the U.S.A., where even the atrocities of General Custer or the KKK seem more innocent and explicable. This isn't my species. This isn't my history, or my tribe. Or perhaps, is it?

III. Searching "Nuremburg Trials" on the Web
<http://www.nijm.ord/Nuremburg%20transcript.htm>
From *The 50th Anniversary of Nuremburg;*
Tape 10 – 11/9/97; statement by M. Berenbaum, PhD

On January 18, 1945, when Joseph Mengele was leaving Auschwitz, he took his notes with him. He thought that his notes would be his key to fame and fortune, stature and status in the post-Holocaust world, and he never understood once that there was an infamy to what he had done. He thought it was good science. There is the famous debate between Robert J. Lifton and Elie Wiesel. When questioned whether the physicians involved in the final solution could possibly be considered 'human,' Lifton answers, "Yes. They were not only human but they were physicians and they were operating out of the 'universe' of the physicians and the world view of the physicians." Wiesel, who situates the Holocaust as a world apart and feels that that world is not our world, commented, "You know it's demonic that they are human." And the demon is found, to my mind, in the fact that what resulted in the Holocaust was an expression in the extreme of elements that are present in the mainstream. I don't only mean the role of physicians but the role of lawyers, the role of all the other elements that contributed to the perpetuation of the crime. This has vast implications to our world, between the allegiance we have to patients and the allegiance we have to state; the allegiance we have to companies that employ us and to the economics of it. Perhaps I would feel much more comfortable if I really believed that that world was not our world. But my own view has been that the Holocaust is the extreme expression of what is common to the mainstream and the major deterrent to it are the values that allow us to draw boundaries.

IV. Boston: Hemingway's Centennial

Spring, 1999, I am in the audience for a lavish and lavishly funded hundredth birthday conference for Ernest Hemingway at the John Fitzgerald Kennedy Library on Columbia Point, a bright, clear spring day. This is a ritual homage to an art that has survived the artist and the life by writers at all stages of career, from Nobel winners to mid-career to nonentity. Some here have in their lifetimes known Hemingway, the man. Some, like me, came to the dream of writing, while he, Faulkner, T.S. Eliot, and Robert Frost were still publishing; and felt the shock and loss at news of Hemingway's suicide in 1961. I feel the absence in this company of my friend Andre Dubus, who died only months ago, and who valued Hemingway as Hemingway valued Tolstoy. Many have only known Hemingway's work as canonized, as smothered in commentary and legend, and most recently as condemned for being culturally offensive.

In such gatherings, the more I age, the more I feel inconsequential and detached. The gathering has been organized largely by Askold Melnyczuk, who sits to my left (he is younger than I and I remember when he moved to Boston with a stapled little magazine called *Agni Review* and worked in a Xerox shop; since then *Agni*, supported by Boston University, has come of age, while Askold himself has published a well-received novel, taught at B.U. and Emerson, married a novelist and served for several summers as staff at the *Ploughshares* fiction conference in the Castle). Having stepped down from *Ploughshares* and from organizing things, these days I am happy to teach and to write. My marriage holds, children prosper. Love animates.

I can't see the dais thanks to the big hair of Sue Miller sitting in front of me. Liam Rector, younger than I and seemingly fully recovered from cancer, is sitting to my right. Schmoozing with Bob Shacochis, Liam had invited me earlier up to the poshy speakers' lounge where I met Annie Proulx, George Plimpton, and Frederick Busch. I recognize others in the audience. Across the room I see Jim Carroll, who is scheduled to speak on a panel later called "The Ugly American." I have taught Sue Miller's novels, and wonder through the filter of her vision, a vision also concerned with justice, at least as the personal life is filtered by society, where the finalities of war figure.

Frances FitzGerald is moderating a panel about War Writing with Stratis Haviaras, Paul Fussell, Bob Shacochis, and Tobias Wolff, each of who has witnessed war first hand. Paul Fussell quotes Hemingway: "Never allow yourself to believe that war is not a crime." In his seventies, or older, Fussell tells us passionately that war is an attempt by old men to see how efficiently teenage boys can kill the greatest number of other teenage boys.

The NATO bombings of Kosovo are in the news. Stratis, who has published lyrical novels about World War II and the Greek Civil War of his boyhood, now reads aloud a brilliant meditation on war. There is no moral or humanitarian war, he says, reacting against the official statements by NATO and Washington that the bombing is for "humanitarian purposes," to put a stop to Milosevic's genocide, just as Roosevelt had failed to do at early warning of Hitler's Final Solution. When war breaks out, truth is the first casualty. True writing happens only as an afterthought, Stratis says, when it is too late for anything but words. "That's where *we writers* come, as an afterthought over the ruins, telling and retelling the truth. To no avail."

Tim O'Brien is a conspicuous absence. But during the question and answer session with the audience, a young woman asks the panelists about O'Brien.

How do you tell a true war story?

"Maybe the best forms," Wolff says, speaking from his experience of Viet Nam, "are the memoir, or the short story, which concedes the fragmentary experience of war."

"In many cases a true war story cannot be believed," O'Brien himself has written. "If you believe it, be skeptical. It's a question of credibility. Often the crazy stuff is true and the normal stuff isn't . . . In other cases you can't even tell a true war story. Sometimes it's just beyond telling."

How do you tell any true story, bring any experience to mind? Birth? Death? Joy? Despair? Lust? Boredom? Pride? Shame? Reverence and awe?

What is Sisamnes to me or me to Sisamnes?

Was there an old man in a drowning box?

Are the icons of the Nuremburg Trials, those photographs fixed in memory now and viewable on the Web, defenses against and hindrances to imagination, like all clichés? Or are they mirrors, corridors, passages we must explore?

Perhaps something in all of us needs crime, the offense we can't take back, and that no amount of living can make good. Forgiveness, perhaps, is the proof of love. We have our small crimes, all of us; we have an industry of therapists to help us restore perspective, to see small as small and life as large. But the large crimes? The atrocities?

—∞—

I like the idea that art protects in order to expose us. That we can't confront the Gorgons of genocide, of war, of infamy, local and global, except by reflection in Perseus's shield (as Kenneth Burke would have it); for otherwise the prospect would turn us to stone. Dostoyevsky's Grand Inquisitor, on the other hand, whether prophet, judge, politician, or artist, claims to stand between the abyss and the masses, offering us necessary lies.

For me, I only know my failures, my refusals to see, imagine or recall.

I will never grant my father his complexity. I haven't the courage to explore my sister's pain, not only in her husband's betrayal, but in their oldest son's death from AIDS at thirty-four. Though my older brother, Chuck, has forgiven me for patronizing him in my writing, and though he has tried in drunken calls, long distance, to share his pain, I will never fully know nor begin to imagine him as a person: his dreams as a surgeon, his divorce, his heartaches as a father, his loneliness at sixty-six. Though I consider Tim O'Brien, the man, my friend, and we live only eight miles apart, I have had little personal contact with him over time. We co-edited several issues of *Ploughshares* together. I teach his novels and stories, and feel in his art, the stark, fierce mandate to respond in kind. Yet in life, I couldn't bring myself to do anything five years ago, not even a note or phone call, when I read his personal admission in "The Vietnam in Me" in *The New York Times Magazine*: "Last night suicide was on my mind. Not whether, but how. Tonight it will be on my mind again . . . If war is hell, what do we call hopelessness?" This wasn't my business, I thought, and didn't like the thought.

I am squeamish.

I am selfish.

I am stupid of heart.

My wife of twenty-six years, whom I love, lies with her back turned, sobbing in the night, same bed, so close we feel each other breathe. She is afflicted by the deaths of friends, and most recently, by the death of her mother, by worries for her job, and for her own health, for her aging, and for her loneliness as our children grow. I can afford no comfort. In fact, I feel resentful, as if her love for others, even in grief, deprives and indicts me. I am not free of heart.

I am just as guarded towards myself, perhaps.

I think again of O'Brien's description of combat: "You feel an intense, out of the skin awareness of your living self—your truest self, the human being you want to be and then become by the force of wanting it. In the midst of evil you want to be a good man. You want decency. You want justice and courtesy and human concord, things you never knew you wanted."

James Baldwin's writing admonishes me: "Sentimentality, the ostentatious parading of excessive and spurious emotion, is the mark of dishonesty, the inability to feel; the wet eyes of the sentimentalist betray his aversion to experience, his fear of life, his arid heart; and it is always, therefore, the signal of secret and violent inhumanity, the mask of cruelty."

Who are we in this room, I think, *we writers*?

Is literature the cathedral, and do the people who work there, worship there?

Are those who ignore the experiences of others (to paraphrase Santayana) doomed to relive them?

What am I to you?

Dress Rehearsal

I felt a stabbing chest pain on my left side as I worked out at the gym, doing sit-ups. I continued my usual regimen, more work on another machine, bending forward, and then the treadmill for thirty minutes, when the pain grew worse and I had to gasp in open mouth and slowly blow out, as I would to ease a runner's stitch. The rest of the evening I felt fine, but when I lay down to sleep, the pain was so sharp that I couldn't sleep. I still thought it was a muscle spasm, took aspirin, finally got some fitful hours of sleep at dawn. The next day I napped. I took a break from the gym, ran on land for only two miles, and had the same pain. That night, Friday night, again the pain kept me from sleep. I tried massaging my ribs. I tried shallow breathing. I worried about angina and looked up the symptoms on the web. This pain was not intense enough or radiant or in the center of my chest, but distinctly under my ribs, under my left breast. I thought it must be a pulled lateral muscle, or maybe a rib stress fracture, but worried if it weren't that I could be having a heart attack and might damage my heart. I tried and tried to sleep, thinking I would check with the health plan the next day. 2 am. 3 am. 4 am. I tried to breathe so shallowly that there would be no pain, and the tension would relax, but my shallow breaths left me dizzy and short of oxygen.

At 5:30 am I called to Connie. She had been struggling for her own sleep as I tried sharing our bed, before I had gotten up finally and gone downstairs. But when I called to her and said, "Call Harvard Health for me . . . I can't. . . ," she was up at once, all alert and caring. I hadn't the strength myself to call or speak on the phone. I was panicking, sure now it was my heart. I couldn't breathe. I would faint.

I heard her voice telling them: "My husband can't talk on the phone. He has chest pain and can't breathe." They said to come right in, now; they wanted to send an ambulance. We had only my stick shift car at home, which Connie couldn't drive (our daughter had borrowed the automatic across town), but when she told them I could drive, they said, "Lady, listen to yourself. You're telling us your husband can't talk. He has chest pains and can't breathe. We're sending an ambulance." She agreed.

In such moments ordinary life splits open, essence certain through the dross. For Connie there was loving fear. She knew these moments. There had been my mother's dying, sixteen years before. Suffering from progressive heart failure, my mother would have an attack, the paramedics would come; she would be carried with oxygen on a stretcher to the waiting ambulance, and one time I rode with her late at night, jolting to the Emergency Room. Connie had tended her own mother's dying in New York. And Connie herself at a family reunion in Chicago, their last with their sick mother, had passed out and been hospitalized over night. She was diagnosed with atrial fibulation. I hadn't been there. My teaching had kept me in Boston, but I felt the panic long distance and I heard it in my daughter's call from the hospital. Back home, Connie had tests, and was given medication.

Then just months ago last March, I was back from a visit to Los Angeles with my older sister, and in bed late at night, Connie complained of stomach pain, which she thought might be heartburn or gas. She was brave, but I grew increasingly worried. The symptoms sounded like appendicitis, though I always forgot whether the pain should be on the lower right or the lower left side. Connie's was on the right. We called from the bed and they told us to come to the Emergency Room immediately. I drove. I held Connie sleepless, gray, and trembling for what seemed hours after an x-ray: indeed, it was appendicitis and she was operated on. "Garden variety," her woman surgeon told us—me, my daughter and son—when we were allowed to visit later that day.

Now it was my turn.

I panicked that I couldn't breathe. I needed breath. I thought of my brother Jack, whom I just had visited in Colorado. Asthmatic all his life, he had settled in Colorado for the high, dry climate, but at seventy-three, he now suffered from Chronic Pulmonary Disease and was tethered by a long cord in his house to an oxygen pump, which ran constantly. In 1999, our doctor brother Chuck (two years younger than Jack, ten older than me) had died of lung cancer in the New Jersey hospital where only I had been able to visit him. He had lain gasping oxygen. He told me that because of smoking he had more cancer now than he had lung tissue. His surgeon friend took me aside and told me that his death would not be pretty. At best he would be unconscious, but he would strangle to death, unable to get oxygen.

My friend, Richard Yates, had strangled also; in 1992, after months of long distance calls from Tuscaloosa, Alabama, where he would gasp and wheeze oxygen as we spoke (emphysema and TB had ruined his lungs), a mutual friend had called to say he had died, and just recently a researcher shared the grisly details: "After a hernia operation in an understaffed VA hospital, he had a coughing fit and began to choke/suffocate. He apparently tried to get out of bed and was found dead on the floor the next morning."

This was my panic, my experience of needing breath; my gasping, my tripping heart. First a police car had pulled up under a streetlight in the predawn and a tall, burly officer had taken a bag out of the trunk, then hurried up our walk and into our small parlor, where he questioned me as I sat on the couch and Connie stood nearby; while he was checking my pulse, two firemen came in. Same questions. Same answers. Chest pain, can't breathe. Couldn't sleep. Dizzy. Age sixty-one. Was working out in the gym, when I first felt the pain two days ago. A fireman wrapped my arm in a blood pressure sleeve, pumped it up, let it out. "Blood pressure normal. It's not his heart," he said. They were talking on radios, repeating my story. Someone slipped a nose clip on me with oxygen flowing. Two or three additional men came in, crowding our house, these from the ambulance. They made me get on a stretcher. I couldn't lie down, so I sat up Buddha style, grasping the sides as they lifted and carried me out my vestibule, then rolled me down the walk. A small fire engine was parked at the corner, idling loudly, lights flashing. And the ambulance was parked behind the police car. Connie was following close by, too worried to return my eye-rolling mockery at all this spectacle; and what the neighbors must think. The ambulance driver was our neighbor, in fact, I learned later. We had never spoken to him. He lived some four houses down the street. He would walk his two Dalmatians in the playground across from our house. He did a major remodeling of his three-bedroom Cape, the clone of ours and all other the houses in this tract, adding a side room with a basement under it; and lifting the dormers for a full second floor. Construction had taken months. He got in the town newspaper for the Halloween display he put on his lawn each year—skeletons gripping beer cans and gravestones with legends about drunk driving. I was unaware of his wife or kids. He seemed young, mid-thirty's, black hair. My wife rode up front in the ambulance as he drove and later she told me that they had talked. His name was Mack. He had overheard his partner in back asking my age and when I said sixty-one, he marveled (if he was trying to make me feel good, it worked): "Get outta here, you're kidding. I never had you pegged for sixty-one. I would've said forty-eight. Sheesh, would you believe it?" We were off; me deeply breathing oxygen through the nose clip, holding the sides of the stretcher, and watching the road recede through the back windows. No traffic. But the ride was jolting, swerving, rattling. If indeed it wasn't my heart, I felt embarrassed by the overkill. We arrived at the Emergency Entrance of Mt. Auburn Hospital, they backed in and lifted me out – perhaps 6:20 am by now – and I was rolled into a room and transferred to a bed, my blood pressure was monitored, I was kept on oxygen, and the young doctor's diagnosis was for a skeletal muscular problem. I was rolled out and stood for a chest x-ray. Then back to the room for an EKG and a blood test for a possible clot (I never mentioned that I also worried about lung cancer, because of my brother Chuck, though I had never smoked). Results from the blood test were an hour coming, during which Connie was wonderful, catnapping in a metal chair, while I sat up. The doctor came back at last and said everything looked normal, x-rays, blood test, EKG. He thought it was a muscle tear. I should take pain medication so I could sleep, which they would start me on now. At 8 am, Connie called a friend who agreed to pick us up. No sooner did we get home, however, than the phone rang and another doctor who had just read my x-rays told me excitedly that I had pneumonia. He had seen the small spot on my lung that the others had missed. And yes, that would account for the pain. And he was phoning in a prescription for antibiotics.

⤙⤙⤚⤚

Between the painkillers, the antibiotics, and catching up on my sleep, I was back to normal in a day or two. I quipped to Connie that this had only been a dress rehearsal for the true, eventual emergency to come some other time. Meanwhile, I was reassured by and grateful for the privilege of such emergency care, costing my insurance plan several thousands of dollars, most likely, and I felt stupid for not having called and driven into my doctor during business hours on Friday. In living the prospect, the what if, of heart attack, of lung failure, of dire finalities, all the fret of daily lives had receded. I was blessed in Connie's love, and in our children. I was grateful for my health, for the diagnosis and treatment and for the second chance of nothing serious, this time. My experience had made me more alive to Connie's own heart scares; and to feeling with my brother Jack, whom I called long distance to tell all this.

My panic, my gasp for breath had only been a hint of what he lived with daily. During my visit, we had both tried to treat it as ordinary. His wife Janice spoke to save him breath. He would need to rest and clear his lungs of fluid before he could come out to visit. Antibiotics and other drugs had weakened his immune system, so he lived now like Howard Hughes, terrified of germs, and had suffered life-threatening bouts with colds caught from visiting grandchildren. He trailed his oxygen tether as he moved around their house. He sat at the far end of the dinner table, keeping six feet between us, with the back door open behind him for ventilation. Jan cooked for us, but he had no appetite. She had kept him alive, he said. He had always loved her, but he never knew how much until now. They spoke of his frustration. He had always been active, out in the world, working, hunting, building things. Living isolated in the house depressed him; he couldn't find a doctor he could trust. Jan spoke of getting a self-propelled trailer, so they could travel. He could rest in back and have his oxygen and she would drive. The irony, he said, was that he had come to high country and thin air for his asthma, but now that his lungs were failing, if he lived in Florida at sea level, he would breathe more easily. Occasionally during my visit, he was able to unhook the oxygen for short periods. We traded family stories. When we parted and the thought lay heavily in both our minds that we might not see each other again; I wanted to hug him goodbye, to touch him, and could only keep my six-foot distance and wave.

He was concerned now with my call, relieved to hear I was okay.

Later, independently, Jan emailed me that he had been sick again. The doctor had put him back on steroids, which he hated taking, but they were seeing a pulmonary specialist in Greeley the next week. She added, "After you left, Jack told me how he had wanted to hug you."

On Aging

The ninety-four-year-old Johnny Kelley is the patron saint of the Boston Marathon. Richard Wilbur once mentioned him in a poem called "Running." Every year for the decade of the 1990s, at least, he has appeared on the local news coverage at the start of the race in Hopkinton, beaming and in apparent good health, singing "here is the best part; you have a head start, if you are among the very young at heart." Several years ago a statue was unveiled in his honor at the foot of the renowned Heartbreak Hill, at mile sixteen, where Center Street crosses Commonwealth Avenue. The statue depicts an eighty-year-old, shrunken, stringy Johnny Kelley running and holding hands high with a twenty-one-year-old Johnny Kelley in his prime, and is called "Forever Young." I find this inordinately moving, and on the eve of my sixty-first birthday, I had my son take a picture of me standing on the pedestal with one arm around each Johnny's shoulder.

⸺

Between the ages of fifty-one and fifty-seven, I struggled to run the Boston Marathon each year.

I was encouraged the first time by a younger colleague who had finished it the year before and told me it was an unforgettable experience. I had been running only five-, then ten- mile loops around the Charles River bike path, but I started training day by day, week by week, and discovered that I could go farther and longer. From my home in Watertown, the river as it meanders into Boston is punctuated by a series of bridges. The Harvard Bridge marked a twelve-mile loop. The BU Bridge marked a sixteen, the MIT Bridge an eighteen, and all the way around the Science Museum and back to my house was twenty-five miles. I trained and trained, the longer runs taking me three hours. My friend told me that the adrenalin of the event, of the crowds, and of the other runners in the marathon would carry me the 26.2-mile distance even if in my longest run before the race I had only reached eighteen miles.

I'm not a natural athlete, and certainly not a gifted runner. The goal here wasn't competition. I took as gospel the sentences from *Galloway's Book of Running*: "In your first marathon, don't worry about time. Just run to finish. Staying on your feet for twenty-six miles is a feat in itself." On my long training runs, I would sometimes hit my wall five miles from home, falter to a painful walk, call and ask to be picked up; or once, I actually had to take a bus. I was sweaty and given berth by the other passengers.

Race day, my friend and his wife picked me up at 9 am. Another young friend of his, Ray, was in the car. My colleague himself wasn't running, as I had thought he would be, but this other man, Ray, had run the marathon twice before and would be running. They drove us out the turnpike to Hopkinton, then dropped us off and took our picture. I was wearing a red poncho that I would never take off and later would regret, with a bag of jellybeans in the bib. Ray led me from the drop-off point. Hundreds of other runners seemed to materialize, walking the mile or two with us.

I didn't realize it then, but Boston was the only marathon anywhere with qualifying times. Those who met those demanding times in another legitimate marathon were eligible to be "official runners," paid an entry fee, were given a bib number, and were bussed from downtown Boston to Hopkinton. The thousands of others who were "unofficial" were so-called "bandits," unable to qualify, but attempting to run off the record. As we had, they had made their way to Hopkinton under their own power.

Ray was friendly, but distracted. He had his own race to think about. He was looking out for friends. As my guide, he would at least show me to the start. He reassured me that the dreaded Heartbreak Hill wasn't as bad as everybody said. He said to start out slow, and not to let the crowd force my pace. Everyone around us seemed nervous, some bragging and protesting too much; others taciturn. We passed a parking lot where some Canadian college kids joined us, first timers also. I worried that the trek to the starting point was sapping my reserves. People were leaving the road to go pee among the trees on either side. Gradually we came to Hopkinton Common, filled with commotion. Free samples of yogurt and sports drinks. Vendors with pennants, caps and balloons. Newscasters with cameras and microphones. Long lines of runners waiting to use a battery of portable toilets. Runners sitting or lying on public lawns. Runners practicing elaborate stretch routines.

Ray explained that we were jumping in. I should follow him and do just as he did. There were temporary aluminum barriers along Main Street. The official runners were already lining up in pens, according to pace (6 or 7 or 8 minute miles), and wearing their race bibs with numbers. Ray nudged and shouldered his way forward with me behind him as far forward as he could. Near the starting line, the elite runners were warming up; wiry, lean-muscled, small-boned. They were famous, although I didn't recognize any of them. They wore bright colors and sponsor trademarks along with their race bibs, with two-digit numbers. Some were just returning from warm-up runs off a stretch of side road cordoned off for them; others sat cross-legged, waiting. The better runners gathered and packed behind them, hundreds, thousands, followed by a multitude of others stretching far up Main Street.

The day was chill and overcast, perhaps forty-five degrees at late morning. Over the crowd from an elevated, sheltered platform, officials told us the clouds would clear off and that we would have a tailwind. A high school band was playing. Johnny Kelley made an appearance to cheers and applause and sang his song. The wheel chair entrants lined up and, with a shot of the starter's pistol and the crowd's cheer, they were off downhill for their early start. Runners started peeling off whatever disposable layers they had been wearing, trash bags, extra shirts, old jackets, and tossed them to the side. The officials announced ten minutes to the runners' start, then five. A TV news helicopter hovered loudly overhead. Ray pressed close to the barrier. "Come on," he told me. "When they start, you just climb over and jump in. Just do what I do."

Suddenly the loud speaker barked "They're off!" Like water through a broken dam, the elite runners spilled. I couldn't see them. Just the shuffle in front of me, as the press of bodies pushed forward, quickening. There was a mounting cheer from the runners themselves, hats tossed. Ray heaved his ass up on the barrier, swung over one leg, then the other, jumped down. "Good luck! Come on!" he yelled. I did the same, though immediately I lost sight of Ray. I jogged and bobbed, working my way in, keeping pace behind, alongside, and in front of others, all those arms swinging, all those running shoes drumming. I was in a living river and as far ahead as I could see, bobbing heads, colors, human motion flowed. Racers filled the road across, from side to side, and all the way ahead, already rising at a distant crest, and again at the crest beyond that. The pack began to loosen, picking up from a jog to a full running pace, some runners in my way, so I had to veer and weave to pass them, but mostly others jockeying to pass me, hundreds it seemed. Before long, I settled into my run. After three or four miles, there seemed to be about twenty-five runners at my pace, sometimes ahead, sometimes falling back. We were a constant. Others still might pass us, and we might overtake slower runners. There were bodies of every type, every age. Tall and short, overweight and lanky, men and women, college kids, roommate girls, midlife Moms, a number of people wearing Dana Farber Cancer Institute tee shirts, some paunchy Boston policemen, a scattering of white-haired seniors. Some runners were in pairs or in groups, supporting each other. There was casusal chatter. There was even an element of clowns, as if running the race were no chore. One guy was dressed as Groucho Marx, bushy eyebrows, cigar and all. Spectators would call out as we passed. "Hey, Groucho!" or "Go, Mom!" or "Go, Dana Farber!" Since I had no identifying marks, the best I heard a few times was "Go, Red Poncho!" Whatever our pace, we were the "back of the pack," and behind us were hundreds of others, maybe thousands, whether bandits or official runners.

That first time, everything was a surprise. The mile signs came and went. I was running as well as I did around the Charles. Out of Ashland, alongside a lake, then into Framingham, with a depot station and train tracks to the left for miles and an engineer blowing a whistle to us and waving. Clusters of spectators; now and then water tables, where I swerved to catch a cup on the run, managed a gulp or two, then tossed it with the litter of cups underfoot. Little kids reached out to slap palms. Other kids or spectators offered orange slices or cups of Gatorade. Along some stretches residents stood with hoses, spraying runners who wanted to cool off. My friend and his wife surprised me at mile ten, waiting on a bridge I crossed in Natick, and calling out: "Go, DeWitt! Hey! You're looking great!"

I had no idea that there were really five serious hills. The first was just after mile twelve up past Wellesley College, where a gauntlet of students loudly cheered everyone, even us, even me. Then Route sixteen through Wellesley past parks and suburban blocks stretched on and on, a flat two miles, until a surprise downhill into Newton Lower Falls and then the second hill (was this Heartbreak I wondered?), a steep, ¾-mile grade that crested over Route 128 at the Wellesley Hospital. By this point runners were straggling. Instead of the inspiration of collective possibility, there was now the breaking of ranks, admissions of defeat, which were demoralizing. Footsore and cramping, clammy with sweat, mouth pasty from jellybeans and Gatorade, I continued down to the turn at the Newton firehouse onto Commonwealth Avenue, and was stunned to see a third steep hill, which I managed to climb, concentrating on my feet and passing scores of walkers, but after the downgrade, faced with a fourth hill at mile eighteen, I faltered to a walk, just to catch my breath, then ran, then walked, and cleared that crest, ran painfully downhill again past Newton City Hall, then had to struggle the mile up Heartbreak Hill, while others ran past me. When I was half way up, I was overtaken by a man not only running, but running while pushing his grown, paraplegic son ahead of him in a special wheelchair–these were the legendary Hoight's, I would later learn, who had been running the marathon for years. Bystanders exhorted me, along with the multitude of other walkers: "Keep running. C'mon, you can run. Don't walk! It's the last hill. You are almost over the top. It's all downhill from here." I mustered a stagger run for ten yards, then faltered. The uphill felt so steep that I could reach forward and touch the ground rising ahead of me. At the top, I started to run again, letting gravity pull me. I would finish this way, I reasoned; walking up the hills, running down. Boston College fraternity kids were swilling beer on the sidelines and yelling. Rock music blasted from their open windows. There were more and more stretches of walking, but never without running too. A long stretch from Boston College to Cleveland Circle, and then the turn on Beacon Street, and more sudden rises, mile twenty-three, and coming into Kenmore Square, mile twenty-five. I trudged up and over the punishing rise over the Massachusetts Turnpike, then ran some more, determined to finish. I finished the last mile at an agonized run, turning the corner on Hereford, and then onto Boylston, and even found a desperation burst for the finish line, at last, only to be passed and pushed over to the bandit exit where no one noticed or greeted me, except for a few Red Cross helpers asking if I needed water.

The race had taken me four and three-quarter hours. If my friends had waited for me at the finish, they had long since given up. I was stranded, exhausted, wet with sweat and chilled, cramping in downtown Boston. Among the crowds, the official finishers seemed to be everywhere, weary, but smiling, wearing Mylar capes and their finisher medals and surrounded by friends. I had to walk another mile from the finish around the streets, and made my way finally to my college administration building, which I hoped would be open, at Massachusetts Avenue and Berkeley. Walking there was as painful as the worst of the marathon course. Worst of all was I was nobody; I had no money, even for a phone call or a cab. Though it was almost 5 pm, I found the door open, luckily, and as I stepped in I saw the President, Jackie Liebergott, sitting in a conference room at day's end ease with the Chief Academic Officer, Phil Amato. We had our history as colleagues and friends, and as a Chairperson, I reported to them both and felt like a teammate. I walked over, clammy, fatigued in my poncho, and blurted, "Well, here I am, the first Chair to finish the Boston Marathon! Can I sit down a second?" Jackie countered with "Not the first— Dave Luterman used to run it." I went on to explain to their tolerant amusement that I was marooned, had no money, and wanted to use the phone to call my wife and have her come pick me up. "Sorry to interrupt your meeting. . . ." They offered me a chair and a bottle of sparkling water; then I called my wife, thanked them, and went to wait outside on the building's front steps, shivering now. Eventually my wife came.

Subsequent Boston marathons, I knew what to expect. But even though I trained fanatically, even though I knew the Wellesley hills, still the following year I hit my wall at Mile sixteen, the Wellesley Hospital, even before I reached the turn onto Commonwealth Avenue. Many runners were dropping out because of the humidity and heat. I was running near one of the only African Americans I had seen in the pack, a woman, and she was faltering too (one of the cops directing traffic called after, "Way to go, sister!"). We would walk, then stagger run, trying again, but the fatigue and the soreness of our feet brought us back to a crestfallen walk. I forget the words we exchanged, finally, but it was the hopelessness of finishing today, and we decided to catch the trolley in from the T-stop down the block. I had to teach that night, and I had arranged with a colleague, who had an apartment on Newbury and Hereford Streets, near the finish line, that I keep a change of clothes there, show up, shower and change and make my night class. The T on Marathon Day proved to be free (I only had a couple of dollars with me in my shorts). I was glad for the woman's company, which normalized the humiliation of publicly quitting. A few other riders said a few words to us. The Chestnut Hill stop came and went. I got off at Mass. Ave., only to find myself barricaded from watching the runners finish, or looking for friends. Again, fatigued and sore, I must have walked another two miles around the blocked streets to make it to my colleague's. He was sitting on his stoop smiling, "Hey, how'd you do?" As if he thought I had finished. I explained what had happened, and he graciously invited me in for a cold drink then let me go off to shower and dress. I made my night class, aching and sore.

⸺

The Boston Marathon or any marathon is not the distinct occasion that it appears to be, the mark of uncommonness that compels respect from other, un-athletic mortals, other runners, and from oneself. The training itself is the mark, the way of life. For each marathon, the four months or more of managing time, of managing relationships, of managing work, of managing nutrition, spirituality and health. The accretion, daily, of seven to ten to fifteen, to eighteen, to twenty-mile runs, in my case, around the Charles River bike path. Runs at all times of day, all seasons, all weathers. The accretion too of one hour, to two, to three, to four sometimes each day, six days a week (one day for rest): dawn runs, midday in winter for the heat, twilight or darkness in summer heat waves. Where does such time come from? What gets displaced? The empty time? The brooding time? The television time? Spared injuries, the setbacks of hard colds or flu. The shoes run down, replaced. The running shorts and tee shirts and sweatbands and socks. The daily laundries. The gradual weight loss and muscle development.

⸺

I enjoyed the personal and tribal distinction. The passion to run comes from confusion, fear, anger, and stress, unresolved emotional tensions. In my case those had to do with fear of aging, with frustrations in my teaching and writing careers. Runners can be like dancers, expressing lives through movement. Runners have styles and different styles at different moments. There are aggressive, angry runs, raging against limits. There are light, ecstatic runs, the runner's aura joyous, glad for life, for youth and strength. There are searching runs. There are lost runs.

⸺

My fifth and last Boston Marathon is the 99th, March 23, 1995. I am still a bandit, incapable of making the qualifying time. I have, in fact, only finished one marathon running all the way, my first Bay State, in Lowell, the fall of 1992, for my personal best of three hours and fifty minutes. In other different runnings of both the Vermont and Ocean State marathons, I have hit my wall at mile twenty and had to walk and run to finish, 4 hours, 4:15, 4:35. My third Boston, I had dropped out at mile seventeen and limped home. My fourth, likewise, at mile nineteen. My wife has driven me from Watertown out the Turnpike to Hopkinton and we are directed, bumper-to-bumper to a drop-off this time at a state park, where there I climb on one of a series of school busses ferrying runners, nervous and pretentious, to the Hopkinton Common. At the Common there are thousands and thousands of runners (over 30,000 will run the course). More than deja vu, I have a procedure by this point. I stretch on the lawn in front of a church. Though I look for familiar faces in the crowd, perhaps someone from Emerson, or regulars from around the Charles River bike paths, I recognize no one. I am anonymous here. I am simply a runner, an un-bonded bandit. I tell myself to relax; nothing is at stake, just treat this like my week's long run. I have been training for four months on the Wellesley hills, until I know all five of them, landmark by landmark, in both directions. The temperature is prime, not hot like last year, not cold like the year before, or raining like the year before that. Forty-two degrees, a tail wind blowing. Clear skies. Countdown. Ten minutes to go! A loud speaker announces. I get up and edge through the crowd to the barriers. I glimpse again the elite, world-class runners, athletes incomparable to me. They will finish the course in two hours and four to eight minutes, or four minutes per mile, nearly equal to the world record miles back in my high school track days.

There is the wheelchairs start. More countdown. Then the plunge of starting, the surge. I wait for a minute then climb the barrier and jump in, joining the shuffle, which as we start downhill, moves to an impatient, mincing jog. There is the drum and pounding of the herd. When the pack sorts itself out I am running with a group faster than some, much slower than most, with ample elbowroom. Three girls chatting with each other. An older, heavy man wearing Mickey Mouse ears and a Farber Cancer Institute tee shirt. A duded-out twenty-something guy in colorful spandex, new shoes, wrap-around sunglasses and a sloshing water bottle. We will keep company for hours, sometimes abreast, sometimes falling back or working ahead by fifty or more yards. Ashland, Framingham, Natick. The first Wellesley hills stretch ahead, with Wellesley College students cheering without letup, so that each runner feels suddenly special, and however silly, the cheers invigorate me and the others around me. I know from my other Boston runs and from training, that the killer hill for me is in Newton Lower falls, the sudden steep downhill, followed by the long grade up to the Wellesley Hospital. I try to save myself for it. I faltered here the year before, as others ahead and around me are now. Walkers had begun as early as mile twelve. But here, in my group, suddenly there are scores of walkers, exhausted, hands on hips. My feet are hurting and fatigue has set into my legs and hips, but I run steadily up and over the crest. So far so good, but now there is the long downgrade to mile seventeen and the turn at the firehouse. The next five miles include the three hills I have trained on, back and forth. The first steep hill is from here to mile eighteen, then a dip and second hill and just after mile nineteen, the steep up, then flat, then steep up again of Heartbreak Hill, peaking at mile twenty-one. In training, memorizing the terrain, I had been fresh, but now I am hitting my wall. I feel it happening. I know that once I stop running, my muscles will stiffen and I will have to walk, then run, then walk, then run, then walk. Give or take the crowded start, we began at noon; now it is three. My blood sugar is low. My feet refuse more pain. My legs cramp. What am I doing here? With that question, I falter. Starting up the incline, I have to walk, just to the crest, maybe; then I will run again.

This time, mostly walking to the crest of Heartbreak Hill, I feel that I can run and walk to the finish in something over four hours, but that I would then be exhausted and marooned in downtown Boston again. Nobody knows me. I have nothing to prove. Except I do, or why else would I join the ceremony of this race and all its company and public spectacle? Why not run alone around my river path? I reason that veering left from the crest of Heartbreak Hill, and mostly running the five miles to Newton Corner, Galen Street, and then the mile up river to home, will count as a completed 26.2. I do veer off and run the five miles home alone. But it isn't the same. I haven't kept to the course. I haven't had the strength, or passion, or body of all those who have.

—◦◦◦—

Running has its morality. Lessons that I needed to rehearse.

There is the lesson of self-awareness and acceptance, beyond unrealistic ambition. You need to settle within your capacity and perform there as well as you are given to perform, this time. This is a different matter from being better than you are, or can be, by accident or miracle.

There is the lesson of rehearsing a death: the callisthenic of having to falter, to fail against your will and dream and achieving. The mortification, literally. All the coaching advice about dealing with "the wall" and about psyching yourself beyond the wall doesn't apply for me. My lesson is in reaching and honoring limits, not in ignoring them.

There is the lesson that all activities, teaching, parenting, writing, sex, have their distinct karma and the point is to immerse will and effort into its inevitable nature. If it is given for the run to be ten miles, fifteen, twenty, then it is. If it is not given, then it is not. It is not for me to force or will the outcome. Strength is not the issue. The run itself is the issue.

There is the lesson of celebrating, from your individual limits, the glory of full human possibility. The constant flow of runners, thousands and thousands of others—not just the elite, but the good, the average, the lucky, the dogged (each has a life, each has negotiated a way to spend two or more hours for training each day for four months while still parenting and still holding down a job, each has fought snows and freezing temperatures through the hard winter)—as they continue up and over the hills and close the last six miles to the finish.

—

The year of the 100th Boston, I was a spectator for my first time, stationed midway up Heartbreak Hill. I was with my wife Connie and family friends, the Farren's, Pat Farren, the father, groggy and weakened by his chemo treatments. Far off, we saw the red television blimp, following the leaders. Portable radios up loud announced they were near, nearer. Then we saw the wheelchairs. And fifteen minutes behind them, the motorcycle cops, the television car, and the elite men, first the tight pack of Luiz Dos Santos, Cosmas Nedeti, Lameck Aguta, Sammy Lelei, Johan Kagwe, Moses Tanui, Ezekiel Bitok, all of whom passed my watching, running in rhythm as if choreographed and never slowing from their five-minute pace. Perhaps a few minutes behind them came scattered more of the elite men, and more, and more. I recognized Bill Rodgers, a small, slender man, who waved and smiled at the crowd. They streamed by, topping the hill, three and four abreast for ten minutes, and then we saw another TV car and motorcycles coming for the leading women runners, in amongst the men. Word was out on the radio that Uta Pippig, the favorite (and my idol), was in trouble; she was suffering from flu, diarrhea and menstrual bleeding. Tegla Loroupe, her rival, had a lengthy lead, perhaps one hundred yards. As Uta approached and passed our vantage point, Connie said, "God, look, she has blood on her legs!" Uta looked as if she would drop out. She was drenched, haggard, and she shook her head apologetically in our direction, mouthing, "I can't!" After she passed, we stayed for half an hour, perhaps, watching throngs of men and then men and women, all sizes, all running styles, all shapes, a constant stream, each cresting the hill and destined to finish in under three hours. Before we left, we heard the excited radio reports, first that Moses Tanui had won in 2:09:16, and second that Pippig was overtaking Loroupe, then passing, then far ahead for a third win in 2:27:12.

Amazing! Humanity itself!

In recent years I have only managed one 10K race each April, the James Joyce Ramble in Dedham, and this year I haven't even managed that. I work out in the gym with weights and abs machines for half an hour, then half an hour on the treadmill. I developed problems last summer with my hip and spent months in physical therapy. I can no longer run thirty straight minutes on the treadmill at my nine-minute pace. I need to stop every three or five minutes for water then start again. I do run seven miles around the river path without stopping once or twice a week, but I doubt I could make ten anymore. And in other ways, my life has changed. Others have taken over the stress of leadership at school and now I only teach. After years of struggle and rejection, my work is being published. My daughter at twenty-four flourishes on her own; my son at sixteen is coming into his own. He is a sprinter, and when we have tried to run together, he takes off alone and by the time I struggle home, he is showered, settled and watching TV. My marriage is sound. I love my wife. We've all lived life's losses of parents and friends, and the death of my older brother three years ago.

Still each spring marathon fever fills the air. I see runners pushing for distance around the Charles as I drive to school. Come Marathon Monday, I watch the coverage on TV, beginning in Hopkinton. I feel the anticipation. And there again is Johnny Kelley, no longer able to run even the final mile of the race, and barely able to make it to the microphone, but he does, one more time, singing "Young at Heart." The announcer recounts Johnny's sixty-one appearances in the Boston Marathon, his two wins, his seven finishes as second.

As the race gets underway, with cameras following the leaders, I am in fact in the gym, on my treadmill with a TV console at eye level and earphones plugged in. I am remembering. The sights, the smells, the company, the pain, the dream. I watch the leaders, the men passing familiar landmarks, then the women. I can feel the race happening. And even as I drive home, I listen on the radio.

This is aging. Life itself is our glory and ordeal, our measure of heart, and of passion. We do our best. There is no finish line.